Settle Your Tax Debt

Settle your Tax Debt

Sean P. Melvin

Dearborn
Financial Publishing, Inc.®

This publication is designed to provide accurate and authoritative information in regard to the subject matter covered. It is sold with the understanding that the publisher is not engaged in rendering legal, accounting, or other professional service. If legal advice or other expert assistance is required, the services of a competent professional person should be sought.

Editorial Director: Cynthia A. Zigmund
Managing Editor: Jack Kiburz
Project Editor: Trey Thoelcke
Interior Design: Lucy Jenkins
Cover Design: Salvatore Concialdi
Typesetting: Elizabeth Pitts

Library of Congress Cataloging-in-Publication Data

Melvin, Sean P.
    Settle your tax debt : how to save thousands using the IRS
offer in compromise program / Sean P. Melvin.
        p.   cm.
    Includes index.
    ISBN 0-7931-2836-6
    1. Tax compromise—United States—Popular works.   I. Title.
KF6316.Z9M45   1998
343.7305′2—dc21   98-8158
                                                             CIP

Dearborn books are available at special quantity discounts to use as premiums and sales promotions, or for use in corporate training programs. For more information, please call the Special Sales Manager at 800-621-9621, ext. 4384, or write to Dearborn Financial Publishing, Inc., 155 North Wacker Drive, Chicago, IL 60606-1719.

Dedication

To my mother, Winifred E. Melvin (1929–1995), and my father, Joseph P. Melvin

CONTENTS

PREFACE

The biggest advantage that the Internal Revenue Service (IRS) has over the average American taxpayer is the fear factor. It is a simple theory: the more one fears the IRS, the more likely one is to comply with its demands. The IRS instills this fear in several ways. A mass of auditors, agents, computers, lawyers, and seemingly unlimited resources and time, all create the illusion that the odds of beating the IRS are overwhelmingly against the taxpayer. This fear grows partly out of ignorance. Most taxpayers' lack of knowledge of tax laws available to protect the rights of average taxpayers are not well known (and certainly are not publicized by the IRS!).

The most important thing to remember when dealing with the IRS is that most people who owe back taxes are not criminals. Rather, they are ordinary, law-abiding taxpayers from all walks of life who simply didn't know about one or more provisions of the voluminous tax code and whose errors were caught by IRS computers or auditors. But if you owe back taxes, is there any way to avoid paying the entire tax, penalties, and interest owed? You bet! It's known as the Offer in Compromise (OIC) program and it allows taxpayers in certain situations to settle their past tax debts for pennies on the dollar! In 1996, Congress passed the Taxpayer's Bill of Rights 2, which expanded the scope of the original program to cover even more taxpayers. But don't expect your local IRS agent to sit you down and explain the program. Beyond giving you a pamphlet (IRS Publication 1, *Your Rights as a Taxpayer*), which includes a brief explanation of the program, the law doesn't require an IRS agent to recommend or even mention the OIC alternative. Indeed, some citizens who are inclined to judge the IRS harshly would say that because IRS revenue officers (those agents charged with collecting the tax assessments) are rated by their superiors by how much money they collect from taxpayers, revenue officers actually have a *disincentive* to tell taxpayers about the OIC alternative. Until very recently, the IRS officially denied that revenue officers are evaluated solely on tax dollars collected, but it acknowledges that dollars collected is one of many criteria used to judge the performance of revenue officers.

Although learning about the OIC program is itself a challenge, a far more difficult challenge is trying to maneuver through the confusing IRS explanations and submit all the right forms completely and properly filled out (called the OIC package). Typically, once a taxpayer gathers the information necessary to submit an Offer in Compromise package to the IRS, he or she gets lost in the tax jargon and administrative requirements and the OIC is submitted with some defect that ultimately results in rejection. The result is a frustrated taxpayer who feels at the mercy of the IRS.

This book will *empower* you by providing a straightforward, easy-to-understand method for preparing your own Offer in Compromise package. After suffering through an audit (or even a back tax assessment), this book provides the debt-ridden taxpayer a fresh start without an embarrassing and costly bankruptcy filing. Utilizing the 10-step method in this book will save you countless hours of aggravation and money (in legal and accounting fees) while allowing you to wipe out your back tax debt and settle with the IRS once and for all.

In *Step 1* you will learn to determine how much the IRS claims you owe it by interpreting IRS correspondence. The level of importance in each of the most common letters used in the tax assessment and collection process is explained. Step 1 also helps you understand what types of collection methods the IRS will use and how to protect yourself against them until you can submit your OIC package. Step 1 also explains how to contact the IRS. Equally important, it gives a straightforward summary of how IRS agents are categorized (their specific duties), and what they can and cannot legally do.

Step 2 describes the process of using the federal Freedom of Information Act (FOIA) to find out everything the IRS has said or written about you (or your company). You will be armed with information about the government's responsibility in responding to your FOIA request. Information gained through your FOIA will give you an inside view of how the IRS views your case.

Step 3 gives information on spotting inconsistencies in the IRS's assumptions and calculations. It summarizes how, if you think the IRS has made a mistake, to figure your actual tax liability, and when and how to file an amended tax return.

Step 4 provides you with information on IRS collection methods. It explains the IRS's levy process, lists preventive measures, and explores the dangers of hiding assets from the IRS.

Step 5 leads you through the process of determining which OIC category fits your particular circumstances.

Steps 6 and 7 illustrate how to draft a simple personal financial statement, and then transfer that information onto the IRS forms required in an OIC package.

Steps 8 and 9 explain the rules of the OIC program and will guide you through filling out the IRS forms and other documents needed for a successful OIC package.

Step 10 gives advice on rejection-proofing your OIC package and offers specific information on preparing, filing out, and following up on your Offer In Compromise package.

The *Appendixes* feature all of the necessary forms for preparing your own Offer in Compromise and a sample of a fully completed Offer in Compromise package. They also feature excerpts from the *Internal Revenue Manual* used as a guidebook by IRS employees for accepting an Offer in Compromise package.

Settle Your Tax Debt will give you all the necessary tools to help you cut your back taxes and penalties. Perhaps equally important is knowing that there is help available and that the IRS must abide by the same rules as the taxpayer. Eliminating fear from the IRS's arsenal is the best way to effectively negotiate with it. Deal with your IRS debt as you would any other business matter: calmly, rationally, and informatively. With the right attitude and the right information, you can achieve the peace of mind that comes with settling your past taxes with the IRS once and for all.

ACKNOWLEDGMENTS

All good books are the collaborative effort of many people, and this book is no exception. I am very grateful for the assistance and expertise of the following people:

- The professionals at Dearborn Financial Publishing for transforming hundreds of manuscript pages into a perfect product, and especially for the patience and diligence of my editor Cynthia A. Zigmund
- The partners at Fox, Rothschild, O'Brien & Frankel, LLP, for their support and allowing me access to the abundant resources of the top law firm in the Philadelphia region, and especially the Exton partners for setting a standard of excellence for me to follow
- My agent, Wendy Keller, and her staff at ForthWrite for discovering me and pushing me to keep writing
- Finally, to my wife, Joanna M. Melvin, Esquire, for her support, patience, editing, and encouragement during this yearlong project

Determine How Much the IRS Claims You Owe

First, let's make sure that both you and the IRS agree on how much the IRS *claims* you owe the government. This amount is not the same as what you *actually* owe the government. This figure represents what the IRS auditors have calculated, based on the information they have gathered and assumptions they have made in your case. It is also important to know what phase your case is in at this point. If the IRS has levied your bank accounts and/or seized your property, for example, it will be more difficult to get a refund than it would be if you had submitted an Offer in Compromise earlier. Step 1 will show you how to interpret the IRS's sometimes confusing letters and notices and gives you information on the IRS's operating procedures so you can understand what phase of the process your case is in from the IRS's perspective.

Gathering and Interpreting IRS Correspondence

This may sound a lot simpler than it is. Despite the Treasury Department's attempt to simplify IRS letters and forms, IRS correspondence remains mystifying to the average taxpayer. First, assemble all the correspondence the IRS has sent to you and arrange the letters and notices by date.

1

Check the earliest correspondence and look for the word *assessment*. Read the correspondence carefully and pay particular attention to the section that begins:

According to our records, you have not paid the Federal Tax you owe for the tax period shown above. Please pay it today.

The amount our records show you owe is $25,616.42

We figured this amount by adding:
Amount unpaid from prior notices	$24,100.00
Late payment penalty	$ 600.22
Interest	$ 916.20

This is the critical section of the assessment and/or billing notices. The initial notice and demand required by the tax code is typically followed by three or four computer-generated notices known in IRS talk as "CP notices." In the upper right-hand corner of virtually all IRS notices and letters is an identification box (IRS agents call this the "label"). This provides the reader with the name and number of the notice (i.e., CP-501, CP-502, etc.) and the date the letter was issued. More important, it identifies what tax period the IRS is concerned about. It also tells you what type of tax the IRS believes you owe. For example, if your assessment was a result of the IRS's determination that you owe more personal income tax, this is indicated in the label as "Tax Form: 1040."

Once you have determined how much and what type of back tax the IRS originally assessed you, work through the correspondence until you reach the most recent letter. This letter will undoubtedly reflect a higher amount owed than previous letters because penalties and interest have been added. Many taxpayers ignore these billing notices and letters from the IRS, unaware that interest and penalties are accruing daily and in some cases can increase the size of the tax owed by 70 percent or more over the period of a year. This makes it critical that you begin to get together a game plan to protect your assets and settle your tax debt as soon as possible. In the world of the tax code, time is usually on the IRS's side and delay almost never is in the interest of the taxpayer.

Here's a brief breakdown on the types of letters and notices the IRS commonly uses to notify you about back taxes it is attempting to collect.

CP Letters

As mentioned above, after an assessment letter is issued, the IRS will follow up with billing notices. CP-501 is the simplest and least threatening of all the IRS correspondence and generally carries the label of "Reminder" (see Figure 1.1). If the IRS doesn't hear from you, you'll receive a CP-502, which contains a bit of a more threatening tone. Instead of a reminder, the IRS starts out this letter with "Your Tax Is Overdue" (see Figure 1.2). Again, if the IRS hasn't heard from you, expect to receive a CP-503 letter, in which the IRS begins to use the "L" word—lien (see Figure 1.3). While the IRS still has a few steps before filing a federal tax lien, the IRS has started to pay more attention to your case. This letter will start off with "Urgent—Payment Required" on this notice. Believe it or not, if you ignore the CP-503, the IRS will send you a more threatening letter in the form of a CP-504 (see Figure 1.4). This notice is the final step before the IRS files a federal tax lien (discussed in detail later in this chapter). A CP-504 is also the first round of the IRS's intimidation game. It starts out "We intend to levy—respond now." Realistically, the IRS is still quite far from actually levying (seizing) your assets, so don't panic. But once you have received this letter, you should know that an IRS revenue officer (those agents that are assigned to actually collect the tax) will soon be looking at your case and will be making plans on the best way to collect the money owed to the IRS. While this should not affect your chances of having your Offer in Compromise accepted, it is an indication that the IRS enforcement action is imminent in your case.

Notice of Federal Tax Lien

If the IRS has been unable to collect the tax owed by the conventional method (i.e., voluntary payment by the taxpayer), it will file a Notice of Federal Tax Lien (NFTL) (see Figure 1.5). The IRS views the federal tax lien as the backbone of the collection process and it is a heavy hammer in the IRS's arsenal. Even before you have been notified that a federal tax lien was filed, the lien has *already* been attached. Attorneys and CPAs often refer to the federal tax lien as a "secret lien" because the lien has not yet been recorded. This lien takes priority over almost any other creditors, even though the taxpayer may have no way of knowing that the lien existed in the first place! Eventually, however, when the lien is filed, the IRS will send you a NFTL and record the lien in your local recorder of deeds office (or the equivalent in your state). Liens and levies are discussed in more detail later in this chapter.

Figure 1.1 Sample IRS Form CP-501, IRS Billing Notice

```
                        Sample Form CP-501

                                                004519

   Department of the Treasury        ** IF YOU HAVE ANY QUESTIONS, **
   Internal Revenue Service          ** REFER TO THIS INFORMATION: **
                                     NUMBER OF THIS NOTICE:  CP-501
   PHILADELPHIA, PA  19255           DATE OF THIS NOTICE:   10-03-94
                                     TAXPAYER IDENT. NUM:
                                     TAX FORM:  1040
                                     TAX PERIOD:  12-31-92

        Il..,l.lIl...l.l.lIIl.IIl.,IIl...l...l.l.l.l.IIl...IIll.l


        FOR ASSISTANCE CALL:        804-649-2361 LOCAL RICHMOND
        OR USE THE ADDRESS BELOW.   1-800-829-1040 OTHER VA

   IF YOU WRITE, USE THE ADDRESS ON THE STUB AT THE END OF THIS NOTICE
   AND ATTACH THE STUB TO YOUR RESPONSE.


          REMINDER - YOUR ACCOUNT STILL HAS A BALANCE DUE

   According to our records, you have not paid the Federal Tax you owe
   for the tax period shown above.  Please pay it today.

   The amount our records show you owe is $5,297.64.
   We figured this amount by adding:

        Amount unpaid from prior notices        $5,239.42
        Late payment penalty                       $17.45
        Interest                                   $40.77

   The amount unpaid from prior notices may include tax, penalties, and
   interest you still owe IRS.  It also should reflect any credits and
   payments we received from you since the last notice we sent.

   We computed penalty and interest to the date of this notice.  To
   avoid additional penalties and interest, send your payment for the
   amount you owe so we will receive it by 10-13-94.  Otherwise, we may
   have to charge you additional penalties and interest.

   Make your check or money order for the amount you owe payable to the
   Internal Revenue Service.  Write your taxpayer identifying number
   on your payment and send it with the bottom part of this notice in
   the enclosed envelope.

   If you think this bill is incorrect, send the amount you believe
   you owe and a statement explaining the difference.  Be sure to
   include the bottom part of this notice with your reply.
```

Figure 1.2 Sample IRS Form CP-502, Your Tax Is Overdue

```
                                              003437


     Department of the Treasury        ** IF YOU HAVE ANY QUESTIONS, **
     Internal Revenue Service          ** REFER TO THIS INFORMATION: **
                                       NUMBER OF THIS NOTICE:  CP-502
     PHILADELPHIA, PA   19255          DATE OF THIS NOTICE:  11-07-94
                                       TAXPAYER IDENT. NUM:
                                       TAX FORM:  1040
                                       TAX PERIOD:  12-31-92

 _____

             IIIII.IIII....I..I.IIIII.IIII.IIII....I...I..I.I.I.IIII.III...IIIII.I



          FOR ASSISTANCE CALL:          804-649-2361 LOCAL RICHMOND
          OR USE THE ADDRESS BELOW.     1-800-829-1040 OTHER VA

     IF YOU WRITE, USE THE ADDRESS ON THE STUB AT THE END OF THIS NOTICE
 _____  AND ATTACH THE STUB TO YOUR RESPONSE.


                   YOUR TAX IS OVERDUE

     We previously wrote to you about your unpaid Federal Tax, but
     according to our records you have not paid it.  Please pay the
     amount you owe now.

     The amount our records show you owe is $5,360.86.
     We figured this amount by adding:

          Amount unpaid from prior notices        $5,239.42
          Late payment penalty                       $34.91
          Interest                                    $86.53

     The amount unpaid from prior notices may include tax, penalties, and
     interest you still owe IRS.  It also should reflect any credits and
     payments we received from you since the last notice we sent.

     We computed penalty and interest to the date of this notice.  To
     avoid additional penalties and interest, send your payment for the
     amount you owe so we will receive it by 11-17-94.  Otherwise, we may
     have to charge you additional penalties and interest.

     Make your check or money order for the amount you owe payable to the
     Internal Revenue Service.  Write your taxpayer identifying number
     on your payment and send it with the bottom part of this notice in
     the enclosed envelope.

     If you think this bill is incorrect, send the amount you believe
     you owe and a statement explaining the difference.  Send the
     payment and the statement with the bottom part of this notice in
     the enclosed envelope.

     If you recently sent us payments, please fill out the flap on the
     enclosed envelope to help us identify them.  Send the completed
     flap, your payment and/or statement, and the bottom part of this
     notice in the enclosed envelope.
```

Figure 1.3 Sample IRS Form CP-503, Urgent—Payment Required

Sample Form CP-503

```
                                            ** IF YOU HAVE ANY QUESTIONS, *
  Department of the Treasury                ** REFER TO THIS INFORMATION: *
  Internal Revenue Service             NUMBER OF THIS NOTICE: CP-503
  PHILADELPHIA, PA   19255             DATE OF THIS NOTICE: 04-03-95
                                       TAXPAYER IDENT. NUM:
                                       TAX FORM:  1040
                                       TAX PERIOD:  12-31-93


        Illulllulllllllllllllllullullullull


        FOR ASSISTANCE CALL:           410-962-2590 LOCAL BALTIMORE
                                       1-800-829-1040 OTHER MD/DC
                                       CALLER ID: 042934


                      URGENT - PAYMENT REQUIRED
           * * * THE AMOUNT YOU OWE IS $4,121.57.        * * *

        We previously billed you for your overdue federal tax.  We still
     have not received your full payment.  AVOID ADDITIONAL INTEREST -
     PAY THE AMOUNT YOU OWE IN FULL IN THE NEXT 10 DAYS.

        If you've already contacted one of our offices and we gave you an
     installment agreement for this tax period, please disregard the rest
     of this notice.  We will send you reminder notices of the amount you
     owe on your account.  HOWEVER, IF THIS DOESN'T APPLY TO YOU, CONTINUE
     READING.

        Because you haven't paid the amount you owe, we must now consider
     filing a Notice of Federal Tax Lien.  That is a public notice that
     the government has a claim against your property or any future
     property to satisfy this debt.  A notice of lien can affect your
     ability to get credit in the future.  We also must consider taking
     your wages, property, or other assets to pay the amount you owe.

     THE AMOUNT YOU OWE IS $4,121.57.
     We figured this amount by adding:

            Amount unpaid from prior notices         $4,071.11
            Late payment penalty                        $14.84
            Interest                                    $35.62

        The amount unpaid from prior notices may include tax, penalties,
     and interest you still owe IRS.  It also should reflect any cre
     and payments we received from you since the last notice we sent

        The amount you owe includes penalty and interest we computed
     date of this notice.  If we receive your full payment by 04-13-
     we will stop penalty and interest charges.  Otherwise, we will
     continue to charge additional penalties and interest until the
     amount you owe is completely paid.

        We encourage you to send your payment to us today.  Make you
```

Figure 1.3 Sample IRS Form CP-503, Urgent—Payment Required (Continued)

Department of the Treasury
Internal Revenue Service

```
NUMBER OF THIS NOTICE:  CP-503
DATE OF THIS NOTICE:  04-03-95
TAXPAYER IDENT. NUM:
TAX FORM:  1040
TAX PERIOD:  12-31-93
```

> If too little tax is being withheld from your wages to pay the taxes you will owe at the end of the year, you should file a new Form W-4, Employee's Withholding Allowance Certificate, with your employer to change the amount of withholding.

> 2. ESTIMATED TAX PAYMENTS: If you don't pay your tax through withholding, or don't pay enough tax through withholding, you have to estimate the tax you will owe and make payments during the year directly to the IRS.

> If you need more information about changing your Form W-4 or making estimated tax payments, please call us today. Publication 505 explains both methods in detail. You may request forms and Publication 505 by calling 1-800-829-FORM.

> If you write to us or send additional information (including Form 9465, Installment Agreement Request), use the IRS address on the first page of this notice. Be sure to include your telephone number, the best time for us to call, and any necessary changes to our record of your name and address.

```
     KEEP THE PAGE(S) ABOVE FOR YOUR RECORDS          DETACH BELOW
---------------------------------------------------------------------
     Send this PAYMENT VOUCHER with your payment in the enclosed
     envelope.

                              28211-333-25835-4          9512
                        Number of this notice: CP503
          828 5201       Date of this notice: 04-03-95 9517
                        Taxpayer Identifying Number:
                            Form 1040      30  Tax Period 12-31-93


          30 0 9312 670 00000412157

                              AMOUNT YOU OWE.. $4,121.57
                              Subtract any payments you
                              believe we haven't received
                              ....................
                                  PAY THIS AMOUNT..
```

Figure 1.4 Sample IRS Form CP-504, We Intend to Levy

```
                                                        000157

                    P 900 960 375        ** IF YOU HAVE ANY QUESTIONS, **
     Department of the Treasury          ** REFER TO THIS INFORMATION: **
     Internal Revenue Service       NUMBER OF THIS NOTICE: CP-504
     ANDOVER, MA  05501             DATE OF THIS NOTICE: 04-24-95
                                    TAXPAYER IDENT. NUM:
                                    TAX FORM:  1040A
                                    TAX PERIOD: 12-31-92

        I..I..I..I.III...I..I....II...II.I...I.III.I..II...IIII.I


          FOR ASSISTANCE CALL:          716-685-5432 LOCAL BUFFALO
                                        1-800-829-1040 OTHER NY
                                        CALLER ID: 260855


              WE INTEND TO LEVY - RESPOND NOW
        * * * THE AMOUNT YOU OWE IS  $4,363.80          * * *
        - (AVOID ADDITIONAL INTEREST: PAY THIS AMOUNT IN FULL IN 10 DAYS.)

          THIS IS A FORMAL NOTICE OF OUR INTENT TO LEVY (SEIZE) YOUR
     PROPERTY, OR THE RIGHTS TO IT, TO PAY THE TAX YOU OWE.  WE
     PREVIOUSLY SENT YOU NOTICES REQUESTING THE FULL AMOUNT YOU OWE FOR
     THIS OVERDUE TAX, BUT HAVE YET TO RECEIVE IT.

          The    $4,363.80      you owe includes penalty and interest computed
     to the date of this notice.  If we receive your full payment by
     05-04-95, we will stop penalty and interest charges.  Otherwise, we
     will continue to charge additional penalties and interest until the
     amount you owe is completely paid.

          Send your full payment to us today.  Make your check or money
     order for the amount you owe payable to the Internal Revenue Service.
     Write your social security number or employer identification number
     on your payment.  Tear off the payment voucher stub from the end
     of this notice and send it with your payment in the enclosed
     envelope.

          If we don't receive your full payment by 05-24-95, we may levy
     your property without further notice to you.  This means the law
     allows us to take your property or rights to property such as real
     estate and personal property (for example, automobiles and business
     assets) to collect the amount you will owe on your tax account shown
     on the front page of this letter.  We may also take your wages,
     bank accounts, commissions and other income.  We have enclosed
     Publication 594, Understanding the Collection Process, which gives
     you additional information.

          We may file a Notice of Federal Tax Lien at any time to protect
     the government's interest.  A lien is a public notice to your
     creditors that the government has the right to the interest in
     your property, including property you acquire after we file the
     lien.  When there is a lien on your property, it may be difficult
     for you to obtain credit in the future or sell your property.
```

Figure 1.4 Sample IRS Form CP-504, We Intend to Levy (Continued)

000157

Department of the Treasury
Internal Revenue Service

NUMBER OF THIS NOTICE: CP-504
DATE OF THIS NOTICE: 04-24-95
TAXPAYER IDENT. NUM:
TAX FORM: 1040A
TAX PERIOD: 12-31-92

We don't want to take the actions described above. In fact, we prefer that you call us at the telephone number(s) that are shown on the front page of this notice to make arrangements to pay your taxes voluntarily. By working with us to resolve your tax problem, you can help us avoid the lien and levy actions outlined in this notice. However, if we don't hear from you, we will have no choice but to take these collection actions.

If you can't pay the amount you owe now, CALL US IMMEDIATELY at the number(s) shown on the first page of this notice. We want to help you resolve this bill -- don't delay!

If you think this bill is incorrect, or you want to know how we arrived at the amount you owe, CALL US at the number(s) on the first page of this notice and we can tell you.

If you believe that we didn't apply a payment you made to your account for this tax period, CALL US at the phone number(s) on the first page of this notice. When you call, have the following payment information available:

(1) IF YOU DEPOSITED THE PAYMENT DIRECTLY WITH THE IRS -
   - a copy of the front and back of your canceled check;
   - your money order receipt, the name and address of the issuing station with the amount and date of purchase; or the cash amount, date, and number on the cashier's receipt.

-- OR --

(2) IF YOU DEPOSITED THE PAYMENT WITH A BANK -
   - the deposit amount, the date of the deposit, and the name and address of the bank where you made the deposit.

THE AMOUNT YOU OWE IS $4,363.80
We figured this amount by adding:

Amount unpaid from prior notices	$4,325.42
Late payment penalty	$13.44
Interest	$24.94

The amount unpaid from prior notices may include tax, penalties, and interest you still owe IRS. It also should reflect any credits and payments we received from you since the last notice we sent you.

As of the date of this notice, the late payment penalty increases to 1% of the unpaid tax for each month or part of a month the payment

Figure 1.4 Sample IRS Form CP-504, We Intend to Levy (Continued)

```
                                          000157


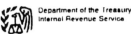  Department of the Treasury          NUMBER OF THIS NOTICE:  CP-504
                      Internal Revenue Service            DATE OF THIS NOTICE:    04-24-95
                                                          TAXPAYER IDENT. NUM:
              _____                                       TAX FORM:   1040A
                                                          TAX PERIOD:  12-31-92
              =====
```

is late up to a maximum of 25% of the unpaid tax.

The federal income tax is a "pay-as-you-go" tax. You must pay the tax as you earn or receive income during the year. There are two easy ways to do this:

1. WITHHOLDING: If you are an employee, your employer will withhold income tax from your pay. Tax is also withheld from other types of income -- including pensions, bonuses, commissions, and gambling winnings. In each case, the amount withheld is paid to the Internal Revenue Service in your name.

If too little tax is being withheld from your wages to pay the taxes you will owe at the end of the year, you should file a new Form W-4, Employee's Withholding Allowance Certificate, with your employer to change the amount of withholding.

2. ESTIMATED TAX PAYMENTS: If you don't pay your tax through withholding, or don't pay enough tax through withholding, you have to estimate the tax you will owe and make payments during the year directly to the IRS.

If you need more information about changing your Form W-4 or making estimated tax payments, please call us today. Publication 505 explains both methods in detail. You may request forms and Publication 505 by calling 1-800-829-FORM.

If you write to us or send additional information (including Form 9465, Installment Agreement Request), use the IRS address on the first page of this notice. Be sure to include your telephone number, the best time for us to call, and any necessary changes to our record of your name and address.

Figure 1.4 Sample IRS Form CP-504, We Intend to Levy (Continued)

000157

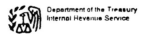

Department of the Treasury
Internal Revenue Service

```
                                    NUMBER OF THIS NOTICE:  CP-504
                                    DATE OF THIS NOTICE:  04-24-95
                                    TAXPAYER IDENT. NUM:
                                    TAX FORM:   1040A
                                    TAX PERIOD:
```

```
    KEEP THE PAGE(S) ABOVE FOR YOUR RECORDS          DETACH BELOW
--------------------------------------------------------------------
   Send this PAYMENT VOUCHER with your payment in the enclosed
envelope.
                                      ACR
            CAF        6020B   08254-472-64010-5          9515
       RPT              Number of this notice: CP504
  608 1601              Date of this notice: 04-24-95 9521
               Taxpayer Identifying Number:
                    Form 1040A     30   Tax Period 12-31-92

        30  0  9212  670  00000000000


                               $4,363.80
                 AMOUNT YOU OWE..
                 Subtract any payments you
                 believe we haven't received
                 ....................
                    PAY THIS AMOUNT..
```

Figure 1.5 IRS Form 668, Notice of Federal Tax Lien

Form 668 (Y) (c) (Rev. October 1993)	Department of the Treasury - Internal Revenue Service **Notice of Federal Tax Lien**	
District	Serial Number	*For Optional Use by Recording Office*

As provided by sections 6321, 6322, and 6323 of the Internal Revenue Code, we are giving a notice that taxes (including interest and penalties) have been assessed against the following-named taxpayer. We have made a demand for payment of this liability, but it remains unpaid. Therefore, there is a lien in favor of the United States on all property and rights to property belonging to this taxpayer for the amount of these taxes, and additional penalties, interest, and costs that may accrue.

Name of Taxpayer

Residence

IMPORTANT RELEASE INFORMATION: For each assessment listed below, unless notice of lien is refiled by the date given in column (e), this notice shall, on the day following such date, operate as a certificate of release as defined in IRC 6325(a).

Kind of Tax (a)	Tax Period Ended (b)	Identifying Number (c)	Date of Assessment (d)	Last Day for Refiling (e)	Unpaid Balance of Assessment (f)

Place of Filing

Total $

This notice was prepared and signed at _____ , on this,

the ____ day of _____ , 19 ____ .

Signature	Title

(NOTE: Certificate of officer authorized by law to take acknowledgments is not essential to the validity of Notice of Federal Tax lien
Rev. Rul. 71-466, 1971 - 2 C.B. 409)

Part 1 - Kept By Recording Office   Form 668 (Y) (c) (Rev. 10/93)

Multiple Matters

Some taxpayers have more than one matter that the IRS is concerned about. For our purposes, it doesn't matter how many different types of taxes you owe. If an Offer in Compromise program is accepted by the IRS, it will settle all tax debt for the individual who has submitted the offer so long as it is properly identified in the offer package (more on that later). However, for organizational reasons, keep each different matter's correspondence in a separate pile.

Types of Taxes Owed

Because not all tax liabilities may be assessed to you as an individual, it is important to recognize what type of tax the IRS claims you owe.

- *Personal income taxes* result from income you reported on your individual income tax return (Form 1040). You are fully and personally liable for such taxes and your assets are fair game when the IRS begins enforcement action to collect the taxes.
- *Corporate income taxes* result from income earned by a corporation. If you are a shareholder of this corporation, you are generally *not* personally liable for its tax debt to the IRS (including "matching" taxes for employees) so long as the corporation is legitimate.
- *Employment taxes* are those taxes deducted from employee paychecks and deposited with the government by the employer on behalf of the employee taxpayer. For officers, directors, shareholders, and others who are responsible for deducting the taxes and depositing them (known as "trust fund taxes"), the IRS may hold those individuals *personally* liable for those taxes. However, shareholders of a corporation who are not involved in such day-to-day operations as depositing employment taxes are generally *not* personally liable for the employment tax debt of a legitimate corporation.

Enforcement Mode: Where You Stand with the IRS

After you have collected the IRS correspondence and figured out what the IRS claims you owe, it is important to know where you stand with the IRS (see Figure 1.6). If you have already received your notice that the IRS will be filing a NFTL, but you have not been subject to any IRS enforcement procedures (such as levying your bank account), there is still time to submit an Offer in Compromise. It is very important to learn what the IRS can and cannot do after they have assessed you back taxes. Let's examine some of the IRS's alternatives.

Tax Lien

As we have seen earlier in this chapter, the first *enforcement* action the IRS will use is the federal tax lien provisions in the tax code. A lien is much different from a levy. A lien is simply a device used to protect the government's interest in your assets. A federal tax lien is known as a "secret" lien because this particular lien attaches to all of the taxpayer's property . This means that even though the lien is not yet recorded in the public record, the IRS has the right to step ahead of certain creditors and even the taxpayer! So if the IRS assesses you back taxes and you then sell your home, you can expect the IRS to be at the settlement table waiting for its cut of the money. Once the IRS has a federal tax lien in place, it will "perfect" the lien by filing the Notice of Federal Tax Lien (NFTL). "Perfection" is a legal concept that determines the order of priority of creditors. It is accomplished by filing a document with the appropriate government official. Once the IRS has perfected its lien by an NFTL, it becomes the highest priority creditor. The only exception to this is when a creditor has already perfected its lien in your property *before* the NFTL was filed. The most common example of such a creditor is the mortgage company that holds the lien on your home or the bank that holds a perfected security interest in a car you financed through it.

Tax Levy

A tax levy is the actual seizing of your assets to satisfy your back tax liability. A federal tax lien is the first step to using a levy. A levy is a particularly lethal weapon in the IRS's arsenal for collecting taxes. The levy commands a third party (such as your bank) to pay any money they are holding for you directly to the IRS.

Because the levy is such a powerful weapon, the tax code spells out certain procedures for the IRS before it can file a levy.

In order for the IRS to legally enforce a levy, first, two notices are required to be sent to you. The first notice is the actual notice of tax owed and demand for payment from the IRS. Generally, the IRS has already met this requirement by sending out the CP letters and/or a tax bill during the initial phase of your case (see above). The second notice required is the IRS's 30-day notice of its intention to levy. This notice formally sets in motion the levy procedure. The IRS will send notices to you and to any third parties who they believe may be paying you money (including your employer or banks) to inform all of you that the money must be paid to the government instead of to you. The notice spells out the tax due and contains an onerous message for any third party that refuses to honor the levy: personal liability. For example, if the local vice president at your bank decides not to honor the levy in order to not lose your business, the IRS can hold that person *personally liable* for the amount that was in your bank account that should have been turned over to the government. Obviously, most third parties honor IRS levies.

The notice of its intention to levy is the warning sign that the IRS has reached the end of its rope with your case. If you have simply ignored all of the notices, letters, and calls from the IRS about resolving the matter, the IRS will quickly act to levy your bank accounts and seize your property if necessary. This is why it is critical to file your Offer in Compromise *before* the IRS has begun such drastic enforcement measures. If the IRS already has seized property or levied bank accounts, you are going to have to file a petition for refund and the waiting time and frustration involved in a refund case are mind-boggling and expensive. If you have submitted an Offer in Compromise, generally the IRS will *not* take the drastic measures outlined above unless it suspects that the offer is merely a delaying tactic.

If the IRS has issued a levy and/or seized property from you, it is required to take certain administrative steps. The requirements are somewhat complex and you should consult a competent attorney or CPA to ensure that the IRS has properly followed the procedures and to initiate a refund suit (if appropriate).

Jeopardy Assessments

In theory, jeopardy assessments are designed to be used only in special circumstances when the IRS has a good faith belief that the taxpayer may be ready

CONSIDER THIS...

What the IRS Can Take to Satisfy Your Tax Debt

The laws that govern liens and property rights can vary greatly from state to state and because this book contains the laws of the majority of states, you should find a competent attorney or CPA to verify the laws in your state. Generally, here's what the IRS can and can't take (either by lien or levy) after it has assessed you back taxes.

- *Real property.* As a general matter, the IRS can place a lien on all of a taxpayer's real property, including the primary residence. If the property is owned jointly (known in legalese as "joint tenants" or "tenants in common"), the IRS lien only attaches to the taxpayer's interest in the property. If you are married and own the property jointly (known as "tenancy by the entirety"), your protection from the IRS lien is even greater. If the IRS assessed one or the other spouse back taxes, the IRS cannot file a lien on the entire property. However, if the tax assessment is against both you and your spouse (which is sometimes the case when a joint return is filed), the IRS may attach a federal tax lien to the entire marital property.

- *Salary and wages.* The IRS may levy your wages so long as it has met the notice and demand requirements in the tax code. This means that the IRS can notify your employer that you owe back taxes and that a percentage of your paycheck must be sent directly to the IRS to satisfy the tax liability. This includes compensation for services such as fees, commissions, bonuses, and the like. In order to levy wages on a continuing basis, the IRS will issue Form 668-W(c) to your employer. Once your employer receives this form, it must pay part of your wages to the IRS every pay period until the IRS notifies it otherwise.

- *Insurance policies and proceeds.* IRS liens attach to your life insurance policy and any cash value it may have. This includes anything that you own, regardless of whether or not you are the insured under the policy. Proceeds of a life insurance policy are generally not subject to attachment. Proceeds from a casualty insurance policy, however, are subject to attachment. This means, for example, if your car is damaged, the IRS will have a lien on any of the money the insurance company pays you.

- *Bank accounts.* IRS liens attach to your personal bank accounts, including shared accounts in a credit union. The lien also attaches to any deposits made after the date of the tax assessment. For joint accounts, how the account is formally titled is a critical distinction that may be the deciding factor in whether a tax lien attaches to that account. If the IRS lien is a result of an assessment against one of the owners/signers of the bank account, and the account requires both signatures, then the IRS lien does not attach. If, however, either of the two owners/signers of a joint bank account are allowed the unrestricted right to withdraw the funds from that account, then the IRS lien does attach and the bank account is subject to levy.

- *IRAs, pension plans, and Social Security benefits.* Technically, IRAs can be attached by an IRS lien. But the manual used by IRS employees for internal guidelines and procedures advises revenue officers against seizing IRA funds unless the taxpayer has flagrantly disregarded the IRS's request for payment. Be aware, however, that the manual is not the law and, in fact, the tax code permits the IRS to place a lien on and levy your IRA money. With some minor exceptions, pension plans and profit-sharing plans—such as a 401(k) or a Keogh—are all subject to an IRS lien attachment. Believe it or not, IRS liens also attach to most of your Social Security benefits.

- *Alimony and child support.* Alimony payments made to the taxpayer are subject to an IRS lien. Child support payments, however, are not subject to the lien because these payments are the property of the child and not the taxpayer parent.

- *Other types of assets.* IRS liens also attach to the following:

  - Licenses and franchise rights, as well as other intangibles such as trademarks and the like

  - Assets in custody of a court

  - Royalties

  - Inheritance proceeds (although some states do not recognize a tax lien in some inheritance contexts)

to flee the United States in order to avoid the IRS, or when the IRS believes the taxpayer may be moving assets outside of the United States. Normally the IRS must give several notices and jump through some procedural hoops before it can take any enforcement action. This procedure can be lengthy, taking months or even years before a tax assessment is effected. The tax code requires that all types of taxes require a 30-day waiting period between assessment and enforcement measures (such as a tax lien or levy). However, a "jeopardy" assessment allows the IRS to immediately collect all taxes owed without waiting the required 30 days. Unfortunately, as a recent case that was brought against the IRS revealed, overzealous agents have misused the jeopardy assessment procedure in order to harass a taxpayer who they believed to be particularly troublesome.

Using the Statute of Limitations to Your Advantage

In nearly every field of law, a deadline is set for the government (or plaintiff in a civil case) to take some action of enforcement. This is known as the statute of limitations and although the length of time varies from field to field, the law prescribes a certain time frame for certain actions. The tax code is no exception to that rule and the statute is perhaps the most powerful and least expensive method to stop the IRS from collecting back taxes.

Figure 1.6 Flowchart: Where You Stand with the IRS

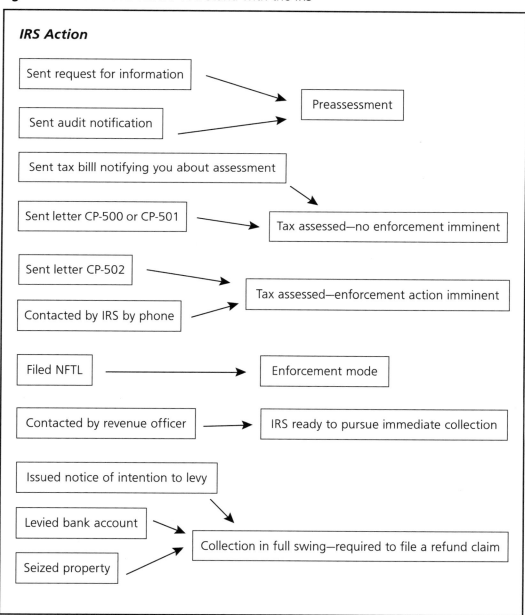

The tax code sets forth a general rule that taxes must be assessed within three years after the relevant return was filed. This means that if the IRS has assessed you back taxes, penalty, and interest more than three years after you filed the return, they cannot legally collect the tax owed. Although the IRS does have mechanisms in place to prevent a statute of limitations error, it does still happen that an agent will miss the statute of limitations deadline and the taxpayer benefits from this error immensely.

Check your correspondence for the date of assessment and which tax years are in question. If you think that the IRS is barred from collecting the tax because it missed the statute of limitations deadline, contact the person whose name is on the latest letter you have from the IRS. If he or she denies that the statute stops the IRS from collecting the tax, contact a tax attorney as soon as possible for clarification of the statute of limitations and possible legal action. One note of caution! The statute of limitations does not apply in cases where the IRS makes a good faith determination that you have purposefully attempted to evade paying taxes. In those cases, the statute of limitations generally cannot be raised as a defense.

Who's Who in the IRS: How, When, and Who to Contact at the IRS

The most important player in the collection process is the revenue officer. He or she has a broad range of authority and discretion in collecting accounts, but is also bound by the tax laws and the *Internal Revenue Manual.* Once you have been sent your notices advising you of the assessment, your local IRS service center eventually sends an internal form to the "field office" responsible for collecting taxes in your area. This office is where the revenue officers are located and eventually your case will be assigned to one of them.

Once assigned a case, the revenue officer has the authority to file a Notice of Federal Tax Lien (NFTL), to serve levies, and to seize property to collect unpaid taxes. Most important, the revenue officer has the authority to not institute collection activities. It is important to recognize the role of a revenue officer because he or she is the contact person with whom you will be dealing (almost exclusively) if your case is in the collection stage.

Revenue officers are supervised by a collection group manager. He or she is typically a senior revenue officer with a good amount of experience within the IRS. The group manager is actually stationed in the field with the revenue officers and is generally aware of most of the larger collection cases being worked on at any one time. As with any federal agency, there are multiple layers of supervision that roughly fall along the following lines:

Commissioner of Internal Revenue

↓

Regional Commissioner

↓

Assistant Regional Commissioner

↓

District Director

↓

Chief, Collection Division of District

↓

Branch Manager

↓

Collection Group Manager

↓

Revenue Officer

CONSIDER THIS...

Dealing with IRS Personnel

Many taxpayers have distorted views of the best way to deal with IRS agents and other IRS personnel. Your real advantage is acting in a professional, businesslike manner about your case. In general, IRS personnel deal with taxpayers, attorneys, and CPAs who are angry, aggressive, rude, and insulting during the course of phone and letter communication. Sometimes the anger is a legitimate response to aggressive or rude IRS agents. However, even if this attitude by the taxpayer is justified, it is foolish to antagonize the IRS when you are fighting to have your tax bill cut. Follow these guidelines when dealing with IRS personnel:

- Be courteous and polite, but do not engage in small talk. Most revenue officers have heavy caseloads and are usually anxious to resolve your case and move on to other matters.

- Tell the IRS agent that you are serious about resolving your tax bill as soon as possible. Many revenue officers become quickly annoyed at obvious delaying tactics. Your sincerity and cooperation (to a point) will benefit you greatly when it comes to the revenue officer's discretionary decisions.

- Don't overpromise what you can pay or when you can pay it. With the knowledge from this book, you may be able to settle with the IRS for pennies on the dollar. If you promise to pay the full amount, the IRS may interpret any other action you take (such as submitting your Offer in Compromise) as a sign of bad faith or even a delaying tactic.

- Keep phone contact to an absolute minimum. It is always better to have a letter from the IRS rather than an oral promise. If you don't understand what the IRS employee means, ask him or her (politely!) to put the request in writing.

- If an IRS agent contacts you by telephone (which usually means your case is in collection phase), start a phone log. Keep notes about your conversations and *always* record the name of the IRS employee with whom you spoke. Also, be sure to note the dates and times of the conversations and any deadlines a revenue officer has asked you to comply with.

- If any IRS employee informs you by letter or orally that you may be subject to a "criminal investigation" or mentions fraud, or if you are contacted by an IRS agent from the criminal investigation division (CID), immediately inform the IRS agent that you wish to consult with your attorney and that you will not make any statements until you have done so. *Cease all contact with the IRS and contact a qualified tax attorney as soon as possible!* If the IRS has begun a criminal investigation, you will need an attorney before corresponding with the IRS again.

- If you believe the IRS agent who is handling your case has it in for you, or his or her attitude is not professional, ask to speak to the agent's supervisor. Again, be courteous. Once you have the opportunity to speak, ask the supervisor to reassign your case to another agent and give a brief reason why you believe the revenue officer assigned to your case isn't playing fair. Most supervisors will transfer the case even if it's simply a personality clash between the taxpayer and the revenue officer.

DON'T FORGET...

✔ Collect all IRS correspondence and arrange by date.

✔ Determine whether the IRS is in "enforcement mode."

✔ Check to see if the statute of limitations has run out.

✔ Call the IRS if you cannot understand why you were sent a particular IRS letter.

File a Freedom of Information Act Request

Political consultants call it opposition research. Lawyers call it discovery. Whatever you wish to call it, the most valuable commodity in any negotiation is *information.* Let us now focus on Congress's attempt to give taxpayers open access by passing the Freedom of Information Act (FOIA).

The FOIA allows citizens to access all the information about them in the files of United States government agencies, including the IRS. This means that, with certain exceptions, any and all correspondence, reports, files, internal memos, videos, recordings, or other media that contain information about you is available for your review upon your request. It can take several months to get a response from the IRS. It is of utmost importance that you begin this process as early as possible so that the IRS has adequate time to act on your request before you submit your Offer in Compromise.

Below is a description of how an FOIA request is handled, followed by the specific steps to obtain your information.

What Happens at the IRS When It Receives Your FOIA Request

Once you have filed a request under the Freedom of Information Act, your request will be forwarded to an internal IRS department that is designed to handle all FOIA requests for that district. Often this internal FOIA office is overwhelmed, not so much by the number of requests, but by the volume of paperwork contained in files. Once your request is received in the FOIA office, it must be processed in accordance with federal statutes and regulations governing the disbursement of information.

An IRS employee of a fairly low rank (some federal agencies use college interns) sets the wheels in motion. First, all of the files and paperwork contained in your taxpayer file at the district office are gathered. Once that is completed, the FOIA officer is supposed to search the IRS's computer files for any printouts or other documents not kept in "hard copy" form in your taxpayer file. Finally, an internal notice is supposed to be sent to IRS headquarters in Washington, D.C. The FOIA office at IRS headquarters then checks to be sure that there are no files in any IRS office outside of your district office's jurisdiction. Any files that exist outside of your district's office are supposed to be sent to the FOIA officer who is processing your request.

But wait! The hard part has just begun. The Freedom of Information Act allows federal agencies to withhold certain documents if they fit into one of the FOIA exceptions. Most of the exceptions are very narrowly defined to ensure that the purpose of the act is not undermined by federal agencies that would use the exemptions to deny access to their files. The most general exception is that of attorney-client privilege. If any IRS personnel contacted any IRS lawyer (known in IRS jargon as "regional counsel") or any lawyer for the U.S. Department of Justice about your case, much of that correspondence is considered privileged and the IRS does not have to release that information to you. There also are some "compelling government interest" exceptions such as your discriminant function score (known as your "DIF" score) or factors that led to your audit. Confidential informants (which the IRS uses frequently) also are protected by the exception to the FOIA. As a result, an IRS supervisor will look through all of your taxpayer file and make a determination as to what is and is not exempt. If any questions arise along the way, the process is delayed further while the IRS supervisor consults IRS lawyers as to whether particular documents are exempt or should be released. As you will see in Figure 2.1, you are entitled to know if the IRS has exempted any documents and why.

Once all of the documents have been separated, copies generally are made for you. If your file is voluminous, the IRS will usually request that you come and mark which documents you want copied. In most cases, the IRS will make copies for you (sometimes you get charged for the copies and sometimes not) and send them to the address on your request.

Step-by-Step: How to File a Freedom of Information Act (FOIA) Request with the IRS

1. Call your local IRS district office (the telephone and fax numbers for each IRS district office are listed in the appendix) and ask for the name and title of the person who handles Freedom of Information Act requests. Usually that person is a "disclosure officer" and his or her office is located within the IRS district office.

2. Draft a letter based on the sample letter in Figure 2.1. Be sure to include a request for specific documents as that is a requirement of the act. Your temptation might be to send for all of the records in your taxpayer file, but this may delay the process significantly. You only need the documents related to the tax years for which the IRS claims you owe back taxes. Requesting your whole file will give you information you don't need and the IRS may take up to six months to process such a comprehensive request. If you file a narrower request, you may get the information back in as little as three weeks (but don't count on it).

3. Your Social Security number must be included in your request or it will be administratively rejected.

4. Mail the request via certified mail with a return receipt requested. The Freedom of Information Act requires the IRS to respond within a certain time frame. The return receipt will prove when the IRS received your request.

5. You need not enclose a fee for copying or searches. Although the act allows the government to charge fees for certain FOIA requests (such as when an FOIA request is used for commercial purposes), generally the IRS will not charge a search fee. It may charge copying costs, particularly when the copying is extensive. If there is a charge, it will bill you for the costs. In certain cases, you can even get an exemption from the copying costs. Call your district office's disclosure officer and request the guidelines for a waiver of FOIA costs.

6. In federal bureaucracies the squeaky wheel gets the oil, so telephone the disclosure officer two weeks after you send in your request. Make your initial call as friendly as possible, inquiring if the disclosure officer received your request and when you can expect a response. Ordinarily, he

or she will tell you that you should receive a response within four weeks from the date the IRS received the request. Wait two more weeks and call again. Be sure to speak to the same IRS employee as you did in your first call and again be pleasant about inquiring when you will receive the information you requested.

7. If you have waited six weeks from the date the IRS received your request, call again. You should inform the call taker in a businesslike manner that you have been patiently waiting for the FOIA request response for more than six weeks and you have not been contacted. Ask when the documents will be released and record the date. You may be inclined to threaten the person with a lawsuit or a call to the supervisor, but this rarely has its intended effect, so avoid the threats. Given the time it takes to litigate an FOIA lawsuit, your threats are not credible.

8. Wait one more week and if you still have no response, file an appeal using the sample letter in Figure 2.2. It sounds unusual to appeal something when nothing has been lost, but the act itself directs you to appeal if the IRS tries to stonewall you. Send the appeal via certified mail, return receipt requested, to the same person with whom you have been dealing.

What to Look For in Your IRS File

Getting a glimpse of your IRS taxpayer file may not be as productive as you may think. It is much like drilling for oil where expectations are high and finding that the well was dry. In many cases, you will learn nothing new about your case. But in some cases, an internal IRS memorandum can speak volumes about why the IRS is proceeding in a certain way. Also, the documents that the IRS holds back are generally more important than the ones they've given you. Pay attention to pertinent omissions. Here's what to look for:

- *Jeopardy assessment correspondence.* If you discover any correspondence that even hints that the IRS believes you are a "risk" taxpayer because you have the ability to leave the country quickly, examine the documents carefully. If you see buzz words such as "international," "passport," "flight risk," "frequently travels outside of the country," or the like, you may be seeing indications that the IRS is becoming worried that you may be a taxpayer who would flee the country along with your assets. This may mean

Figure 2.1 Sample Freedom of Information Act Request

January 2, 1998

SENT VIA CERTIFIED MAIL, RETURN RECEIPT REQUESTED

Tina Taxlady, Disclosure Officer
Internal Revenue Service
Philadelphia, PA 19000

RE: Freedom of Information Act Request of Thomas Taxpayer

Dear Ms. Taxlady:

I am requesting a copy of all of my files for tax years 1996 and 1997. This request is made under the Freedom of Information Act, 5 U.S.C.A. 552. Please adhere to the statutory deadlines imposed by the law to make determination within 10 days of your receipt of this letter.

The information you need for this request is:
Thomas T. Taxpayer
100 E. Main Street
Exton, Pennsylvania 19004
SS# 123-45-6789

If your determination results in any portions of my files being declared exempt, please identify the portions you determined to be exempt and explain the specific exemption provision which you used as a basis to determine that they are exempt. I am aware of my administrative appeal rights.

I am willing to pay the reasonable costs of copying and sending the documents. If those costs exceed $50, you should first call me to obtain permission to exceed the costs. Please send the documents to my address as listed above. I may be reached during the day at 215-555-1221.

Sincerely,

Thomas T. Taxpayer

Figure 2.2 Sample Appeal Letter

February 22, 1998

SENT VIA CERTIFIED MAIL, RETURN RECEIPT REQUESTED

Tina Taxlady, Disclosure Officer
Internal Revenue Service
Philadelphia, PA 19000

RE: Freedom of Information Act Appeal of Thomas Taxpayer

Dear Ms. Taxlady:

I am appealing a Freedom of Information Act denial based on a nonresponse from my letter of January 2, 1998, whereby I filed a Freedom of Information Act request. This appeal is made under 5 U.S.C.A. 552(a)(6).

I am enclosing a copy of my initial Freedom of Information Act request letter dated January 2, 1998, for your information. Additionally, I called on January 16, 1998, and spoke with Mr. Agent from your office. I called again on February 1, 1998, and spoke with Mr. Agent once again. To date I have not received any response to my request.

I requested all of my files for tax years 1996 and 1997. The information I provided was:

Thomas T. Taxpayer
100 E. Main Street
Exton, Pennsylvania 19004
SS# 123-45-6789

Please comply with the statutory time limit for a response to an appeal under the Freedom of Information Act of twenty (20) days.

If you do not comply with the act, I will be forced to instruct my attorney to file a Freedom of Information Act lawsuit. I will be more than happy to discuss this case with you. I may be reached during the day at 215-555-1221.

Sincerely,

Thomas T. Taxpayer

Enclosures: FOIA Request Letter

that you will be the target of a "jeopardy assessment," in which the IRS can clean out your bank accounts and attach a lien on all of your property without following procedures under the law or giving notice to you. It is supposed to be reserved for international tax criminals, but the IRS has used it in many other circumstances. While you may believe that you could not possibly be considered a candidate for a jeopardy assessment, you should take note of the story of a Colorado Springs woman who was victimized by an IRS jeopardy assessment. She was a mother and owner of a small children's clothing store; after a routine audit, she was subjected to a jeopardy assessment without warning. Eventually, the IRS gave back the money (because they had overassessed her to the tune of more than $300,000), but they never apologized for the improper assessment, stating that because the woman had a passport, that alone was enough to justify the assessment! This is wrong, of course, but the IRS doesn't like to admit that it is wrong. Eventually, a judge awarded the woman $350,000 in a verdict against the IRS (the largest award ever against the IRS!).

- *IRS memoranda.* Internal IRS memoranda are valuable for determining what the IRS thinks about your ability to pay tax and whether it believes there was any fraud committed. You may find that some portions of the memoranda are marked out with black marker on the basis that those particular portions of the document are exempt from the FOIA request. Do some detective work trying to reconstruct the deleted wording. It could tip you off to what the IRS is planning to do next. The IRS might have discovered something you didn't even think about, such as a trust fund that you will receive after the death of a relative or insurance proceeds that you may be entitled to in the next few months. Knowing what the IRS agent knows gives you a decided advantage when dealing with the IRS in general and when submitting an Offer in Compromise in particular.

- *Work papers.* If any IRS agent has performed calculations relating to your tax return, or if any agent has audited you, there should be a set of "work papers" used by the agent in determining your liability. These papers may be very useful to your CPA or tax lawyer in Step 3 when calculating your actual tax liability. You may or may not understand the figures and notes, but a good CPA or tax lawyer will. They often show the assumptions used by the agent when calculating your back tax liability. In order to figure your actual tax liability, it will be helpful to see what IRS assumptions were used.

CASE STUDY

The FOIA Advantage

Joanna filed a Freedom of Information Act request after she received a notice of back taxes assessed against her. She received her taxpayer file in approximately four weeks. While going through the file, she noticed the notes of the auditor who examined her tax return. He made an assumption that cost her $25,000 in unwarranted back taxes. She checked her original return and saw that she mistakenly omitted the income from proceeds from the sale of some of her stock on her tax return.

Rather than trying to find out what Joanna's "basis" was (i.e., how much she paid for the stock) in the asset, the IRS auditor simply assigned a zero basis. Because her basis was well above zero for the stock, the resulting tax liability was wrong. While she still owed some tax, the FOIA request opened Joanna's eyes to the fact that IRS auditors often use erroneous assumptions in their calculations. She called the auditor immediately and then followed up with information about her basis. The tax liability was reduced from $43,000 to $18,000.

Now that Joanna had come to an agreement with the IRS on how much was actually owed, she could proceed with the next steps to see if she qualified for the Offer in Compromise program.

Eventually she determined that she would submit an Offer in Compromise, and based on the offer and financial information she submitted, the IRS accepted her Offer in Compromise of $8,000 to satisfy the entire tax debt. Armed with the right information, her persistence, the FOIA request, and the Offer in Compromise, Joanna saved approximately $33,000 and avoided many sleepless nights. Even with the legal fees Joanna incurred (approximately $5,000) she still saved a significant amount over what she originally owed.

- *Criminal Investigation Division (CID).* If you discover any mention of the IRS's CID unit, stop reading and bring the entire file to a tax attorney immediately. The IRS has been known to miss withholding certain documents from you that will tip you that CID may be investigating your case. Again, this is a potentially serious matter, so contact a tax attorney as soon as possible. (See Step 3 for how to select a good tax professional.) If you don't know a tax attorney, ask your CPA for a referral.

DON'T FORGET...

✔ Call the IRS's district office in your area to find out the name and address of your FOIA disclosure officer.

✔ Write a FOIA request letter and send by certified mail.

✔ Seeking information as to the status of your request, telephone the disclosure officer at two-week intervals. If after these calls you do not have a response, file a letter of appeal.

✔ After receiving your file, examine it, looking in particular for the words *fraud, negligence,* and *criminal investigation.*

STEP 3

Figure Your Actual Tax Liability

The IRS uses several ways to determine if you have paid the appropriate amount of taxes. It is not the purpose of this book to detail advice for avoiding audits or how to prepare yourself for and defend yourself in an audit. There are many good books available on those subjects. Rather, this book helps you understand how the IRS assesses back taxes, and what you can do to correct IRS assumptions. The goal of this step is to come to a mutual understanding with the IRS on how much tax you actually owe. Armed with that information, you have the groundwork to cut your tax bill significantly through the Offer in Compromise program.

Computer Audits

The IRS is increasingly relying on computer audits. The computer simply matches the information you provided on your tax return to information supplied to the IRS by another party (such as your employer, a stock brokerage house, etc.). If information is missing from your return that was reported by the source of the income, the IRS will generally send you a CP-2000 notice, commonly known as a Notice of Proposed Changes to Your 19__ Tax Return (see Figure 3.1). Although the original purpose for this computer-matching method was to handle simple mistakes on your tax returns such as math errors, the program of computer matching (known by the IRS as the Information Return Program) has taken on a life of its own.

Figure 3.1 Sample CP-2000, Notice of Proposed Changes to Your Tax Return

SAMPLE CP-2000 NOTICE

DEPARTMENT OF THE TRE   RY
INTERNAL REVENUE SERVICE-UR

TYPE OF   TICE: CP-2000
DATE OF THIS NOTICE: 02/19
SOCIAL SECURITY NUMBER:
TAX FORM: 1040   TAX YEAR: 1989

PLEASE RESPOND TO THIS NOTICE
BY COMPLETING THE LAST PAGE
AND SENDING IT TO US IN THE
ENVELOPE PROVIDED.

FOR GENERAL INFORMATION
PLEASE CALL US AT:

1-800-829-1040

NOTICE OF PROPOSED CHANGES TO YOUR 1989 TAX RETURN

WE ARE PROPOSING CHANGES TO YOUR 1989 TAX RETURN BECAUSE THE INFORMATION ON YOUR TAX
RETURN IS NOT THE SAME AS THE INFORMATION REPORTED TO US BY YOUR EMPLOYERS, BANKS, AND
OTHER PAYERS.

PLEASE READ THIS NOTICE CAREFULLY. IT EXPLAINS WHAT YOU SHOULD DO IF YOU AGREE OR
DISAGREE WITH OUR PROPOSED CHANGES. PAGE 2 SHOWS THE PROPOSED CHANGES TO YOUR 1989
ACCOUNT. WE PROPOSE TO INCREASE YOUR TAX. IF YOU AGREE WITH THIS CHANGE, YOU WILL
OWE US $316.

PLEASE COMPARE YOUR RECORDS WITH THE PAYER INFORMATION SHOWN ON PAGE 3 OF THIS NOTICE.
IF YOU AGREE WITH THE PROPOSED CHANGES ON PAGE 2:
- CHECK BOX A ON THE LAST PAGE OF THIS NOTICE,
- SIGN AND DATE THE CONSENT TO THE TAX INCREASE,
- ENCLOSE YOUR PAYMENT IN FULL, IF POSSIBLE, AND MAKE YOUR CHECK OR MONEY ORDER
  PAYABLE TO THE INTERNAL REVENUE SERVICE, AND
- RETURN THE LAST PAGE OF THIS NOTICE ALONG WITH YOUR PAYMENT IN THE ENCLOSED
  ENVELOPE.

IF YOU DO NOT AGREE WITH THE PROPOSED CHANGES ON PAGE 2:
- CHECK BOX B OR C ON THE LAST PAGE OF THIS NOTICE,
- ENCLOSE A SIGNED STATEMENT EXPLAINING WHY YOU DISAGREE,
- INCLUDE ANY SUPPORTING DOCUMENTS YOU WISH US TO CONSIDER, AND
- USE THE ENVELOPE ENCLOSED TO RETURN THE LAST PAGE OF THIS NOTICE WITH YOUR
  STATEMENT AND DOCUMENTS. PLEASE INCLUDE A TELEPHONE NUMBER, INCLUDING AN AREA
  CODE, AND THE BEST TIME TO CALL YOU.

IT IS IMPORTANT THAT WE RECEIVE YOUR COMPLETED RESPONSE WITHIN 30 DAYS FROM THE DATE
OF THIS NOTICE. YOU HAVE 60 DAYS IF YOU LIVE OUTSIDE OF THE UNITED STATES. IF WE
DO NOT RECEIVE YOUR RESPONSE WITHIN THIS PERIOD, WE WILL ISSUE A NOTICE OF DEFICIENCY
TO YOU FOLLOWED BY A FINAL BILL FOR THE PROPOSED AMOUNT SHOWN ON PAGE 2. YOU MAY
CONTEST THE NOTICE OF DEFICIENCY IN COURT IF YOU BELIEVE YOU DO NOT OWE THE ADDITIONAL
TAX.

PLEASE RESPOND TO US EVEN IF YOU DO NOT UNDERSTAND OUR COMPUTATION OR CANNOT PAY THE
PROPOSED TAX DUE. IF YOU DELAY YOUR RESPONSE, INTEREST ON ANY AMOUNT YOU OWE WILL
INCREASE. INTEREST STOPS ONLY WHEN YOU PAY THE TOTAL AMOUNT YOU OWE. IF YOU SIGN THE
CONSENT TO TAX INCREASE, FULL PAYMENT IS DUE WITHIN 15 DAYS AFTER WE RECEIVE YOUR
SIGNED CONSENT. IF WE DO NOT RECEIVE YOUR PAYMENT BY THEN, WE WILL SEND YOU A BILL.
THIS BILL WILL INCLUDE YOUR TAX, ANY PENALTIES, AND ADDITIONAL INTEREST.

IF YOU AGREE WITH THE CHANGES WE PROPOSE, YOU DO NOT HAVE TO FILE AN AMENDED TAX
RETURN. HOWEVER, YOU SHOULD REVIEW YOUR RECORDS AND RETURNS FILED AFTER THE YEAR
IDENTIFIED IN THIS NOTICE, TO MAKE SURE YOU REPORTED ALL INCOME CORRECTLY.

IF YOU DID NOT REPORT ALL YOUR INCOME CORRECTLY, YOU SHOULD FILE AN AMENDED TAX RETURN
(FORM 1040X) FOR EACH YEAR, AND PAY ANY ADDITIONAL TAX AND INTEREST YOU OWE. IT IS TO
YOUR ADVANTAGE TO CORRECT YOUR TAX RETURNS AND PAY ANY ADDITIONAL TAX AND INTEREST
AS SOON AS POSSIBLE TO AVOID PENALTIES AND ADDITIONAL INTEREST.

THE ENCLOSED PUBLICATION 1383 CONTAINS DETAILED INFORMATION ABOUT HOW TO RESPOND TO
THIS NOTICE. PLEASE KEEP THIS NOTICE FOR YOUR RECORDS. THANK YOU FOR YOUR COOPERATION.

NOTE: WE SEND INFORMATION TO YOUR STATE AND LOCAL TAX AGENCIES ABOUT ANY INCREASE
OR DECREASE IN YOUR TAX AS A RESULT OF THIS NOTICE.

00001966

CP-2000 (REV. 7/91)

Figure 3.1 Sample CP-2000, Notice of Proposed Changes to Your Tax Return (Continued)

SAMPLE CP-2000 NOTICE

SERVICE CENTER   DO 94

OUR PROPOSED CHANGES TO YOUR 1989 INCOME TAX
(DETAILED INFORMATION FOR THESE CHANGES BEGINS ON PAGE 3)

CHANGED ITEM(S)	SHOWN ON RETURN	REPORTED TO IRS BY PAYERS	INCREASE OR DECREASE
TAXABLE WAGES	$ 91,875	$ 92,788	$ 913.00

PROPOSED CHANGES IN ADJUSTED GROSS INCOME

	SHOWN ON RETURN	PROPOSED AMOUNT	INCREASE OR DECREASE
MISCELLANEOUS DEDUCTION	$ 2,330	$ 2,312	$ 18.00
TOTAL INCREASE			$ 931.00

PROPOSED CHANGES IN TAX COMPUTATION

		SHOWN ON RETURN	PROPOSED AMOUNT	INCREASE OR DECREASE
1.	TAXABLE INCOME	$ 61,648.00	$ 62,579.00	$ 931.00
2.	TAX	13,238.00	13,499.00	261.00
3.	TOTAL TAXES	13,238.00	13,499.00	261.00
4.	NET TAX INCREASE..			261.00
5.	INCOME TAX WITHHELD	16,521.00	16,521.00	0.00
6.	INTEREST FROM 4/15/90 TO 15 DAYS AFTER THE DATE OF THIS NOTICE.......			55.00
7.	PROPOSED AMOUNT YOU OWE IRS...$			316.00

Figure 3.1 Sample CP-2000, Notice of Proposed Changes to Your Tax Return (Continued)

```
                                                         DO 94


AMOUNTS REPORTED TO IRS BUT NOT IDENTIFIED, FULLY REPORTED, OR CORRECTLY DEDUCTED ON
YOUR INCOME TAX RETURN FOR 1989.

   1. CHARLES SCHWAB & CO. INC.        ISSUED FORM W-2
                                       FOR TAXABLE WAGES              $       913
                                          SOCIAL SECURITY WITHHELD             68
      ACCOUNT NUMBER                      SOCIAL SECURITY WAGES              913
      EIN /4-1737782
                                                                           0002

                         EXPLANATION OF CHANGES

DISCLOSURE AUTHORIZATION STATEMENT

   IF YOU WISH TO AUTHORIZE SOMEONE, IN ADDITION TO YOU, TO DISCUSS THIS NOTICE
   WITH US, PLEASE SIGN AND DATE THE AUTHORIZATION STATEMENT ON THE LAST PAGE OF THIS
   NOTICE.  ALSO INCLUDE THE NAME AND ADDRESS OF THE PERSON YOU AUTHORIZE.

   THE PERSON YOU CHOOSE MAY ONLY GIVE AND RECEIVE INFORMATION ABOUT THE TAX YEAR IN THIS
   NOTICE.  HE OR SHE CANNOT SIGN FOR YOU, OR REPRESENT YOU IN AN INTERVIEW OR IN
   U.S. TAX COURT.  IF WE NEED MORE INFORMATION, WE WILL ASK FOR IT THROUGH THE PERSON
   YOU CHOSE.  PLEASE HAVE THAT PERSON:
        - WRITE TO US AT THE ADDRESS SHOWN ON THIS NOTICE,
        - SEND ANY SUPPORTING DOCUMENTS TO US, AND
        - GIVE US A TELEPHONE NUMBER, INCLUDING AN AREA CODE, AND THE BEST TIME TO CALL.

   YOU MAY CHANGE OR CANCEL YOUR AUTHORIZATION BY SENDING A SIGNED STATEMENT TO THE RETURN
   ADDRESS ON THIS NOTICE.  PLEASE STATE THE TAX YEAR FOR WHICH YOU WISH TO CHANGE OR
   CANCEL YOUR DISCLOSURE AUTHORIZATION.

   YOUR STATEMENT SHOULD INCLUDE THE NAME, ADDRESS, AND TELEPHONE NUMBER OF THE PERSON WHO
   WILL NO LONGER BE AUTHORIZED TO DISCUSS THIS NOTICE AND THE NAME, ADDRESS, AND TELEPHONE
   NUMBER OF ANY NEW PERSON YOU ARE AUTHORIZING.

MISIDENTIFIED INCOME

   IF ANY OF THE INCOME SHOWN ON THIS NOTICE IS NOT YOURS:
   - SEND US THE NAME, ADDRESS, AND SOCIAL SECURITY NUMBER OF THE PERSON WHO RECEIVED THE
     INCOME, OR SEND US A COPY OF THE INCOME TAX RETURN WHERE THE INCOME WAS REPORTED,
     IF YOU HAVE IT,
   - CHECK BOX B OR C ON THE LAST PAGE OF THIS NOTICE,
   - RETURN YOUR SUPPORTING DOCUMENTS AND THE LAST PAGE OF THIS NOTICE IN THE ENCLOSED
     ENVELOPE.

CHILDREN'S INCOME

   IF THE INCOME BELONGS TO YOUR MINOR CHILD AND THE LAW DOES NOT REQUIRE YOUR CHILD TO
   FILE AN INCOME TAX RETURN:
   - SEND A SIGNED STATEMENT TO US EXPLAINING THIS, AND
   - NOTIFY THE PAYERS TO CORRECT THEIR RECORDS TO SHOW THE NAME AND SOCIAL SECURITY NUMBER
     OF THE PERSON WHO ACTUALLY RECEIVED THE INCOME, SO THAT FUTURE REPORTS TO US ARE
     ACCURATE.

INTEREST PERIOD

   INTEREST HAS BEEN FIGURED FROM APRIL 15, 1990 TO 15 DAYS AFTER THE DATE OF THIS NOTICE
   ON THIS PROPOSED CHANGE ONLY.  IF A FULL PAYMENT WAS RECEIVED, INTEREST IS FIGURED FROM
   APRIL 15, 1990, TO THE DATE OF THE PAYMENT.  WE ARE REQUIRED TO CHARGE INTEREST AS
   PROVIDED BY LAW, ON THE UNPAID TAX FROM THE DUE DATE OF THE RETURN, TO THE DATE THE TAX
   IS PAID.

MISCELLANEOUS DEDUCTIONS PERCENTAGE LIMITATION

   YOU CAN ONLY CLAIM YOUR MISCELLANEOUS DEDUCTIONS THAT ARE OVER 2% OF YOUR ADJUSTED
   GROSS INCOME ON LINE 31 OF YOUR TAX RETURN.  WE REFIGURED YOUR MISCELLANEOUS
   DEDUCTIONS BECAUSE WHEN YOUR ADJUSTED GROSS INCOME CHANGED, YOUR 2% LIMIT CHANGED.

                         PAGE   3

                                                        CP-2000
```

Figure 3.1 Sample CP-2000, Notice of Proposed Changes to Your Tax Return (Continued)

SAMPLE CP-2000 NOTICE

```
                                              1989    DO 94              02/19/92
                                              FSC
   290*00261/8u6*    /764*    0*    /170*    /310*    /IN  .0055/680*    /   *   /

              RESPONSE TO OUR PROPOSED CHANGES TO YOUR 1989 INCOME TAX
            PLEASE COMPLETE THE SECTION BELOW THAT APPLIES TO YOU AND RETURN THE ENTIRE PAGE
   IN THE ENVELOPE WE ENCLOSED.  BE SURE THE INTERNAL REVENUE SERVICE ADDRESS SHOWS
   THROUGH THE WINDOW.  IF YOU ARE MAKING A PAYMENT WITH THIS NOTICE, WRITE THE AMOUNT
   OF YOUR PAYMENT ON THIS LINE $_____.  PLEASE MAKE YOUR CHECK OR MONEY ORDER
   PAYABLE TO THE INTERNAL REVENUE SERVICE.

                                    CHECK ONE

   A) [ ]   TOTAL AGREEMENT, CONSENT TO TAX INCREASE - I CONSENT TO THE IMMEDIATE ASSESSMENT
            AND COLLECTION OF THE INCREASE IN TAX AND PENALTIES SHOWN ON THIS NOTICE, PLUS
            INTEREST.  I UNDERSTAND THAT BY SIGNING THIS WAIVER, I WILL NOT BE ABLE TO
            CONTEST THESE CHANGES IN THE U.S. TAX COURT FOR THE TAX YEAR SHOWN ON THIS
            NOTICE UNLESS ADDITIONAL TAX IS DETERMINED TO BE DUE FOR THIS YEAR.


   _____   SIGNATURE                          DATE        SPOUSE'S SIGNATURE
                                                           (REQUIRED IF YOU FILED A JOINT RETURN)

   _____

   B) [ ]   PARTIAL AGREEMENT WITH PROPOSED CHANGES - I AGREE TO A PORTION OF THE PROPOSED
            CHANGES TO MY INCOME, DEDUCTIONS, TAXES AND/OR CREDITS SHOWN ON THIS NOTICE.
            I HAVE ATTACHED A SIGNED STATEMENT EXPLAINING WHICH ITEMS I DISAGREE WITH AND
            WHY I DISAGREE, ALONG WITH MY SUPPORTING DOCUMENTS.


   C) [ ]   TOTAL DISAGREEMENT WITH PROPOSED CHANGES - I DISAGREE WITH ALL OF THE PROPOSED
            CHANGES ON THIS NOTICE.  FOR EACH PROPOSED CHANGE, I HAVE ATTACHED A SIGNED
            STATEMENT AND SUPPORTING DOCUMENTS EXPLAINING WHY I DISAGREE.


                                AUTHORIZATION STATEMENT
   IF YOU WISH TO AUTHORIZE SOMEONE, IN ADDITION TO YOU, TO DISCUSS THIS NOTICE WITH THE
   INTERNAL REVENUE SERVICE, PLEASE SIGN BELOW.
   I AUTHORIZE_____
                       NAME                           ADDRESS
   TO GIVE AND RECEIVE INFORMATION FROM THE INTERNAL REVENUE SERVICE ABOUT THIS NOTICE.


   _____                    _____
            SIGNATURE OF TAXPAYER                                        DATE
                                                                              CP-2000
   ..........................................................................................
                                PLEASE DO NOT DETACH

                   PLEASE BE SURE OUR ADDRESS SHOWS THROUGH THE WINDOW




   123283928 XY ALEX 30 0 8912 640 00000031600

            I..,III.I.II..I..I.I..III.II..,IIIII.I.,I.II.I.II..III..,IIII.I

   INTERNAL REVENUE SERVICE




                                PAGE   4

                                                                     CP-2000
```

Unfortunately, these automatic adjustments are notorious for being wrong. A national publication reported that up to 50 percent of CP-2000 notices contain errors. Most commonly, the errors result from the IRS computers looking for income reported on your return to match a Form 1099, and because the taxpayer simply entered the income information in the wrong box on the return, the IRS computers spit out an automatic, but erroneous, adjustment.

Receiving this notice can be upsetting. Often, the CP-2000 notice assesses back taxes, interest, and penalties, and gives only a vague explanation of why the IRS assessed more tax. You have 30 days to respond.

To figure your actual tax liability, check the section of the CP-2000 (usually page 3) that starts "AMOUNTS REPORTED TO IRS BUT NOT IDENTIFIED, FULLY REPORTED, OR INCORRECTLY DEDUCTED ON YOUR INCOME TAX RETURN FOR [Year]." This will generally give the source of the information reporting your income and what form was filed that conflicts with your income tax return. Compare that information to your tax return for the year in question. Do your own matching program and see if the IRS computers looked in all of the right places for your income. Gather all of your Form 1099s and W-2s and try to resolve the discrepancy. Then turn back to the CP-2000 notice section beginning "OUR PROPOSED CHANGES TO YOUR [Year] TAX RETURN" (usually page 2 of the notice), and compare the "PROPOSED CHANGES IN TAX COMPUTATION" to your return.

If you figure out the discrepancy, you will have arrived at one of two conclusions:

1. you owe the tax because you didn't report it properly (or at all); or
2. the IRS has made a mistake and you either do not owe any tax or do not owe all of the tax the IRS claims you owe. Before you pursue an Offer in Compromise program, you must come to an agreement with the IRS about how much tax you actually owe. If the CP-2000 notice is correct and you owe the tax, you should still recheck your return to see if you missed any deductions to which you may have been entitled. If the CP-2000 notice is wrong, respond immediately. You will lose your rights to disagree with the IRS computer if you don't respond within 30 days.

If you are to be successful in having your tax bill cut through the Offer in Compromise program, you must come to a mutual agreement on how much tax is owed. The only exception is when the IRS has taken an unreasonable position on a certain deduction. In those rare cases, your offer will be based on doubt as to liability.

Step-by-Step: Correcting Your CP-2000 Notice

1. Fill out the final page of the CP-2000 notice and check the appropriate box. In this case you'll check either "B" (I agree to a portion of the proposed changes) or "C" (I disagree with all of the proposed changes).
2. Photocopy the entire CP-2000 notice and write a letter explaining why the adjustment is wrong. Keep it brief and to the point and attach copies (never originals) of any supporting material to your letter. The letter should contain:

   - Your name (and your spouse's name if the liability is from a joint tax return), your address, and your Social Security or tax identification number.
   - A brief statement of where the IRS erred. For math errors, show how you calculated the amounts and on what data you based your numbers. For matching errors, include a copy of the matching form that will show the IRS its error and explain why there is a discrepancy (e.g., my employer reported my wages incorrectly).
   - Any necessary documentary support for each statement, such as letters of correction from your employer, an amended Form 1099, and the like.
   - A final statement requesting specific action. Use the IRS term *abate* when requesting that your tax bill be adjusted downward. Also, if your calculations show that you still owe back taxes, but not the amount by which the IRS computer adjusted the return, state the amount you believe you owe.
   - Your signature and the date on the letter that includes a phone number where the IRS can reach you during the day.
3. Send your letter, a copy of the CP-2000 notice, and any supporting documentation to the IRS service center listed on the CP-2000 notice (usually your local service center) by certified mail with a return receipt requested.
4. If you get another notice or additional letters from the IRS after you have sent in your dispute letter, don't be alarmed. It sometimes takes several months for your dispute letter to be entered into the IRS computers. If the notices continue after 60 days, simply resend your correspondence to the IRS with a brief cover note stating, "This was sent to the IRS on [date sent] and I am still receiving notices to respond," with your signature and date.

CASE STUDY

Disputing an Adjustment to Your Tax Return

Two years ago, Richard worked as a police officer in a local municipality. In addition to his duties as a police officer, Richard also worked at the local hospital two nights a week as a security guard. The hospital would pay Richard as an independent contractor and would send him a check every month without withholding for taxes. One year ago, Richard left the police department and entered another profession. Because his new job required him to move, Richard never got the Form 1099 sent to him by the hospital. By the time Richard filed his tax return, he forgot all about the hospital income and omitted it from his tax return.

This year Richard received a CP-2000 notice from the IRS stating that he owed back taxes and penalties based on unreported income from the hospital in the amount of $25,000. Although he did not have the Form 1099 that the hospital sent, Richard dug up his check stubs from the hospital and totaled them up. By his calculations, the hospital only paid him $15,000.

Richard wrote the following letter:

August 1, 1998

IRS ADJUSTMENTS
IRS Service Center, Philadelphia, PA 19000

Dear Sir/Madam:
    I received your notice dated [date] adjusting my account to assess $25,000 in additional income for tax year 1996. The notice is wrong. The hospital only paid $15,000 to me in tax year 1996. The hospital never sent me a Form 1099, but I am enclosing copies of all check stubs that the hospital sent to me during tax year 1996. The total is $15,000.

Kindly abate all taxes, penalties, and interest you have proposed as a result of this error. I may be reached at 215-555-1234 during the day.

Sincerely,

Richard _____

(SS# 197-11-2940)

Enclosed: IRS notices
           Pay stub copies

Other Audit Methods

Depending on the amount of tax owed and the complexity of your tax return, the IRS may utilize one of several methods to audit you. These include a mail audit, an office audit (where you bring your records to a local IRS service center), and field audits (where the IRS comes to your office or home). After the audit, the IRS will send you an examination report. Your careful attention to the details of the examination report is critical to determining to figure out your actual tax liability. Again, the goal here is not necessarily to cut your tax bill (that's for later), but rather to agree with the IRS about how much you actually owe in back taxes.

Generally your examination report will be mailed to you in one package containing three parts:

1. A standard cover letter describing your options within 30 days of the report
2. IRS Form 1902-B, Report of Individual Tax Examination Changes
3. IRS Form 886-A, Explanation of Items

Carefully look at each item "changed" on your Form 1902-B (see Figure 3.2). Each row of entry has an "explanation number" (an internal IRS code for a

Figure 3.2 Sample Examination Report

SAMPLE EXAMINATION REPORT

Report of Individual Income Tax Examination Changes						Department of the Treasury — Internal Revenue Service

| Name of Taxpayer | | Year 19 | Form 1040 | Filing Status Single | In Reply Refer To: OOO IRS 222 | |
| Authorized Representative | | Date of Report | | Social Security Number :123-456-7890 | Examining District 000-00 | |

Income and Deduction Amounts Adjusted

Explanation Number (See attached)	Item Changed	Amount Shown on Return or as Previously Adjusted	Corrected Amount of Income or Deduction	Adjustmer Increase (Decrease)
6102	Net Operating Loss	23226	0	23226
5605	Sch-C Rentals Loss	13757	0	13757
5605	Sch-C Acting Loss	17246	0	17246
0101	Gross Receipts Rentals	—	—	—
0101	Gross Receipts Acting	—	—	—
8203	S.E. Tax	—	—	—
8138	Negligence	—	—	—
8120	Substantial Understatement	—	—	—

A. Adjustment in income and deductions — increase (decrease) (See explanation of adjustments attached.)		54229
B. Adjusted gross or taxable income shown on return or as previously adjusted		17660
C. Corrected adjusted gross or taxable income		71889
D. Tax figured	Tax Rate Schedule	16261
E. Tax credits (general business, child and dependent care, foreign, etc.) (If adjusted, see explanation attached.)		—
F. Other taxes (self-employment, alternative minimum, tax from recapture of investment credit, etc.) (If adjusted, see explanation attached.)	S.E. Tax	667
G. Corrected tax (line D less line E plus line F)		16928
H. Tax shown on return or as previously adjusted		4197
I. Deficiency (increase in tax before credit adjustments—line G less line H)		12731
J. Overassessment (decrease in tax before credit adjustments—line H less line G)		—
K. Adjustments to prepayment credits		—
L. Balance due — this does not include any interest charges (line I or J as adjusted by line K)		12731
M. Overpayment—this does not include any interest due you (line I or J as adjusted by line K)		—
N. Penalties, if any (See explanation attached.)	Negligence 3.6653 (a)(1) 636.55 Substantial Understatement 3 6661 =	3182.86

Although this report is subject to review, you may consider it as your notice that your case is closed if you are not notified of an exception to these findings within 45 days after a signed copy of the report or a signed waiver, Form 870, is received by the District Director. If you agree, please sign one copy of this report, and return it in the enclosed envelope. Keep the other copy with your records.

Consent to Assessment and Collection - I do not wish to exercise my appeal rights with the Internal Revenue Service or to contest in the United States Tax Court the findings in this report. Therefore, I consent to either:
(1) The immediate assessment and collection of the balance due shown on Line L, plus any interest due on this tax, and also any penalties shown on line N, or
(2) The overpayment shown on line M, plus any interest and adjusted by penalties shown on line N.

Your signature	Date	Spouse's signature, if a joint return was filed	Date
(See notices on the back)			Form 1902-B (Rev. 1-87)

Figure 3.2 Sample Examination Report (Continued)

SAMPLE EXAMINATION REPORT

FORM 886-A (REV APRIL 1968)	EXPLANATION OF ITEMS	SCHEDULE NO. OR EXHIBIT A
NAME OF TAXPAYER		YEAR/PERIOD ENDED

6102 You did not sustain a net operating loss in the tax year within the meaning of section 172 of the Internal Revenue Code because your loss was attributable solely to non-business expenses. Therefore, there is no net operating loss carryback or carryover, and your deduction claimed is disallowed. Taxable income is increased accordingly.

0101 Although not adjusted Gross Receipts are an open audit issue.

8203 We have adjusted your self-employment tax due to a change in your net profit from this self employment

5605 Since you did not establish that the business expense shown on your tax return was paid or incurred during the taxable year and that the expense was ordinary and necessary to your business we have disallowed the amount shown

DEPARTMENT OF THE TREASURY - INTERNAL REVENUE SERVICE

* U.S. GOVERNMENT PRINTING OFFICE 1980 381-561/5160

FORM 886-A (REV. 4-68)

Page____

Figure 3.2 Sample Examination Report (Continued)

SAMPLE EXAMINATION REPORT

FORM 886-A (REV APRIL 1968)	EXPLANATION OF ITEMS	SCHEDULE NO. OR EXHIBIT B
NAME OF TAXPAYER		YEAR/PERIOD ENDED

8138 Since all or part of the underpayment of tax you were required to show on your return is due to negligence or intentional disregard of rules and regulations, you are being charged a penalty under Internal Revenue Code Section 6653(a). For tax returns due, without regard to extensions, after December 31, 1988, this penalty is 5% of the underpayment. The interest on the penalty is calculated according to Internal Revenue Code Section 6601(e)(2)(B) from the due date of the return (including extensions) until the additional tax is paid.

8120 Since there is a substantial understatement of income tax you are liable for a penalty of 25 percent of the amount of any underpayment attributable to such understatement. This applies to tax not assessed prior to October 21, 1986. In addition, interest is figured on the penalty from the due date of the return (without regard to extensions). See Internal Revenue Code Section 6661 and 6601(e)(2).

DEPARTMENT OF THE TREASURY · INTERNAL REVENUE SERVICE   FORM 886-A (REV. 4-68)
*U.S. GOVERNMENT PRINTING OFFICE 1989 381-561/5140   Page____

particular change), then the box next to it that gives a brief description of the item that was changed. The three final boxes in each row show what you reported, then what the IRS claims is correct, then the adjustment made. Compare your tax return and supporting documents to the IRS's changes. What exactly did IRS change ? Look for the IRS to be obsessed with the following:

1. Home office deductions
2. Independent contractor versus wage employee deductions
3. Business expenses that could be construed as personal expenses
4. Asset sales
5. Real estate rental income and deductions

Most back taxes are assessed in these five categories, and the IRS auditor examining your return will generally not give you the benefit of the doubt in these cases.

Recheck the numbers in items A through N on the Report of Individual Income Tax Examination Changes. This section is a minitax return and sometimes the IRS auditor will make a simple math error in this section. If you realize that the IRS examination report has touched on something legitimate (such as failing to disclose income or an improper deduction), you are generally better off using that back tax assessment amount as your "actual tax liability."

IRS Form 1902-B is accompanied by a narrative report that details the auditor's findings. It is organized according to the IRS internal code numbers found on Form 1902-B as the explanation number. Examine these explanations to be sure that the auditor understands the situation correctly. This is easier than it sounds because the auditor will generally keep the comments brief and to the point without giving weight to your view of the adjustment.

If you find that the adjustment was unwarranted, you should call the auditor and tell him or her what findings you disagree with and what additional proof you intend to offer that may change the report. You may request an appointment with the auditor or you may mail in the additional documentation. If you still cannot get the problem resolved, call the auditor's supervisor. Do not get into auditor-bashing, as the auditor's supervisor will then be placed in the position of defending his or her employee's actions. Rather, get to the point and have your case ready to present. In any case, if you are ultimately unsuccessful, you will have to make a judgment as to whether it is worth the time and expense to appeal the audit through the IRS's appeals unit or in U.S. Tax Court.

CONSIDER THIS...

Your Second Bite at the Apple

While you may dread the notion of being assessed back taxes, there may be a silver lining to that cloud: adjustments in your favor! After your auditor has completed the review, bring up your adjustments. Check your tax return for some of the most commonly missed deductions:

1. Fees for preparation of your return by a CPA or tax preparer
2. Cleaning and laundry when traveling
3. Employee's moving expenses
4. Employment agency fees
5. Gambling losses to the extent of gambling gains
6. Depreciation of home computers used for business
7. Hearing aids
8. Mortgage prepayment penalties
9. Points on a home mortgage
10. Theft or embezzlement losses
11. Worthless stock or securities
12. Penalty on early withdrawal of savings
13. Fees for safe deposit boxes to hold investments (securities)
14. Unreimbursed business expenses such as cellular phones
15. Self-employment tax

Do You Need a Tax Professional?

If you receive a notice that you have been selected for an audit, it is always a good idea to sit down with a qualified tax professional to go over the nitty-gritty of your return. Having a CPA check your work is a less expensive alternative to hiring your CPA to handle the "nuts and bolts" of putting together your Offer in

Compromise. I always recommend having a good tax professional looking over your shoulder, but if you are in any of the following circumstances, a tax professional is not just a good idea, it's a must.

- Your return is complex or deals with an emerging area of tax law.
- You are self-employed and take a large number of business deductions.
- You believe that you committed a tax crime or tax fraud.
- You failed to file a return for the year being audited.
- IRS agents have mentioned the word *fraud* or *negligence*.
- You have been contacted by the IRS's Criminal Investigation Division (even if just by phone).
- You filed a gift tax return, took a home office deduction, or sold a major asset during the year being audited.

There are several different types of tax professionals from which to choose. Here's a rundown:

- *Certified public accountant (CPA).* A CPA is probably the most qualified person to review your tax return for mistakes or adjustments. CPAs are well versed in tax law (particularly income taxes), and often have an edge when it comes to spotting potential IRS inconsistencies during the audit. CPAs are required to have taken a certain level of college courses in accounting and are then tested in a series of fairly grueling examinations. Once they have passed the CPA exam, CPAs are required to earn continuing professional education credits.
- *Tax attorneys.* Tax attorneys are also well versed in tax law and deal with the IRS often. If the IRS has mentioned the word *fraud* or *illegal* or you have received any calls from a special agent in the IRS's Criminal Investigation Division (CID), you need to consult a tax lawyer as soon as possible. Perhaps the biggest advantage that tax lawyers have over other professionals is the protection of attorney-client privilege. Anything you say to your attorney is confidential and that attorney cannot be compelled to testify against you. While there are rumblings in Congress about extending that same privilege to CPAs, for now attorneys are the only tax professionals to which the privilege extends.
- *Accountants and enrolled agents.* These tax professionals are ones who have had some training in the tax laws, but generally do not have the depth to be able to flush out complicated tax situations. Enrolled agents are

tested and certified by the IRS (a great many enrolled agents are former IRS agents), but it is difficult to verify any of their credentials (some are not college graduates, for example), and you may end up with a marginal enrolled agent looking at your tax returns. Don't assume because the enrolled agent is a former IRS agent that he or she possesses some magical power to unlock IRS mysteries. There is very little help afforded to former agents by current agents.

Step-by-Step: Finding a Tax Professional

1. Ask your colleagues at work, or others in the community, for a recommendation. Generally, try to get a recommendation from those who use professionals on a regular basis. If you are in a small business, ask your business lawyer for a referral. Financial planners, real estate brokers, and non-tax-attorneys are often the very best source for finding a good candidate. Do not pick a candidate based on his or her ads in the yellow pages. These ads are virtually unregulated and reveal virtually nothing about a particular professional.

2. Compose a list of three candidates and phone each of them for a ten-minute conversation. Make it clear that you are looking for a tax professional to assist you in the review, preparation, and filing of your tax return and ask what his or her hourly rate is. Most CPAs charge between $90 and $200 per hour, while tax lawyers will charge slightly higher fees. Ask how long each has been practicing and how long with his or her current employer (this flushes out job jumpers). Be aware, however, that CPAs and tax attorneys are very busy from mid-January through April 15. If you need to speak with a CPA during that period, be brief and patient when waiting for a return phone call.

3. Select a candidate based on his or her experience, stability, and general attitude. You should also take into account the professional's hourly rate, but don't let that be the sole factor. In selecting a professional, you very often get what you pay for.

4. Once you have selected your professional, mail in your documents for review before your meeting, and then schedule an appointment with him or her. This will save you and your tax professional time reading your return during your meeting.

5. Before you begin to discuss your tax return, get a fee agreement hammered out. One of the most difficult subjects to discuss with any professional is fees. But it is critical for you to understand what the professional's hourly rate will be and approximately how many hours he or she will spend working on your project. This will avoid surprises at the end of the month when the bill arrives.

Once you have finished calculating how much you owe the IRS, and you and the IRS agree on the amount owed, you have taken a giant step towards resolving your past tax debt for good and for pennies on the dollar through the Offer in Compromise program.

D O N ' T   F O R G E T . . .

✔ Check any notices from the IRS marked "CP-2000" for what the IRS believes your tax liability to be.

✔ Compare the information the IRS gives you with your own tax return for the year(s) in question.

✔ Write a letter to the IRS to explain the difference (if any) between the two numbers and request an adjustment in taxes owed.

✔ Select and contact a tax professional if your return is complicated or if you have been assessed a negligence penalty.

Protect Your Assets

Now that you have determined exactly what the IRS claims you owe it and now that you figured your actual tax liability, it is important to take some intermediate steps until you are able to submit your Offer in Compromise package. First, let's take a closer look at the IRS revenue collection process.

The Collection Process

If you owe the IRS money, you're not alone. According to the government, between 15 and 20 percent of taxpayers owe back taxes at any one time. Add the number of people who never file tax returns at all, and as many as 40 percent of the American population may owe back taxes. Generally, you file your tax return every year and pay what you have calculated your tax to be. There are some very legitimate (and some not so legitimate) reasons why taxpayers owe back taxes.

If you prepared and filed a return, you ended up with a back tax bill for one of the following reasons:

1. *Audit.* The IRS found that you did not pay the correct amount of tax because of a disallowed deduction, credit, or math error. This is the most common reason you end up with a back tax assessment, but if you let the appeal time pass or you signed the audit report, your back tax bill is now

a fact and you must either settle it through the Offer in Compromise program, pay it in full, or enter into an installment agreement. If you fail to pay your back tax bill voluntarily, the IRS will eventually seize your assets and sell what it can to satisfy your tax bill. It also will garnish your wages and step to the front of the line to collect some payments due you (such as an insurance policy payout.)

2. *Automatic adjustment.* If you failed to report income that was detected by the IRS computer matching system, the IRS has simply adjusted your return without an audit and sent you notice of its intent to assess you additional back taxes. If you haven't filed a protest letter (see Step 3 for more on how to file a protest letter) within the specified period of time, you have again lost your right to appeal and your choices are limited to settling the debt through full payment or the Offer in Compromise program.

The IRS collection process consists of a rather long chain of bureaucrats. At any particular point, you may well be able to settle the tax owed, but in other cases it will take a while and you must wait until you get to the final person on the chain. IRS officials are experts at passing the buck, and nowhere is that truer than in the Collection Division. Despite the IRS's attempts to become more warm and fuzzy, the fact is that the IRS is a "supercreditor" and when you owe money to the IRS, it will have weapons at its disposal unlike any other creditor. Typically, if you owed a creditor, such as a credit card issuer, it would send you notices, threats, warnings, and knock your credit rating down. If you failed to respond to your creditor or if you refused to pay because you believe it is not entitled to the money, it will eventually have to sue you in court to recover its money. After it has taken you to court, your creditor would have to then follow special rules about forcing you to pay the court judgment (known in legalese as "execution of a judgment"). But when the IRS is the creditor, it need not worry about the procedures of taking you to court. The law gives it instant judge and jury power. If the IRS records a Notice of Federal Tax Lien, your credit may be ruined for years. This information is not meant to seem overblown nor intended to scare you into action. It is a reality and if you simply ignore your IRS problems, or if you are not armed with all the information you need, your daily life will be consumed by IRS letters, phone calls, visits, embarrassments, and the like.

This book is intended to empower you with current information and inside information on how the IRS is approaching your case. Even with the potent resources of the IRS, you can exert taxpayer influence and level the playing field by being aware of how to eliminate your back tax bill forever.

Nuts and Bolts of the Collection Process

The IRS has ten years from the date of assessment to collect the taxes owed. This may seem like a long time, but when you consider the volume of people with whom the Collection Division must deal, it is actually quite a challenge for the IRS. The main objective of the IRS Collection Division is to collect the maximum amount of dollars using the least amount of effort. In keeping with that goal, the IRS utilizes a variety of methods. Computers and agents are the bulk of the Collection Division's power. Generally, the IRS starts out by notifying you that you owe some back tax. By the time you receive these computer-generated collection notices, you will have either been assessed back taxes after an audit or had your taxes adjusted automatically (see Step 2). In theory, these computerized collection notices should never be a surprise. You will have been assessed and had an opportunity to appeal by the time the IRS computers start spitting out notices intended to collect the taxes owed. Once these notices start arriving, the fact that you will pay some tax is pretty much carved in stone. The challenge becomes carving down that tax bill through the Offer in Compromise program and delaying the IRS's collection efforts until you can properly submit an offer that has a chance of being accepted.

The computer-generated notices are called 500 series notices because they bear the internal IRS codes of Notice CP-501, Notice CP-502, and so on. They will come about once a month (see Step 1 for examples of these notices) and will become increasingly threatening. Usually your case will be turned over to an IRS revenue officer.

As we learned in Step 1, the IRS agent whose job it is to collect taxes owed is known as a revenue officer. If you have not already received a phone call from the IRS, most assuredly you will receive one soon after the revenue officer gets the case. The revenue officer will not be overly friendly, but also will probably not be aggressive at this point. If you flagrantly disregard his or her attempt to collect the tax or you simply refuse to pay, the revenue officer will file a federal tax lien against your property and probably proceed to empty out your bank accounts and/ or seize your property until such time as the tax bill is satisfied.

The IRS Computer-Automated Collection System (ACS)

After you receive your warning letters in the 500 series, your account is automatically sent to the IRS supercomputer section—the automated collection system (ACS). The ACS section of the IRS has the authority to collect most overdue tax bills and to issue notices to taxpayers who have not filed a return at all. As you may guess, the IRS doesn't exactly advertise the internal dealings of the ACS branch, and the speculations of many so-called tax experts on what the IRS's ACS branch will be doing in the future is pure guesswork. One thing that is known about the ACS branch is its "Q" scoring system. It sounds devious, but it's really just a score given to every taxpayer who owes back taxes, and it is based mainly on the amount of back taxes you owe. If your "Q" score is sufficiently low, then your case will probably stay in the ACS branch until the ten-year collection period is close to running out. At that point, the ACS collector will probably send your file to the revenue officer in your home district. If you start out with a high score (usually a high back tax debt and a poor history of tax compliance), your file is usually sent from the ACS to a revenue officer fairly quickly.

If your file is still at the ACS, you probably are still pretty far from having your assets seized. The ACS unit has been called the "Ma Bell" section of the IRS because most of its work is done on the phone. The ACS computer uses facts taken from your tax returns and other tax filings (such as Form 1099 or Form W-4) to analyze your account. Then an ACS collector will phone you. ACS collectors are trained to stick to their written scripts, collect as much as possible in back tax debt, and sometimes grant an extension of time or other special request. ACS collectors listen to long and sad stories from taxpayers every single day. They are subjected to insults, threats (the IRS allows many ACS collectors to use on-the-job aliases), and taxpayer lies on a regular basis, and some ACS collectors return the insults in kind. Most just cast them aside, but it also hardens the collectors to the real travails of taxpayers who are telling the truth about why they cannot pay. The result is that you usually won't get anywhere with an ACS collector unless you are ready to pay the full amount or agree to go on an installment plan. The ACS collector usually will agree to a taxpayer's paying off any debt less than $10,000 in 36 or fewer months in installments. Much of the ACS's responsibility is to follow up on the phone calls demanding payment from taxpayers and responding to taxpayer requests (usually for additional time).

At the IRS, the ACS unit is staffed by a number of ACS collectors in a group. The group is composed of five to seven collectors who work as a team handling a batch of cases assigned to that particular group. Although the official IRS line is that each ACS collector will give the same answers to your questions and will act the same to a given set of circumstances, human nature indicates otherwise. Some are willing to cut you some slack on payment terms, while others in the exact same circumstances will not cut any taxpayer any slack other than delaying a federal tax lien filing. Keep this in mind if you speak with an ACS collector in a particularly foul mood. You can simply give an excuse to hang up, and call back later. More than likely, you will speak to another ACS collector who may be more sympathetic to your plight. Remember, however, that ACS collectors are not known for their sympathetic tendencies.

Revenue Officers

If you are a habitual tax delinquent, you owe a large amount of money to the IRS, or you simply refuse to acknowledge any IRS correspondence and phone calls (or so they claim), your case will eventually wind up on the desk of a revenue officer. Revenue officers generally are handling large caseloads but are perhaps the most efficient agents in the IRS. They will evaluate each case, then map out a plan of action to collect the taxes. In some cases, a revenue officer will simply call you and ask you to fill out IRS Form 433-A (Collection Information Statement [see Step 7]). If you cannot be contacted by phone, or if you ignore the calls, the revenue officer will show up unannounced at your home or office! Depending on the revenue officer and what your file contains, he or she may request that you give some information about your assets then and there. An officer who already has your assets/liabilities information may try to get you to sign an already prepared installment agreement on the spot. Don't be intimidated. You should have your CPA or tax attorney review all documents before you sign them. When the revenue officer asks you for information or for you to sign any documents, requesting to see your CPA or attorney will probably result in the revenue officer's simply setting up an appointment for you to come to the local IRS office for an interview. This gives you time to collect all of your data, do some research, and consult an expert before disclosing any information to the IRS.

Do I Have to Give the IRS Information?

Technically, you don't have to give the IRS any information about your financial situation just because it asks for it. Refusing to give information to an IRS agent is not a crime unless the IRS has obtained a subpoena. But as a practical matter, being known as an IRS troublemaker is generally not helpful to your cause. If you refuse a revenue officer's request for information, he or she will probably issue a collection information summons, a legal order to bring your records to a local IRS office and give information to the appropriate IRS official. The IRS will generally issue the summons before taking further collection action, but if the revenue officer has knowledge about your assets (remember he or she has access to your tax returns, which disclose most of your assets), he or she may simply seize the known assets or attempt to garnish your wages. Never lie to a revenue officer about your assets (or anything else). You may get away with it in the short term, but if the IRS finds out that you gave false information to it, you will be in for rough sailing and you have significantly reduced your chances of resolving your tax debt through the Offer in Compromise program.

Keeping the Tax Man Waiting

If your situation with the IRS is critical because the IRS has threatened to attach a lien on your property, there are several methods to slow the IRS down while you prepare the Offer in Compromise package. Intentionally lying to the IRS to slow down your case (or for any other reason) is illegal and unwise. The temporary stay you receive if you lie to the IRS about certain assets will most assuredly come back to haunt you. If the IRS wants to actively pursue you, it will send your file to the Criminal Investigation Division (CID) for review (although this is admittedly rare). However, there are certain legal ways to delay the collection of taxes.

If your case in still at the ACS, you're in luck. Upon your reasonable request, the ACS collector usually will give you a short-term extension of up to 30 days. A "reasonable request" can be as simple as "I need another month to come up with some money." Depending on the circumstances, the ACS collector will input a particular "hold" identification number into the computer file containing your case. Once the case is assigned a hold number, the computer automatically holds

CASE STUDY

The Reluctant Taxpayer

Amanda is a 30-year-old professional who leads a busy life. A single mother of one, Amanda's family and job responsibilities left her with little time to do the housekeeping and household finances. Two years ago, she prepared her own tax return and took some improper deductions based on what one of her colleagues told her one day in the office. After an audit, the IRS disallowed the deductions and assessed Amanda back taxes, penalties, and interest.

When she received a notice that the IRS had assessed back taxes against her, she became annoyed and intended to appeal the auditor's determination. But her daughter caught the flu and she was assigned a big project at work, so Amanda let a few months slip by without sending in a protest letter or even calling the auditor. Eventually, the IRS began to send letters to Amanda requesting that she pay the tax in full. The tone of the letters was friendly, so Amanda wasn't worried about the IRS trying to collect the money. She again put it on her list of things to do, but it never got done. Several more months went by and whenever Amanda tried to focus on getting things straightened out with the IRS, some other responsibility came along that caused her to put the IRS problem aside. The more time that passed, the more Amanda tried to convince herself that the IRS would simply drop the whole thing and go away.

One day Amanda arrived home to find a message from an IRS collector on her machine. The collector left her name and number for Amanda to call and, again, Amanda put it off, promising herself that she would call and straighten out this mess. Soon after, Amanda received a CP notice from the IRS demanding payment. The letters were threatening, but Amanda simply had no money to pay the back taxes owed and she decided to wait until she could talk to her mother about a family loan. More weeks went by, and more letters were disregarded until one day a revenue officer from the IRS showed up at Amanda's office. Amanda was terrified and embarrassed. She signed the installment agreement request form because she figured that was the easiest way to get the revenue officer out of her office.

The revenue officer left and mailed a copy of the installment agreement to Amanda at her home, and another month went by without any IRS attention. Amanda paid the first month's installment but missed the second month. Again, the IRS called and left messages that Amanda never returned. The revenue officer deemed Amanda a reluctant taxpayer and filed a federal tax lien on all of her property and issued a notice to Amanda that if her taxes were not paid in full in ten days, the IRS would levy her bank accounts and begin to seize assets.

After Amanda consulted a tax attorney, they figured out that the IRS had incorrectly assessed some of the tax and that Amanda did not owe as much as the IRS claimed. If Amanda had consulted the tax professional earlier, a simple protest letter could have avoided more than $4,000 in penalties and interest. Instead, Amanda paid more money than she should have, suffered embarrassment at her workplace, and lost a lot of sleep over a simple tax bill. Amanda learned the hard way that ignoring IRS notices ends up costing time, money, and aggravation. All unnecessary!

This case does have a happy ending. Amanda's attorney convinced the IRS to drop the installment agreement and Amanda filed an Offer in Compromise based on doubt as to liability and collectibility. The IRS agreed to accept 60 cents on the dollar and eventually Amanda settled her past tax debt with the IRS once and for all.

your case for a certain number of days before it's sent to collections again. If the IRS determines that you cannot pay anything right now, it will hold your case for about 90 days and then check again. The IRS doesn't make public the number of days effected by a particular hold number, but such numbers basically fall into short-term holds (less than 12 months) and long-term holds (18 months and up).

It is difficult to get a long-term hold. You must convince the ACS collector that your financial situation is dire. No assets and no extra income are the two major factors used by the ACS in delaying your collection for a longer period of time. But if you're preparing an Offer in Compromise, you'll not need more than a month or so to get your package together and you won't need a long-term extension. As a practical matter, the IRS will suspend collection activities if you have submitted an Offer in Compromise in good faith. From a purely legal perspective, however, the IRS can continue to try to collect the tax. If the IRS believes that your Offer in Compromise package is submitted in "bad faith," the revenue officer assigned to your case will continue collection efforts (usually with a bit more fervor). Therefore, submitting an Offer in Compromise package simply to buy more time is generally a bad idea. A better way is to simply inform the revenue officer that you are consulting with your accountant or lawyer and that you will be submitting an Offer in Compromise package in the next four weeks. Generally, the revenue officer will give you a deadline and agree not to collect the tax unless you fail to submit your Offer in Compromise.

If your case has not yet reached the ACS, you still have some time to gather information and focus on submitting an Offer in Compromise package. You should begin to receive the 500 series of letters soon after you receive an assessment of back taxes. This is the best opportunity to slow down the wheels of the IRS collection system if you need more time to line up funding to make a down payment with your Offer in Compromise package. A word of caution though: Don't obtain extensions and then let the time pass without taking any action. In the beginning of the collection process, extensions are relatively easy to come by. But the farther along you are in the collection chain, the harder it will be to get extension time. Moreover, if an ACS collector or a revenue officer gave you a deadline, generally the IRS will follow up on the deadline. However, if you continue to send in requests for extensions of time in the beginning of the collection process, the IRS will rarely follow up on the deadline you have proposed. Depending on the tax owed and the efficiency of your local service center, your request for an extension may buy you up to six months of time or more before the case is sent to someone for collection. Once you receive a series 500 letter, respond to the IRS in writing by requesting a 60-day extension. Any future 500 series letters should also be met with a request in writing for a 60-day extension. Sending in a payment with each letter (the amount should be small, perhaps as little as .5 percent of the total tax requested) will also help you get more time to prepare your Offer in Compromise.

Keeping the IRS Happy While You Put Together Your Offer

One of the most important prerequisites for a successful Offer in Compromise package is keeping current with your taxes as they accrue. This means that if your back tax assessment was from 1996 and you submit an Offer in Compro-

CONSIDER THIS...

Penalties and Interest

Remember that while you may be stalling the collection out of a procrastination instinct or for a more legitimate reason (such as trying to obtain sources of funding to pay the tax), the interest on your tax debt is still accruing even if you have entered into an installment agreement. If you did not pay your taxes on time, the IRS will charge you interest as if you are borrowing the money from it. The interest rate is set by Congress and is adjusted every fiscal quarter. Interest is compounded so you are paying interest on interest!

From this perspective, the clock is against you. You should not try to submit a less-than-reasonable Offer in Compromise simply to avoid paying additional interest. In fact, the interest accrues until the time that the total tax debt is satisfied. This means that all during the collection process and all during the investigation phase of your offer, interest is being added to your tax bill. If you delay just for the sake of delay, it will cost you even more money.

---

mise in late 1998, the first thing the IRS will check will be to see if you have filed a 1997 tax return. But what if you can't pay the tax due when it is time to file your return? Pay as much money as you can towards your current tax bill and submit IRS Form 9465—Installment Agreement Request—with your tax return (see Figure 4.1). This will allow you to extend the payment period for up to 36 months (but no longer) and will prevent the IRS from initiating additional collection activities related to your current or past tax years. Even if you can't send any money with your return, it is important to file your return anyway. Otherwise, you will be charged a penalty for failing to file the return and your Offer in Compromise will be jeopardized.

Form 9456 gives information to the IRS that allows it to evaluate how much you can afford to pay every month on your tax bill. Remember, however, that you still pay interest on any money that is owed to the IRS. In 30 days (or so), the IRS

Figure 4.1 Form 9465, Sample Installment Agreement Request

Form **9465**
(Rev. January 1996)
Department of the Treasury
Internal Revenue Service

Installment Agreement Request

▶ **See instructions below and on back.**

OMB No. 1545-1350

Note: *Do not file this form if you are currently making payments on an installment agreement. You must pay your other Federal tax liabilities in full or you will be in default on your agreement.*

If you can't pay the full amount you owe, you can ask to make monthly installment payments. If we approve your request, you will be charged a $43 fee. **Do not include the fee with this form.** We will deduct the fee from your first payment after we approve your request, unless you choose **Direct Debit** (see the line 13 instructions). We will usually let you know within 30 days after we receive your request whether it is approved or denied. But if this request is for tax due on a return you filed after March 31, it may take us longer than 30 days to reply.

To ask for an installment agreement, complete this form. Attach it to the front of your return when you file. If you have already filed your return or you are filing this form in response to a notice, see **How Do I File Form 9465?** on page 2. If you have any questions about this request, call 1-800-829-1040.

Caution: *A Notice of Federal Tax Lien may be filed to protect the government's interest until you pay in full.*

1	Your first name and initial	Last name	Your social security number
	Amanda P.	Reluctant	101 20 3333

	If a joint return, spouse's first name and initial	Last name	Spouse's social security number
	N/A		

Your current address (number and street). If you have a P.O. box and no home delivery, show box number. — 100 E. 1st Avenue   Apt. number

City, town or post office, state, and ZIP code. If a foreign address, show city, state or province, postal code, and full name of country. — Maintown, PA 19355

2 If this address is new since you filed your last tax return, check here . . . . ▶ ☐

3 (610) 123-4567   After 5:00 p.m.   4 (610) 123-0000   100   After 9 A.m.
  Your home phone number   Best time for us to call   Your work phone number   Ext.   Best time for us to call

5 Name of your bank or other financial institution: 6 Your employer's name:
  Best Bank   Awful Employer, Inc.
  Address   Address
  100 E. 11th Avenue   100 E. 21st Avenue
  City, state, and ZIP code   City, state, and ZIP code
  Maintown, PA 19355   Maintown, PA 19355

7 Enter the tax return for which you are making this request (for example, Form 1040). But if you are filing this form in response to a notice, don't complete lines 7 through 9. Instead, attach the bottom section of the notice to this form and go to line 10 . . . . ▶ 1040

8 Enter the tax year for which you are making this request (for example, 1995) . . . . ▶ 1998

9 Enter the total amount you owe as shown on your tax return . . . . ▶ $ 2,000

10 Enter the amount of any payment you are making with your tax return (or notice). See instructions ▶ $ 200

11 Enter the amount you can paym each month. **Make your payments as large as possible to limit interest and penalty charges.** The charges will continue until you pay in full . . . . ▶ $ 800

12 Enter the date you want to make your payment each month. Do not enter a date later than the 28th ▶ 15th

13 If you would like to make your monthly payments using **Direct Debit** (automatic withdrawals from your bank account), check here . . . . ▶ ☐

Your signature   *Amanda Reluctant*   Date 4/15/98   Spouse's signature. If a joint return, BOTH must sign.   Date

Privacy Act and Paperwork Reduction Act Notice.—Our legal right to ask for the information on this form is Internal Revenue Code sections 6001, 6011, 6012(a), 6109, and 6159 and their regulations. We will use the information to process your request for an installment agreement. The reason we need your name and social security number is to secure proper identification. We require this information to gain access to the tax information in our files and properly respond to your request. If you do not enter the information, we may not be able to process your request. We may give this information to the Department of Justice as provided by law. We may also give it to cities, states, and the District of Columbia to carry out their tax laws.

Cat. No. 14842Y ·   Form **9465** (Rev. 1-96)

will write to you to let you know whether or not your request has been accepted. Sometimes the IRS will require you to submit additional information, but if your tax bill is less than $5,000, you shouldn't have any trouble getting the IRS to approve your payment terms.

For short extensions, the IRS has also greatly improved its automated telephone system in recent years. This can be used in a variety of circumstances, but it seems to work best for simple requests such as additional time to pay. Have all the information about your case at hand, including the amount and dates of your proposed payment schedule. Generally, if your request is to pay in 60 days or less, you can use the automated telephone system. Requests for longer extensions require you to fill out Form 9465 and file it with your tax return.

Protecting Your Assets

Once you have given the IRS all of your financial information, you are an open book. The IRS now knows where you bank, where you work, where you live, and how much money you have (in general). It even knows who some of your family members are so that they can contact them in the event that you are unable to be located (why else would they ask for that information on their forms?). This is exactly where the IRS wants you. Some revenue officers are known to be overly aggressive and the information you give them allows them to seize your assets with relatively little effort.

Bank accounts and the like (brokerage accounts, etc.) are easy prey for the IRS and you should be careful that not too much is left in your bank accounts that were disclosed to the IRS. Despite what an IRS employee may tell you, the information you disclose to the IRS must be true on the date you give it. Occasionally the IRS will ask for updates, and you must disclose any new accounts you opened since your last disclosure. If you are diligent in following the steps in this book, you will not need to move accounts around because you will be submitting an Offer in Compromise and the IRS will suspend collection activities while they investigate. But if you're nervous that an overly enthusiastic revenue officer will seize your assets before you can submit an offer, many tax professionals recommend moving the majority of the most vulnerable assets (such as bank accounts) out of the original account and into a new account at a new place. Simply reduce your balance to a minimum and move the majority of assets to a new bank or brokerage house. Remember that the IRS may still find the assets if you make one of the following common mistakes:

- Moving your bank account and then paying a tax bill with a check from the new account. The IRS records your bank account number in its records for just such an occasion. Be sure to pay your tax bills out of your old account.
- Moving your account to another bank close to your home or work. Revenue officers have the ability to do a "bank search" in your local area to try and locate your assets. The two starting points for many revenue officers are banks close to your home or banks close to your workplace.
- Moving your bank account (or brokerage account) to an interest-bearing account. For the time that you are trying to solve your problems with the IRS, you will probably be better off placing the majority of your assets into an account that does not pay interest. Any interest earned on your bank account is reported to the IRS and will allow it to identify your account easily.
- Depositing more than $10,000 in cash in your new bank account. Again, the IRS receives notice of such transactions and this provides it with the information it will need to seize the account. Rather, write out a regular check to your new bank. It should only take a few days to clear and the IRS will not have to be notified.

If the IRS requests that you update your information (either written or orally), then you will again have to make a judgment call as to whether you want to move your assets again or not. In any case, don't lie about assets! Hiding assets is a crime, but the more practical result is losing your credibility with the revenue officer. This inevitably leads to harsher treatment for you.

D O N ' T   F O R G E T . . .

✔ Become aware of where you are in the collection process and how soon it will be before the IRS tries to levy your property.

✔ If your case is in the ACS and you need more time, request a 60-day extension directly from the ACS collector who contacts you.

✔ Don't make mistakes that will allow the IRS to easily locate all of your assets.

Choose an Offer in Compromise Category

Now that you have done the footwork to establish some of the basics in your case and have an understanding of the IRS collection process, as well as the Offer in Compromise program, we can begin to examine how to submit a successful Offer in Compromise to the IRS.

The Offer in Compromise program has two classes of offers:

1. Doubt as to liability
2. Doubt as to collectibility

The majority of those eligible for tax forgiveness will be filed under the second category, but there are advantages to filing under the liability category as well.

Doubt as to Liability

Doubt as to liability exists when you have some legal basis for believing that you simply do not owe the tax. Before you can take advantage of the doubt-as-to-liability category, you must have some tangible evidence that you do not owe the tax due. The most common type of case eligible for the liability category involves a taxpayer who is audited and assessed back taxes based on erroneous or missing information. For example, if you filed a tax return that failed to report a capital gain on the sale of investment property and it was discovered during an audit, there is a reasonable chance that the auditor will assess you the maximum amount of capital gains liability by giving you a "zero" basis in your asset. Although clearly most properties must have a higher basis than zero, the IRS often assigns a zero basis when there is no information about what was the basis in your house.

If it is a clear case of "I don't owe the tax," an Offer in Compromise based on doubt as to liability will be very effective. If the liability is subject to differing views of the tax law (i.e., the IRS interprets the law differently from Tax Court), then an offer based on liability has less of a chance of success.

Doubt as to Collectibility

This category is simply boiled down to "I know I owe, but I can't pay." Most Offers in Compromise are in this category and the two simple requirements are

1. your inability to pay the tax assessment in full and
2. the apparent likelihood that the IRS will not be able to realize the full collection potential in the future.

Doubt-as-to-collectibility offers must include a written statement that explains why the IRS could not collect more than is being offered and also must explain what other collection factors may impact on collection potential. The IRS investigates this type of Offer in Compromise thoroughly and with a close eye. You should expect to be able to verify your income, living expenses, debts, value of your existing assets, and all other information that you disclose to the IRS.

Installment Agreements

When there is doubt as to collectibility, you can expect the IRS to first try to initiate an installment agreement with you. An installment agreement allows for payment of back taxes over time. The Taxpayer's Bill of Rights requires the IRS to consider an installment agreement so long as the agreement facilitates the collection of the tax. You do not have an absolute right to an installment agreement. Most revenue officers, however, will be very cooperative in offering you an installment agreement if he or she realizes that you have a steady source of income from your employer or some type of trust. Remember that the revenue officer's respon-

sibility is to get as much of the total tax debt paid as possible as soon as possible. On the other hand, from the IRS's perspective, getting the entire amount owed paid over ten years is much better than getting half of it all at one time. This means that a revenue officer is more inclined to draw up an installment agreement to have you pay small amounts over a long period of time until the collection statutes run out. But your goal is to settle the tax debt once and for all and for less than the full amount. Therefore, an installment agreement may sound like an attractive alternative when the revenue officer offers it, but it really should be used only in the event that the IRS will not accept any Offer in Compromise proposals.

You may be in a situation where the IRS is threatening to levy your bank account because you have delayed your response or have not responded at all. In this situation, you need some time to put together your Offer in Compromise package at the same time as you need to stop the levy before you submit the package. At this point, an installment agreement is a good option until you can adequately prepare your offer. Don't submit a slipshod Offer in Compromise because of the threat of an IRS levy! This will appear to be a delaying tactic that may push your revenue officer to pull out all plugs and start aggressive enforcement action. If you do enter into an installment agreement, remember the following points:

- An installment agreement is more of a contract between you and Uncle Sam than an IRS enforcement tool. You are required to perform certain obligations (paying the installments on time is the principal obligation) and the government is agreeing to accept that payment instead of pursuing enforcement, such as levying bank accounts or seizing property.
- The tax code authorizes the IRS to enter into an installment agreement so long as that agreement facilitates collection of the tax. This subjective standard allows the revenue officer a wide range of discretion with respect to whether or not to offer an installment agreement. This is yet another good reason not to antagonize the revenue officer on your case.
- Once the installment agreement is executed, the IRS is not permitted to alter, modify, or terminate the agreement during its term unless
  1. you gave false information to the IRS and it discovers that the information is false after the agreement is executed,
  2. the IRS determines the tax collection is in jeopardy (e.g., the IRS believes that you or your assets are planning a permanent trip out of the United States), and/or
  3. you breach one or more of the terms of the installment agreement.

- An important part of the installment agreement is your promise to keep up on all current tax liabilities as they become due and that all tax returns due during the term of the installment agreement must be timely filed.
- If your financial condition materially improves (IRS jargon for "hit the lottery"), the IRS can terminate the agreement and start the collection process all over again.
- If the IRS has already filed a Notice of Federal Tax Lien, it will generally not release the lien during the term of the installment agreement. It will, however, usually agree to allow you to transfer or sell assets so long as you have faithfully met the terms of the installment agreement.

Your Rights under the Taxpayer's Bill of Rights and Other Taxpayer Laws

In 1988, Congress passed the Taxpayer's Bill of Rights (TBR) in response to complaints of overzealous actions by revenue officers. In July 1996, the Taxpayer's Bill of Rights 2 (TBR2) was passed. These laws added a number of provisions to clarify and strengthen the rights of taxpayers in their dealings with the IRS.

Notice Rights

Under TBR and TBR2, the IRS is now required to provide a written statement of the refund, collection, and appeals rights of the taxpayer and must also describe what the IRS can and cannot do when trying to collect the tax. The IRS now mails Publication 1, *Your Rights as a Taxpayer,* as a standard procedure in order to comply with this notice requirement. If the IRS is in collection mode in your case, you should review the publication carefully. If you have not received one, call the IRS's toll-free number to order the publication or download the publication from the IRS's Web site (both the toll-free number and the Web address are located in Appendix A). In addition, the TBRs require the IRS to provide additional notice and information before serving a levy on you. Most important, the IRS also must provide you with your options to prevent the levy, including appeal, payment and refund, release of lien, and so on.

CASE STUDY

Death, Bagels, and Taxes

Abel, Baker, and Cain were three equal-share owners/shareholders in The Bagel Shop, Inc., a popular bagel, sandwich, and coffee shop located in a busy corporate center. Abel was the operational manager of the business. He hired and fired the personnel, kept an eye on the register, monitored and ordered inventory, handled day-to-day problems with customers and vendors, and performed all of the functions of a general manager. Abel also worked as a waiter when the restaurant was shorthanded and kept all of the tips he earned that day. Baker took care of the business end of the company, including calculating daily cash receipts, paying bills, preparing weekly cash flow reports, and doing the payroll for the wait and kitchen staff. Cain was purely an investor and rendered some strategic business advice. However, Cain was rarely on-site, never worked in the restaurant, and had no check-signing authority.

The Bagel Shop, Inc., was very successful in its start-up years, but then began to run into some cash flow shortages around payday. Usually, the cash flow would improve in a few days, but the fact remained that there often wasn't enough to pay all the employees on time. Because Baker, acting as the book-keeper, didn't want to be blamed for missing a payroll, he started to take the money that was to be deposited as withholding taxes from employee paychecks and used it to cover the cash shortage. He didn't tell his partners this fact and hoped that income from the restaurant would improve shortly. However, business did not improve and Baker failed to deposit employment taxes for two straight quarters. As a further stroke of bad luck for the company, Baker died suddenly of a heart attack and the business was left without a bookkeeper and in serious debt.

Abel and Cain tried to keep the business afloat for several more months, but because Abel could not support himself on tips alone, he left the business for a better-paying opportunity. Cain had lost most of his investment and didn't want to pay any legal fees to properly dissolve the corporation, so he simply sold the equipment and stopped paying rent.

Several months later, the IRS sent letters to Abel and Cain telling them that they were still officers of the corporation and, much to Abel and Cain's surprise, that their corporation owed employment taxes to the government to the tune of $42,000 with penalties and interest. After Abel and Cain met with the IRS agents handling the case, they were informed that because these taxes were employment taxes, known as "trust fund" taxes, the IRS intended to hold each of them personally responsible for payment of the full amount of the tax. They were shocked and angry at their now deceased partner and explained that it was he who had taken the trust fund taxes. In addition, the IRS announced that Abel would be assessed an additional $8,000 since there was an indication that he had not reported his tips properly.

Abel consulted his CPA. They determined that:

- Abel had little or no personal assets. He and his wife had a jointly owned family home with about $10,000 in equity. Abel also had a small Keough account (pension fund) worth about $1,000.

- Abel was making $2,000 per month at his new job.

- Abel was a signer on the payroll checks when Baker was away, and therefore he would be a responsible party under the tax code. He was liable for the trust fund taxes.

- Abel had underreported his tips and therefore he was liable for underreporting his income.

Abel's Case

Based on the above facts, Abel decided to file an Offer in Compromise based on doubt as to collectibility. The facts that Abel has very few assets and even fewer within the reach of the IRS (his principal asset was a marital home, which is exempt from IRS levy) and that there is very little question as to liability makes this a clear-cut choice in favor of an offer based on doubt as to collectibility.

Cain's Case

Cain's facts are quite different:

- Cain had substantial assets and, in theory, the IRS could satisfy the entire trust fund liability by one levy to one of his larger bank accounts.

- Cain's annual income is around $100,000 per year and it has been so for several years.

- Cain had never signed any paychecks, nor was he an active player in the business, and therefore some doubt existed as to whether he could be held liable for the trust fund taxes as a responsible party. Generally, one must have an active role in the business to be classified as a responsible party for payment of trust fund taxes.

- Cain has always filed a timely income tax return and does not owe back taxes.

Cain's inclination is to appeal the assessment for the trust fund taxes based on the fact that he's not liable for any of the amount due under the tax code. But Cain is a smart and shrewd businessperson and he realizes that there are no guarantees that he will prevail unless he goes to court. He decides that rather than pay thousands of dollars for an attorney and CPA to fight the IRS through litigation, he will simply file an Offer in Compromise based on doubt as to liability. He also knows that he must act fast because his assets are substantial and the IRS has threatened to file a Notice of Federal Tax Lien.

Liability of The Bagel Shop, Inc.

Both Cain and Abel were concerned that while Baker was alive he may not have paid the required corporate taxes and that they may now be liable for the corporate taxes! Consider the following facts:

- The Bagel Shop, Inc., was a registered corporation that was properly incorporated before it opened for business.

- Baker was diligent about keeping minutes up-to-date and following all corporate formalities.

Based on these facts, neither Cain nor Abel will be personally liable for any corporate taxes. Because the business was properly incorporated and adhered to corporate formalities, it existed as its own legal entity separate and apart from its shareholders Abel, Baker, and Cain. Therefore, although the IRS can attach a lien on all of the business assets of the corporation, it cannot pursue Abel and Cain (or even Baker's estate) individually for the corporate income tax debt. This, however, does not get Abel or Cain off the hook for employment trust fund taxes (as described above) because the tax code makes a special provision for certain people to be held individually responsible for trust fund taxes.

Interview Rights

Congress also provided taxpayers with rights during one of the most nerve-racking processes of dealing with the IRS: the dreaded IRS interview. You have the following rights:

- You may make an audio recording of the interview so long as you provide the IRS with advance notice. The IRS also may record the interview with the same advance notice to you. As a practical matter, most IRS agents will opt not to record the interview. However, if the IRS does tape the interview, you have a right to purchase a transcript from it. Although professional opinion is split on the subject of whether or not taxpayers should record IRS interviews, many attorneys and CPAs recommend that you not record the interview unless the revenue officer has shown some evidence of bad faith in your case (such as threats, intimidation, or lying). The reason given by many professionals is that recording an interview flies in the face of the cardinal rule not to antagonize the IRS agent. It is usually best to make notes during the interview to refresh your recollection if it becomes necessary.

- The IRS is required to terminate the interview immediately if you ask to speak to your attorney or accountant during the interview. This can be a powerful tool, but it can only be utilized if you show up at the interview unrepresented (i.e., without counsel or a CPA). If you believe that answering any of the questions the IRS agent is asking will hurt your case or your ability to submit an Offer in Compromise, ask to speak with your attorney or CPA. The agent will suspend the interview. He or she may ask you to contact your attorney or CPA from the IRS office, or simply to reschedule the interview after you have consulted your tax professional.

- The IRS is required to conduct the interview at a reasonable time and place. Reasonable usually means that you will be required to appear at the field office closest to your home. The IRS is no longer allowed to conduct an interview at the taxpayer's place of business if the business is so small that it would require you to close the business for the interview. This does not restrict the IRS from visiting your business in order to verify facts about your business assets.

Automatic Abatement of Some Penalties

The Taxpayer's Bill of Rights allows for automatic abatement of penalties (IRS jargon for elimination of penalty sums) if the following three conditions are met:

1. You have made a specific written request for IRS advice.
2. An IRS employee gave you wrong advice.
3. The penalty is later imposed because you relied on the IRS agent's advice.

So long as you gave the IRS employee adequate and accurate information in your advice request, any penalty the IRS imposed is eliminated automatically.

Appeal for Liens

Another provision allows the taxpayer to file an administrative appeal when there is a question about the legality of filing a Notice of Federal Tax Lien on behalf of the government. You may request that the IRS lift the tax lien so long as it was filed in error (before the tax assessment, for example). If the lien was erroneously filed, the IRS must issue a release of the lien within 14 days. If the IRS fails to do this in that time period, it may be subject to a lawsuit by you for damages related to its collection activities.

Abuse of Taxpayer by IRS Agents

Congress recognized that when IRS agents step over the line, taxpayers are often left without redress for their trouble with the IRS and related expenses. Consequently, Congress authorized taxpayer lawsuits against the IRS in certain instances. You may recover damages for money spent by you because of the IRS's unauthorized (or illegal) collection efforts. If the IRS wrongfully refused to release a lien, for example, you may be able to recover the expenses (including legal fees in some cases) you incurred due to the IRS's actions.

But the TBR provisions that give you the right to sue the IRS sound a lot better than they work in practice. First, you must have exhausted all of the administrative avenues (which may delay the process significantly) before you file suit. Second, the problem with suits against the IRS is the problem with litigation in general: it is expensive, risky, and time consuming. If you believe that you have a potential lawsuit against the IRS for overstepping its boundaries, contact a qualified tax lawyer to discuss the case. There are some cases where you simply cannot afford to "absorb" the expenses that the IRS has caused you and you will be left with no choice except to sue. Also, remember that you generally cannot recover money for mental anguish or other types of psychological damages from the IRS unless the IRS has acted recklessly.

On the brighter side, federal courts have been much more willing to make awards to victims of overly aggressive IRS tactics. Recently, a federal judge in Denver, Colorado, awarded a $325,000 judgment to a woman victimized by the IRS. If the IRS does not appeal the verdict, it will be the largest award ever levied against the IRS. But this is not a common occurrence. If you have a legitimate case, don't be afraid to pursue it, but don't set your expectations too high.

D O N ' T   F O R G E T . . .

✔ Decide which Offer in Compromise category you best fit into.

✔ Consider an installment agreement if you don't fall in the guidelines for an Offer in Compromise.

✔ Know your rights under the Taxpayer's Bill of Rights (and the Taxpayer's Bill of Rights 2) in case you are the victim of an overly aggressive revenue officer.

Draft a Personal Financial Statement

Reporting your personal finances to the IRS is a bit more difficult than many people expect. The IRS has designed special forms that allows it to plug the information in from the forms to a formula it then uses to evaluate whether or not you are eligible for an Offer in Compromise or any other type of program. The problem is that the forms are not very user friendly, and many times the information required is either misplaced or misinterpreted by the taxpayer. The result is that the IRS will make assumptions based on less-than-accurate information.

This step is designed to be a more user-friendly method of compiling personal financial data. You can then use these data to assist you in completing these special forms known as IRS Form 433-A and Form 433-B (collection information statements). Step 7 in this book tells you how to fill out these collection information statements, but for now let's focus on creating a financial snapshot of your personal balance sheet.

Sources of Income

List sources from which you receive money (see Figure 6.1). Usually, your job is the major part of your income. Dig out your W-2 form or some recent pay stubs to help you verify these data. Remember to include income from your mutual funds, investments, or interest-bearing accounts. Collect your last year's

1099-I forms which will give you a good idea of what your income is from these various sources. Also, consider income from rental properties, insurance proceeds, pension proceeds, child support, alimony, and any other source of income (whether regular or not). Figure 6.2 shows a sample completed form.

Expenses

Your total monthly expenses include more than the IRS is willing to give you credit for (more on that in Step 7). Although we will not list all of these expenses for your Offer in Compromise package, for purposes of this step assemble your bills, receipts, and checkbook ledger to figure how much you spend for rent (or mortgage payments), home equity loans, utilities, maintenance of your home, food, clothing, transportation, taxes (including your state, local, and federal income taxes), automobile payments, household expenses, credit card payments, professional expenses, and other miscellaneous expenses. (See Figures 6.3 and 6.4)

Current Assets and Liabilities

Many people do not know their true net worth because they have never bothered to figure out their assets and liabilities.

Assets

First, you need to know what assets and liabilities are. Your assets include: cash in the bank; your investments in mutual funds, stocks, bonds, government securities, and money market funds; partnerships or closely held businesses; your home and other property you own; cash value of your life insurance policies; your automobiles; and your personal property such as jewelry, furniture, and collections. Figure 6.5 shows the types of assets you want to list. Figure 6.6 shows a sample completed list of assets.

Figure 6.1 Sources of Income

List Your Income Sources:

Source	Gross Annual Income	Net Income per Month
Wages		
Investments: a. Mutual Funds/Stocks b. Partnerships/S Corporations c. Rental Property d. Interest-Bearing Accounts	— — — — —	
Child Support	N/A	
Alimony	—	
Pension Payments	—	
Insurance/Settlement Proceeds	—	
Sale of Any Assets	—	
Other Income 1		
Other Income 2		

Total Monthly Income . . . .$

Figure 6.2 Sample Sources of Income

List Your Income Sources:

Source	Gross Annual Income	Net Income Per Month
Wages	*$40,000*	*$2,613*
Investments: a. Mutual Funds/Stocks b. Partnerships/S Corporations c. Rental Property d. Interest-Bearing Accounts	*1,100* *-0-* *-0-* *500*	*92* *42*
Child Support	*-0-*	
Alimony	*-0-*	
Pension Payments	*-0-*	
Insurance/Settlement Proceeds	*-0-*	
Sale of Any Assets		
Other Income 1 *Royalties from magazine article*	*500*	*42*
Other Income 2 *N/A*		

Total Monthly Income *$2,789*

Figure 6.3 List of Monthly Expenses

Nature of Expense	Monthly Payment Due
Housing: a. Rent or Mortgage b. Maintenance of Home c. Home Equity Loan d. Utilities e. Other Household Expenses	~~805~~ ~~60.00~~ **840** ~~366.00~~ ~~365~~ — **50** — 300 *PHONE* 140.00-200.00 30 30
Food: a. Groceries b. Other (Meals Out, etc.)	400 250.00 120 115.00
Clothes: a. New Clothes b. Cleaning/Laundry	~~60~~ **SS** ~~38~~ **25**
Transportation: a. Auto Loan Payments b. Gas, Maintenance, Parking, and Tolls *INSURANCE*	—0— **398** 200 **300**
Credit Cards: a. [Issuer] *VISA* b. [Issuer] *MASTERCARD* c. [Issuer] *AMGX*	200.00 ~~40~~ *Master*
Professional: a. Medical — *CATE FARING* 400/mTH b. Dental 5000/total estimate c. Attorney/Accountant	~~█████~~ 400 200 125 30.mth

Figure 6.3 List of Monthly Expenses (Continued)

Nature of Expense	Monthly Payment Due
Insurance: a. Homeowners or Rental Insurance b. Car c. Life and Disability d. Other *ASS of 40 year Medical*	− *32.00* *80* *200*
Taxes: a. Property b. State Income ✓ c. Municipal or School Taxes d. Other *Federal*	*120.00 ?*
Other Expenses: a. College Tuition b. Alimony/Child Support c. Medications/Prescriptions d. Student Loans e. Other Loans f. Entertainment/Travel g. Miscellaneous	*30.00* *100 mth*
Total Monthly Expenses . . . . $	

Figure 6.4 Sample List of Monthly Expenses

Nature of Expense	Monthly Payment Due
Housing: a. Rent or Mortgage b. Maintenance of Home c. Home Equity Loan d. Utilities *(Electricity, Water, Trash)* e. Other Household Expenses *(Cleaning Supplies)*	$725 15 125 300 10
Food: a. Groceries b. Other (Meals Out, etc.)	600 150
Clothes: a. New Clothes b. Cleaning/Laundry	50 25
Transportation: a. Auto Loan Payments b. Gas, Maintenance, Parking, and Tolls	250 50
Credit Cards: a. [Issuer] *Visa* b. [Issuer] *MasterCard* c. [Issuer]	125 70
Professional: a. Medical b. Dental c. Attorney/Accountant	200 100 150

Figure 6.4 Sample List of Monthly Expenses (Continued)

Nature of Expense	Monthly Payment Due
Insurance: a. Homeowners or Rental Insurance b. Car c. Life and Disability d. Other *Jewelry*	$ 90 100 25 20
Taxes: a. Property b. State Income c. Municipal or School Taxes d. Other **Federal**	1,000 120 140 **600.00**
Other Expenses: a. College Tuition b. Alimony/Child Support c. Medications/Prescriptions d. Student Loans e. Other Loans *Private loan* f. Entertainment/Travel g. Miscellaneous	-0- -0- 20 -0- 100 150 75
Total Monthly Expenses $4,550	

Figure 6.5 List of Assets

List Your Current Assets:

Asset	Fair Market Value
Cash: a. Held in Checking b. Held in Savings c. Held in Certificates of Deposit d. Held Elsewhere	(For cash items, fill in actual balance in account) — #2000 *to pay bills*
Mutual Funds (List): a. b.	—0—
Stocks (List): a. b.	—0—
Government Securities (T-Bills)	—0—
Bonds	—0—
Money Market Funds	—0—
Automobiles	*auto 4000 down, 18500 owned ... 200,000 miles ... 6500*
Property: a. Principal Residence b. Other	B. 0
Personal Property (Furniture, Jewelry, Clothing, and Collections)	

Total Monthly Income . . . . $

Figure 6.6 Sample List of Assets

List Your Current Assets:

Asset	Fair Market Value
	(For cash items, fill in actual balance in account)
Cash:	
a. Held in Checking	$ 1,800
b. Held in Savings	200
c. Held in Certificates of Deposit	-0-
d. Held Elsewhere	-0-
Mutual Funds (List):	
a. *Vanguard (IRA)*	5,000
b. *Kaufmann*	1,000
Stocks (List):	
a. *ATT*	500
b.	
Government Securities (T-Bills)	-0-
Bonds	-0-
Money Market Funds	-0-
Automobiles	5,000
Property:	
a. Principal Residence	200,000
b. Other	-0-
Personal Property (Furniture, Jewelry, Clothing, and Collections)	15,000

Total Assets **$228,500**

CONSIDER THIS...

Rules of Thumb for Evaluating Assets

You may have a difficult time placing a value on some of the assets you own (such as real estate), so follow these tips for determining the fair market value:

- Real Estate. The price you paid for your house (or any piece of property) is not necessarily the fair market value. Market values fluctuate greatly from year to year and from neighborhood to neighborhood. Try to discover what a house similar to yours in your neighborhood sold for. Looking at the real estate section of your local newspaper is a good way to check the actual transaction price. If that information is not readily available, contact a few real estate agents and ask them for a general appraisal value of your home. If you tell a REALTOR® that you are considering selling your home, he or she will come to your house and give you an estimated price for similar houses in your neighborhood. Discount each number by about 10 percent and average the results, which should be a good indicator of the fair market value of your home.

- Closely Held Business. Evaluating this is a bit trickier. Don't rely on old financial statements as a true indicator of the value of the business. Rather, ask your CPA for a fair market value analysis. A CPA will know what the standard going rate is in your particular industry and will discount or add value accordingly.

Liabilities and Equity

Figure 6.7 shows you how to gather together the information on your assets, liabilities, and equity. For each asset in your list, identify your liability—what balance is still due and owing—to calculate your equity in your assets (asset – liability = equity). If you have trouble, check the sample list shown in Figure 6.8.

Figure 6.7 List of Assets, Liabilities, and Equity

Asset	Liability	Equity
Total		

Figure 6.8 Sample List of Assets, Liabilities, and Equity

Asset		Liability	Equity
Cash	$2,000	-0-	$ 2,000
Mutual Funds	6,000	-0-	6,000
Stocks	5,000	-0-	5,000
Auto	5,000 ~~18~~6,500	2,000	3,000
Principal Residence	200,000	150,000	50,000
Personal Property		-0-	-0-
Total	$218,000	$152,000	$61,500

Transferring Information to Your Offer in Compromise

Now you have identified all your assets and liabilities, as well as your income and expenses. This information makes the process of filling out the rest of the documents related to your Offer in Compromise a great deal easier. Also, if an asset, liability, or expense doesn't fit into one of the categories on the checklist, add it on at the bottom of the proper column.

DON'T FORGET...

✔ Using Figure 6.1, create your income list by collecting documents showing your sources of income, such as your W-2 statement, 1099-I forms, bank records, and the like.

✔ Using Figure 6.3, create your list of monthly expenses by collecting documents showing your expenses including mortgage bills, car loan bills, alimony order, housing, and the like.

✔ Using Figure 6.7, create your list of assets, liabilities, and equity. Use conservative valuation methods when valuing your assets.

Complete Collection Information Statements (IRS Form 433-A and Form 433-B)

An integral part of your Offer in Compromise package is the proper completion of the IRS's collection information statements. The IRS Form 433-A is the statement for individuals and Form 433-B is the statement for businesses. If your tax liability involves individual income taxes, you probably will be required to fill out only Form 433-A. An important exception to that general rule is when you derive much of your income from being self-employed or from a small business that you own (or in which you own the majority of shares). In that case, you must submit both a Form 433-A and a Form 433-B with your Offer in Compromise. (These forms may be found in Appendix C.)

The purpose of submitting these forms in the Offer in Compromise is so the reviewing revenue officer (and any subsequent reviewer from the IRS) may gain a snapshot of your financial picture and be able to evaluate your financial history and lifestyle.

Because these forms are a bit tricky to fill out, be sure you have completed Step 6. This will help you to complete Form 433-A and/or Form 433-B without becoming confused by the overwhelming amount of information requested by the IRS. The IRS often uses terms that have a meaning different than the ordinary use of the word. For example, for Form 433 purposes an "asset" is actually an asset minus your liability. In most accounting circles, an asset refers to an actual asset— the fair market value of your asset. Liabilities are shown in a separate section. "Expenses" also carry a different meaning for purposes of this form. Being aware

Read this

asset — liability = IRS "asset"

of these distinctions will save you a lot of time, so be sure not to assume that any particular term carries the ordinary meaning.

Also, use this step to begin to organize and gather supporting documentation that will be used in submitting your offer package. Such documentation includes: canceled checks, rent or mortgage receipts, utility bills, car lease agreements, car expense bills, credit card receipts, insurance premium invoices, household expense receipts, and the like. Be sure that you have documentation for the amounts you are reporting on the forms. When you list your medical expenses, for example, gather your bills and checks for that item and keep them together in one file. You'll be needing them later to support your Offer in Compromise.

Your Living Expenses

The IRS has its own view of how much money you should spend while you still owe the government past taxes. The IRS is not required to give you "credit" for your actual living expenses, but rather will allow for a certain dollar amount to be spent for those expenses and calculate the excess as if it were available for payment of your tax liability. The *Internal Revenue Manual* sets guidelines for use by revenue officers on how much money is necessary to sustain yourself and your dependents. The standards are updated annually, but the natural bureaucratic lag time between when the standards should be changed as opposed to when they are changed results in a lower-than-average allowance for certain living expenses.

- *National Standards.* For certain categories of expenses, the IRS has established a national uniform baseline (see Figure 7.1). The categories include: meals out and groceries; personal care products and services (haircuts, etc); and housekeeping and lawn maintenance materials.
- *Local Standards.* Expenses that are local in nature are determined by the IRS district office in your area. Although this allows you some flexibility if you live in a part of the country that has traditionally high living expenses, the IRS does not allow standards to differ within a local district (e.g., an expensive suburb and a rural town in the same district) or for your special circumstances (such as a large family requiring a large house). The local standards cover: housing expenses such as utilities, maintenance, and telephone; mortgage or rent payments; and transportation-related expenses (includes your car payments, gas and maintenance, tools, parking at your job, and public transportation).

Figure 7.1   IRS Form 433-A, National Standard Expenses

National Standard Expenses
(Item 42)

Total Monthly Income	Number of Persons in Household				
	One	Two	Three	Four	Over Four
Less than $830	315	509	553	714	+120
$830 to $1,249	383	517	624	723	+130
$1,250 to $1,669	448	569	670	803	+140
$1,670 to $2,499	511	651	731	839	+150
$2,500 to $3,329	551	707	809	905	+160
$3,330 to $4,169	590	840	948	1,053	+170
$4,170 to $5,829	665	913	1,019	1,177	+180
$5,830 and over	923	1,179	1,329	1,397	+190

Expenses include: Housekeeping supplies
Clothing and clothing services
Personal care products and services
Food
Miscellaneous

To find the amount you are allowed, read down the Total Gross Monthly Income Column until you find your income, then read across to the column for the number of persons in your family.

If there are more than four persons in your family, multiply the number of additional persons by the amount in the "Over Four" column and add the result to the amount in the "Four" column. (For example total monthly income of $830 to $1,249 for six persons would equal a monthly national standard of 723 + 130 + 130, or 983.)

Normally, expenses should be allowed only for persons who can be claimed as exemptions on your income tax return.

Dollar amounts are derived from Bureau of Labor Statistics (BLS) Consumer Expenditure Survey. 1992-93. Tables 1. 3. 4. and 5.

"U.S. Government Printing Office: 1995 — 387-109/21884

- *Conditional Expenses.* These are expenses that the IRS considers to not be absolutely necessary for your safety or well-being. You can claim the conditional expenses if you can pay your tax liability in full in three years. Conditional expenses do not help your case in an Offer in Compromise. *Too much money being spent on these types of expenses is fatal to your offer.* The conditional expenses will be disallowed unless you can prove to the revenue officer that the additional amounts are necessary for your health or welfare or your family's. You also may get some conditional expenses allowed by the IRS if there is a likely chance that you will produce income to help pay your tax bill. These conditional expenses are such things as charitable contributions, educational expenses (including college costs and tuition), and unsecured debts, such as credit card debt.

Your Assets

Disclosing your assets to the IRS seems counterintuitive to many taxpayers. Indeed, the real danger of disclosing those assets to the IRS is that you will have given the revenue officer a complete road map to use in the event he or she ever decides to take aggressive enforcement actions. But revealing your assets is essential to having your offer accepted, so follow these guidelines:

- Assets such as cash, stocks, and CDs should match your personal financial statement in Step 6. These amounts may not be estimated; they must be specific dollar amounts. The value of other types of assets such as personal property, jewelry, furniture, and clothing may be estimated within reason. The lower the value placed on property, the less inclined the IRS will be to seize it. Remember that the IRS has to calculate the costs of seizure and sale for each asset and that makes you more secure with assets that aren't worth much on resale (such as a car).
- For valuing your real estate, consult the newspaper for what similar houses in your neighborhood are being sold for. Or ask a local real estate agent or appraiser what the fair market value of your house is and then discount it by 10 percent for costs associated with a sale.

- Group certain personal assets (such as furniture) in one category. Give the estimated value of what those items would sell for at a flea market. Most furniture would be worth about 10 to 15 percent of its original value for a year or two, then drop down to less than 5 percent of its original value.

Nuts and Bolts: Filling Out Form 433-A

1. Fill out boxes 1, 2, 3, and 4 of the form with your personal information (see Figure 7.2).
2. Section I of the form requires you to give employer name and information. You must give this information even if the tax liability has nothing to do with your business. This also applies to the "spouse" sections of the form. Unless you are divorced, single, or widowed, you should fill out the information regarding your spouse whether or not your spouse is liable for your tax payments.
3. Section II calls for your individual information and allows you to input certain information about your dependents. Also, provide your previous address unless you have lived in your current home for more than 15 years.
4. Section III requires you to fill in the names of your banks, credit unions, and any accounts where you maintain a balance of available money (including IRA and pension plans). Be sure that your most recent statement agrees with the balance in box 13. Box 14 allows you to show the IRS what your current credit card liabilities are. List property that you own (if any), including investment properties, and the like in box 16. Again, have your mortgage payment book handy as you will be submitting copies of the mortgage payments to the IRS with your Offer in Compromise. In box 17, you should list all of your policies whether or not they have cash value. Box 18 allows you to fill in your stocks, bonds, mutual funds, other securities or types of investments, or savings. Box 19 requires you to provide more information related to your finances. Check the appropriate box. In box 19(a) be sure to check the "Yes" box if you have even been threatened with litigation recently (including by a bill collector). The other boxes are self-explanatory.
5. Section IV is the heart of the form. Simply take the information you compiled in Step 6 of this book and transfer to the form. Again, double-check the liability amounts to be sure they agree with your bills and receipts. The IRS will examine this section closely.

Figure 7.2 IRS Form 433-A, Collection Information Statement for Individuals

Form **433-A** (Rev. September 1995)	Department of the Treasury — Internal Revenue Service **Collection Information Statement for Individuals**

NOTE: Complete all blocks, except shaded areas. Write "N/A" *(not applicable)* in those blocks that do not apply.
Instructions for certain line items are in Publication 1854.

1. Taxpayer(s) name(s) and address Russell Retired 100 Bay View Road Retired City, FL 33054 County Broward	2. Home phone number (954) 123-4567	3. Marital status Married
	4.a. Taxpayer's social security number 197-00-2947	b. Spouse's social security number 197-01-2947

Section I.   Employment Information

5. Taxpayer's employer or business *(name and address)* Retired Hardware store owner	a. How long employed N/A	b. Business phone number ( ) N/A	c. Occupation Retired
	d. Number of exemptions claimed on Form W-4 N/A	e. Pay period: ☐ Weekly ☐ Bi-weekly N/A ☐ Monthly ☐ _____ Payday: _____ (Mon - Sun)	f. *(Check appropriate box)* ☐ Wage earner ☐ Sole proprietor ☐ Partner
6. Spouse's employer or business *(name and address)* Retired	a. How long employed N/A	b. Business phone number ( ) N/A	c. Occupation Retired
	d. Number of exemptions claimed on Form W-4 N/A	e. Pay period: ☐ Weekly ☐ Bi-weekly N/A ☐ Monthly ☐ _____ Payday: _____ (Mon - Sun)	f. *(Check appropriate box)* ☐ Wage earner ☐ Sole proprietor ☐ Partner

Section II.   Personal Information

7. Name, address and telephone number of next of kin or other reference Mrs. Russell Retired 100 Bay View Road Retired City, FL 33054	8. Other names or aliases N/A	9. Previous address(es) 555 Northeast Drive Philadelphia, PA 19355

10. Age and relationship of dependents living in your household *(exclude yourself and spouse)*

None

11. Date of Birth ▶	a. Taxpayer 12/1/32	b. Spouse 12/1/35	12. Latest filed income tax return *(tax year)* 1997	a. Number of exemptions claimed 1	b. Adjusted Gross Income $12,500

Section III.   General Financial Information

13. Bank accounts (include savings & loans, credit unions, IRA and retirement plans, certificates of deposit, etc.) Enter bank *loans* in item 28.

Name of Institution	Address	Type of Account	Account No.	Balance
Best Bank	1000 Main St., Ft. Lauderdale	check	141-448	$8,000
Northeast Funds	23 Northeast Dr., Philadelphia, PA	Keogh	322-000	$7,300
		Total *(Enter in Item 21)*		

Cat. No. 20312N   Form **433-A** (Rev. 9-95)

Figure 7.2 IRS Form 433-A, Collection Information Statement for Individuals (Continued)

Section III - *continued*   **General Financial Information**

14. Charge cards and lines of credit from banks, credit unions, and savings and loans. List all other charge accounts in item 28.

Type of Account or Card	Name and Address of Financial Institution	Monthly Payment	Credit Limit	Amount Owed	Credit Available
	Totals *(Enter in Item 27)* ▶				

15. Safe deposit boxes rented or accessed *(List all locations, box numbers, and contents)*

16.	**Real Property** *(Brief description and type of ownership)*	**Physical Address**
a.		County _____
b.		County _____
c.		County _____

17.	**Life Insurance** *(Name of Company)*	Policy Number	Type	Face Amount	Available Loan Value
			☐ Whole ☐ Term		
			☐ Whole ☐ Term		
			☐ Whole ☐ Term		
		Total *(Enter in Item 23)* ▶			

18. Securities (stocks, bonds, mutual funds, money market funds, government securities, etc.):

Kind	Quantity or Denomination	Current Value	Where Located	Owner of Record

19. Other information relating to your financial condition. If you check the yes box, please give dates and explain on page 4, Additional Information or Comments:

a. Court proceedings	☐ Yes ☐ No	b. Bankruptcies	☐ Yes ☐ No
c. Repossessions	☐ Yes ☐ No	d. Recent sale or other transfer of assets for less than full value	☐ Yes ☐ No
e. Anticipated increase in income	☐ Yes ☐ No	f. Participant or beneficiary to trust, estate, profit sharing, etc.	☐ Yes ☐ No

Form **433-A**   **page 2**   (Rev. 9-95)

Figure 7.2 IRS Form 433-A, Collection Information Statement for Individuals (Continued)

Section IV. — Assets and Liabilities

Description	Current Market Value	Current Amount Owed	Equity in Asset	Amount of Monthly Payment	Name and Address of Lien/Note Holder/Lender	Date Pledged	Date of Final Payment
20. Cash							
21. Bank accounts (from Item 13)							
22. Securities (from Item 18)							
23. Cash or loan value of insurance							
24. Vehicles (model, year, license, tag#)							
a.							
b.							
c.							
25. Real property (From Section III, item 16) a.							
b.							
c.							
26. Other assets							
a.							
b.							
c.							
d.							
e.							
27. Bank revolving credit (from Item 14)							
28. Other Liabilities (Including bank loans, judgments, notes, and charge accounts not entered in Item 13.) a.							
b.							
c.							
d.							
e.							
f.							
g.							
29. Federal taxes owed (prior years)							
30. **Totals**			$	$			

Internal Revenue Service Use Only Below This Line

Financial Verification/Analysis

Item	Date Information or Encumbrance Verified	Date Property Inspected	Estimated Forced Sale Equity
Personal Residence			
Other Real Property			
Vehicles			
Other Personal Property			
State Employment (Husband and Wife)			
Income Tax Return			
Wage Statements (Husband and Wife)			
Sources of Income/Credit (D&B Report)			
Expenses			
Other Assets/Liabilities			

Form **433-A**   **page 3**   (Rev. 9-95)

Nuts and Bolts: Filling Out Form 433-B

Remember that you need to fill out Form 433-B (shown in Figure 7.3) only if you are self-employed, derive substantially all of your income from a small business, or if the Offer in Compromise involves your business.

1. Fill out boxes 1–6 as appropriate. If you're not sure about any of this information, consult your CPA or tax attorney immediately. Do not estimate: It will assuredly come back to haunt you even if your offer is otherwise processable.

2. In box 7, you must reveal the names of officers, owners, and partners of a business entity. You need not list all shareholders (particularly if a shareholder owns a minority percentage of the business), but you should always list any majority shareholder(s) if you are submitting an Offer in Compromise on behalf of the business.

3. Section I calls for general financial information, including the names of your bank(s) and sources of credit for the business. The IRS is looking for a way to get you to pay the bill off in full with a line of credit, so be sure that you do not overestimate your ability to borrow, even if the bank has already set up a line of credit for you. In many cases, a bank will not advance money if your financial condition has deteriorated since you originally applied. Check with your banker if you're not sure of your status. Section I also requires that you disclose other sources of possible cash for the IRS, such as accounts receivables, loans to shareholders, and the like. While you should never lie or withhold any of this information from the IRS, be very cautious about verifying your accounts receivables to be sure they are still collectible. If you inform the IRS you have $100,000 in accounts receivables, but you know that $20,000 of the receivables are 12 months past due with little chance for collecting, write that amount off as a bad debt. If you are reluctant to do that, attach an addendum to the form explaining why the debt is uncollectible.

4. Ask your CPA for help in filling out the assets/liabilities section for your business. Unless you have a good working knowledge of accounting rules, the calculations called for on the assets/liabilities page can be complex. If the IRS detects a difference in what you've reported and what is actually the case, your mistake may be viewed as bad faith or trying to hide assets.

Figure 7.3 IRS Form 433-B, Collection Information Statement for Businesses

---

Form **433-B**
(Rev. June 1991)
Department of the Treasury
Internal Revenue Service

Collection Information Statement for Businesses

(If you need additional space, please attach a separate sheet.)

Note: Complete all blocks, except shaded areas. Write "N/A" *(not applicable)* **in those blocks that do not apply.**

1 Name and address of business	2 Business phone number ( )
	3 (Check appropriate box)
	☐ Sole proprietor ☐ Other *(specify)*
	☐ Partnership
County	☐ Corporation

4 Name and title of person being interviewed	5 Employer identification number	6 Type of business

7 Information about owner, partners, officers, major shareholder, etc.

Name and Title	Effective Date	Home Address	Phone Number	Social Security Number	Total Shares or Interest

Section I   **General Financial Information**

8 Latest filed income tax return ▶	Form	Tax year ended	Net income before taxes

9 Bank accounts *(List all types of accounts including payroll and general, savings, certificates of deposit, etc.)*

Name of Institution	Address	Type of Account	Account Number	Balance
		Total *(Enter in item 17)* . . . ▶		

10 Bank credit available *(Lines of credit, etc.)*

Name of Institution	Address	Credit Limit	Amount Owed	Credit Available	Monthly Payments
Totals *(Enter in items 24 or 25 as appropriate)* . . . . ▶					

11 Location, box number, and contents of all safe deposit boxes rented or accessed

Cat. No. 16649P   Form **433-B** (Rev. 6-91)

Figure 7.3 IRS Form 433-B, Collection Information Statement for Businesses (Continued)

Form 433-B (Rev. 6-91)   Page **2**

Section I (continued)   **General Financial Information**

12   Real property

	Brief Description and Type of Ownership	Physical Address
a		County
b		County
c		County
d		County

13   Life insurance policies owned with business as beneficiary

Name Insured	Company	Policy Number	Type	Face Amount	Available Loan Value

Total (Enter in item 19) . . . . ▶

14a   Additional information regarding financial condition *(Court proceedings, bankruptcies filed or anticipated, transfers of assets for less than full value, changes in market conditions, etc. Include information regarding company participation in trusts, estates, profit-sharing plans, etc.)*

b   If you know of any person or organization that borrowed or otherwise provided funds to pay net payrolls:

(i)   Who borrowed funds?

(ii)   Who supplied funds?

15   Accounts/notes receivable *(Include current contract jobs, loans to stockholders, officers, partners, etc.)*

Name	Address	Amount Due	Date Due	Status
		$		

Total (Enter in item 18) . . . . ▶ | $

Figure 7.3 IRS Form 433-B, Collection Information Statement for Businesses (Continued)

Form 433-B (Rev. 6-91)   Page **3**

Section II   **Asset and Liability Analysis**

(a) Description	(b) Cur. Mkt. Value	(c) Liabilities Bal. Due	(d) Equity in Asset	(e) Amt. of Mo. Pymt	(f) Name and Address of Lien/Note Holder/Obligee	(g) Date Pledged	(h) Date of Final Pymt.
16 Cash on hand							
17 Bank accounts							
18 Accounts/Notes receivable							
19 Life insurance loan value							
20 Real property *(from item 12)* a							
b							
c							
d							
21 Vehicles *(model, year, and license)* a							
b							
c							
22 Machinery and equipment *(specify)* a							
b							
c							
23 Merchandise inventory *(specify)* a							
b							
24 Other assets *(specify)* a							
b							
25 Other liabilities *(including notes and judgments)* a							
b							
c							
d							
e							
f							
g							
h							
26 Federal taxes owed							
27 Total							

Figure 7.3 IRS Form 433-B, Collection Information Statement for Businesses (Continued)

Form 433-B (Rev. 6-91)   Page **4**

Section III   **Income and Expense Analysis**

The following information applies to income and expenses during the period _____ to _____   Accounting method used

Income		Expenses	
28 Gross receipts from sales, services, etc.	$	34 Materials purchased	$
29 Gross rental income		35 Net wages and salaries (Number of employees ....)	
30 Interest		36 Rent	
31 Dividends		37 Allowable installment payments *(IRS use only)*	
32 Other income *(specify)*		38 Supplies	
		39 Utilities/telephone	
		40 Gasoline/oil	
		41 Repairs and maintenance	
		42 Insurance	
		43 Current taxes	
		44 Other *(specify)*	
33 Total income ▶	$	45 Total expenses *(IRS use only)* ▶	$
		46 Net difference *(IRS use only)* ▶	$

Certification: Under penalties of perjury, I declare that to the best of my knowledge and belief this statement of assets, liabilities, and other information is true, correct, and complete.

47 Signature   48 Date

Internal Revenue Service Use Only Below This Line

Financial Verification/Analysis

Item	Date Information or Encumbrance Verified	Date Property Inspected	Estimated Forced Sale Equity
Sources of income/credit (D&B report)			
Expenses			
Real property			
Vehicles			
Machinery and equipment			
Merchandise			
Accounts/notes receivable			
Corporate information, if applicable			
U.C.C.: senior/junior lienholder			
Other assets/liabilities			

Explain any difference between item 46 (or P&L) and the installment agreement payment amount:

Name of originator and IDRS assignment number	Date

CONSIDER THIS...

Hiding Assets and Other Criminal Acts

During your encounters with the IRS, you may have an urge to disclose only what you want the IRS to know about your assets. However, hiding assets or lying about assets to the IRS is a criminal offense! Depending on your methods, you could face a severe fine and/or jail time. Also, do not take the IRS's ability to locate your assets too lightly. It has a multitude of methods to verify your statements and any information you submit. In the case of an Offer in Compromise, the IRS agent will verify the information you reported on your Form 433-A or Form 433-B by cross-checking the information with the IRS's computer database, interviewing third parties, and even visiting your office or home personally.

Most taxpayers can resolve their debts with the IRS through legal methods (such as the Offer in Compromise program), so don't complicate your case by trying to hide assets. It almost never works.

DON'T FORGET...

✔ Review the IRS's national standards for living expenses and compare your actual expenses to its standards.

✔ Using the information you collected in Step 6, fill out the collection information statements required.

✔ Never hide assets from the IRS. You must disclose those assets that are asked for on the form(s); no more and no less.

Calculate Your Minimum Offer in Compromise

After completing IRS Form 433-A and/or Form 433-B, you have all of the information necessary to calculate your minimum acceptable offer. Remember that the IRS is not interested in very low offers and they do not operate the Offer in Compromise program under the "something is better than nothing premise." Offering too little money is a common reason for rejection and the IRS specifically instructs its employees not to engage in negotiation with the taxpayer who is submitting an offer below collection potential. You must calculate your offer in the same way the IRS will calculate the potential collection amount: through a standard (and simple) formula using certain facts from your collection information statements (Form 433-A and Form 433-B).

The Nuts and Bolts of Offers in Compromise Based on Doubt as to Collectibility

In determining the acceptability of an Offer in Compromise based on doubt as to collectibility, the IRS historically required that the total amount offered had to exceed the total "equity value" of your assets. The current IRS policy is a bit more lenient as it generally will not reject an offer solely on the basis of evaluation of your assets. Rather, the IRS will look to what it refers to as "collection potential" and then compares your offer to that number.

The tool used to submit your Offer in Compromise is IRS Form 656 and the package also must include Forms 433-A and 433-B (discussed in Step 7). But any good Offer in Compromise package also includes other documents that you provide to help support your case. You should begin to assemble these documents now: leases or mortgage payment statements; court orders for support or alimony payments; documents that show that your assets are encumbered by secured creditors (which puts them ahead of the IRS) such as a security agreement or a UCC-1 filing; any real estate appraisals, bank statements, brokerage statements, unpaid notes, bills, or other evidence of your debts; statements from your doctor concerning your deteriorating health problems or your inability to work full-time; titles and records to motor vehicles; and any other documents that support the information you reported on your financial statements. You do not need to attach IRS correspondence to your offer package, but it is usually a good idea to attach your tax returns for the last two years. Some tax professionals see including your tax returns as an unnecessary step as the IRS already has your tax returns. However, as a practical matter, the IRS official who will be evaluating your offer may have to send for your returns through internal IRS channels. This will delay the review of your offer significantly because the internal ordering system for tax returns at the IRS is archaic.

You should also consider making a payment "deposit" with your Offer in Compromise. Although it is not legally required, the IRS will view your good faith deposit as a sign that you are serious about settling the tax liability. It is important to realize that the IRS will not apply the payment unless it accepts the offer or you tell them to accept the payment toward your assessment. This means that even if the IRS has filed a federal tax lien, it will return the deposit if it does not accept the offer. Deposits of from 10 to 20 percent of the total amount being offered is very reasonable, but if you cannot afford that much, try sending in some amount that will evidence your good faith and desire to settle the tax bill. You do not, however, earn any interest on the deposit while it is in IRS hands, so be sure not to submit the whole amount all at once, or even 50 percent of the total amount being offered with your Offer in Compromise package.

Offer in Compromise program payments may be paid in one of three ways:

1. In full, by personal check or certified check when the offer is submitted
2. In "deferred" payments due upon acceptance of the offer
3. At specified and reasonable periods following the IRS's acceptance of your offer

Before your Offer in Compromise actually gets to the examining officer who will make the determination on the offer, it is reviewed by the revenue officer assigned to your case to be sure that the offer is processable. Believe it or not, most self-help offers (offers prepared without professional help) never make it past this first hurdle. Within 14 calendar days of submitting your offer, the IRS will return your offer package if one of the following is true:

- The offer leaves out basic data such as what liabilities and tax years the offer covers.
- You have not signed the appropriate forms.
- The amount offered is zero dollars.
- You fail to provide the appropriate financial information on yourself and/or you fail to submit IRS Form 433-A and/or Form 433-B with your offer package.
- You fail to submit a reasonable offer based on the financial information you have submitted (i.e., your offer does not reflect the collection potential).
- You have used an outdated form or you have altered any IRS forms submitted with the offer package.
- You have failed to comply with current filing and payment requirements.

If your Offer in Compromise package was accepted for processing, you will be notified within 14 calendar days. The IRS's letter will set a time frame to inform you whether or not your offer has been accepted. Although IRS manuals and publications promise to reply in 30 to 45 days, it will be at least three months and could go as long as a year if a complex investigation is warranted by your offer.

Once your offer is deemed processable, it is routed to the appropriate IRS office. Generally, the examining officer makes a determination as to what constitutes an acceptable offer by looking at the amounts that can be collected from your current assets. These include cash in the bank, stocks, mutual funds, real property equity, insurance policy cash values, and so on. The IRS also looks at the liquidation value of your assets and amounts that may be collected from your future income. To this end, a high income stream generally hurts your chances of having your offer accepted. The IRS has ten years for you to accumulate sufficient assets to pay the taxes in full.

— What is a high income stream?
—

CASE STUDY

The Retiree's Nightmare

After 30 years in business, Russell decided to sell his hardware store and retire. He sold the store and its assets for a relatively small amount of money, and he and his wife moved to Florida to retire. Russell went ahead of his wife and bought a condo, using the money from the sale of the store. Because his wife was not available to sign the papers for the house, a real estate agent, anxious for his commission, convinced Russell to simply hold the property as sole owner. One week later, Russell and his wife began their retirement life in the Florida condo. They also kept their house in the Northeast because Russell wanted his only daughter and son-in-law to inherit it after he and his wife were dead. Russell was enjoying his retirement and regularly gave cash gifts to his daughter and son-in-law because the retirees only needed Social Security and Russell's wife's pension check to live comfortably.

One day the IRS sent Russell a notice that he was being assessed back taxes because his tax preparer (who also was now retired) had taken improper deductions on Russell's personal income tax return. But the liability stemmed from his Schedule C filing (income from his business) two years before and therefore it was Russell's liability alone. Russell's wife was not responsible for any taxes. Finally, Russell received his assessment notice: He owed $73,000 in taxes, penalties, and interest.

Russell's assets were as follows (*indicates property held jointly with his wife):

Cash	$ 8,000
Keogh Account	7,300
Home Equity—Northeast*	175,000
Condo Equity—Florida	20,000
Furniture*	10,000
Personal Property	5,000
Autos*	3,000
Life Insurance Cash Value	500
Total	**228,800**
Total (Excluding Jointly Held Assets)	**$ 40,800**

At first glance, it appears that Russell would simply have to sell one of his properties and use that money to pay off his tax bill. But let's take a closer look at the alternatives:

Installment Agreement

Because Russell no longer earns a salary and is retired, it is very unlikely that the IRS would propose or even accept an installment agreement. Remember, installment agreements are agreements to pay tax owed over a period of time. They are primarily a tool for those who are not eligible under the Offer in Compromise program and who have a reasonable income stream that will allow them to pay the installments after paying living expenses.

Offer in Compromise—Doubt as to Liability

This alternative deserves a close look. Russell took his returns and records to a reputable CPA to ensure that the IRS had correctly assessed him the amounts they claimed he owed (as detailed in Step 1). Although he had to pay money to the CPA, it was smart to have the expert advice and a critical eye of a CPA before going any further with the IRS. However, Russell's CPA did not find any errors or false assumptions in the IRS's calculations and therefore an Offer in Compromise based on doubt as to liability was out of the question.

Offer in Compromise—Doubt as to Collectibility

Although a quick look at Russell's balance sheet might lead him to believe that his assets were too high to submit an Offer in Compromise based on doubt as to collectibility, a closer look reveals a possible avenue to cut his tax debt significantly. The most important thing to remember is that the IRS is looking not just at Russell's assets, but also at the IRS's collection potential. In Step 1, we learned that the IRS cannot levy or seize property that is held by both husband and wife (known in legalese as "tenants by the entirety") for any individual tax liability of one of the spouses. That is the case here. Russell's northeastern house and his autos are all outside the reach of the IRS! Therefore, the IRS collection potential drops significantly. Add on to that the impracticality of the IRS seizing and selling Russell's personal property (which probably has a "quick sale" value of significantly less than its original value), and the IRS's collection potential drops even further. But Russell is vulnerable in one area. Because he alone was the sole owner of record of the condo in Florida, that property is within the IRS's reach and could be subject to an IRS lien and seizure for unpaid taxes. With this in mind, Russell begins to calculate his Offer in Compromise amount based on doubt as to collectibility.

How to Figure the Minimum Amount the IRS Will Accept

We have already learned that the IRS traditionally focuses on a two-prong set of conditions to judge the amount you have offered: your total equity value and collection potential. Your total equity value is calculated using the information derived from the financial information statement that you prepared in Step 6. Your Offer in Compromise must be at least equal to the total equity value of all of your property and assets, plus one dollar. For purposes of placing a value on your property, the IRS uses what is known as the "quick sale" value. This works greatly to your benefit because it undervalues your property and makes your financial picture look more bleak (which is what we're trying to accomplish in the first place!). A quick sale value is less than the fair market value, but more than a so-called forced sale value of your assets.

For example, if you have a home with a fair market value of $200,000 and you owe $100,000 to the mortgage company, you have $100,000 in equity. If you stop paying your mortgage and the mortgage company forecloses on the house, this will result in a forced sale that would net about 70 percent of the value of the home: $140,000. Using the IRS's method of quick sale, however, your house has a value halfway between the fair market value ($200,000) and the forced sale value ($140,000). The approximate quick sale value would be $170,000. Because you owe $100,000, the IRS considers this house as representing $70,000 in assets (the quick sale value minus the amount owed the mortgage holder). The IRS uses the same method to put a value on all of your personal property that is not exempt from collection. Simply multiply the fair market value by 70 percent to determine the forced sale value and then calculate the halfway point between the fair market value and the forced sale value used by the IRS.

The second part of the IRS's Offer in Compromise is the "collectibility" test. For this test, the IRS compares how much you have offered with how much it could potentially collect if you entered into an installment agreement. This is a more complex figure and it takes a bit of calculation.

When your offer is submitted, the revenue officer will treat the package as if you were ready to enter into an installment agreement. He or she will do this by examining your collection information statements submitted on IRS Form 433-A and/or Form 433-B and determine what is the maximum amount of money you could pay each month. If, for example, the revenue officer determines you could pay $200 per month, he or she will then plug that amount into an IRS-created formula to determine what five years of monthly payments would yield the IRS. You may think that this means that you would simply multiply $200 times 60 months

CASE STUDY

Russell's Offer in Compromise Calculations

You'll recall that Russell's balance sheet would show only $40,800 in eligible assets because the house in the Northeast, the autos, and most of the furniture was owned by both him and his wife. Russell figured out his total equity using the IRS's quick sale valuation:

Asset	Fair Market Value (FMV)	Forced Sale Value (FSV) (70% of FMV)	Quick Sale Value (halfway point between FMV and FSV)
Condo	$100,000	$70,000	$85,000
Personal Property	5,000	3,500	4,250
Total			89,250
LESS (Mortgage Owed on Condo)			(80,000)
Equity Value of Property			$ 9,250

To that, Russell added his other assets that would be eligible:

Keogh Account	$ 7,300
Cash on Hand	8,000
TOTAL NET REALIZABLE EQUITY	**$24,550**

To meet the first part of the IRS Offer in Compromise test, Russell would have to offer at least $24,551 (eligible assets plus one dollar) (see Figure 8.1). But he also realizes that he must consider the second part of the IRS test to have his offer accepted.

Figure 8.1 Form 656, Sample Offer in Compromise

Department of Treasury
Internal Revenue Service

Form 656 (Rev. 1-97)
Catalog Number 16728N

Form 656

Offer in Compromise

*(If you need more space, use another sheet titled
"Attachment to Form 656", and sign and date it.)*

Item 1

Taxpayer's Name and Home or Business Address

Mr. Russell Retired
Name
100 Bay View Road
Street Address
Retired City, FL   33054
City   State   Zip Code
(Same as above)
Mailing Address (if different from above)

_____

City   State   Zip Code

Item 2

Social Security Numbers

(a) Primary 197-00-2947

(b) Secondary N/A

Item 3

Employer Identification Number (Included in offer)
N/A

Item 4

Other Employer Identification Numbers (Not included in offer)
N/A

Item 5

To: Commissioner of Internal Revenue Service

I/we (includes all types of taxpayers) submit this offer to compromise
the tax liabilities plus any interest, penalties, additions to tax, and additional amounts required by law (tax liability) for the tax type and period
marked below: (Please mark an "X" for the correct description and fill-in the correct tax periods(s), adding additional periods if needed.)

☒ **1040/1120 Income tax**—Year(s) _____1997_____

☐ **941 Employer's Quarterly Federal Tax Return**—Quarterly Period(s) _____

☐ **940 Employer's Annual Federal
Unemployment (FUTA) Tax Return**—Year(s) _____

☐ **Trust Fund Recovery Penalty** as a
responsible person of (enter corporation name) _____

for failure to pay withholding and Federal Insurance
Contributions Act Taxes (Social Security taxes)—Period(s) _____

☐ **Other Federal taxes** (specify type and periods(s). _____

Item 6

I/we submit this offer for the reason(s) checked below:

☐ **Doubt as to Liability**— "I do not believe I owe this amount." You *must* include
a detailed explanation of the reasons you believe you do not owe the tax.

☒ **Doubt as to Collectibility**—"I have insufficient assets and income to pay the
full amount." You *must* include a complete financial statement (Form 433-A and/ or
Form 433-B).

Item 7

I/We offer to pay $ 24,551.00

☐ **Paid in full with this offer.**
☐ **Deposit of $ 10,000 00** **with this offer.**
☐ **No deposit.**
Check one of the following boxes.
☒ Balance to be paid in ☐ 10, ☒ 30, ☐ 60, or ☐ 90 days from notice of accep-
tance of the offer. If more than one payment will be paid during the time frame
checked, provide the amount of the payment and date to be paid on the line below.

$14,551.00 - 30 days from acceptance

☐ Other proposed payment terms. Enter the specific dates (mm/dd/yy format)
and dollar amounts of the the payment terms you propose on the lines below.

_____

In addition to the above amount, IRS will add interest from the date IRS
accepts the offer until the date you completely pay the amount offered, as
required by section 6621 of the Internal Revenue Code, IRS compounds
interest daily, as required by section 6622 of the Internal Revenue Code.

9

Figure 8.1 Form 656, Sample Offer in Compromise (Continued)

Item 8

By submitting this offer, I/we understand and agree to the following conditions:

(a) I/we voluntarily submit all payments made on this offer.

(b) IRS will apply payments made under the terms of this offer in the best interest of the government.

(c) If IRS rejects the offer or I/we withdraw the offer, IRS will return any amount paid with the offer. If I/we agree in writing, IRS will apply the amount paid with the offer to the amount owed. If I/we agree to apply the payment, the date the offer is rejected or withdrawn will be considered the date of payment. I/we understand that IRS will not pay interest on any amount I/we submit with the offer.

(d) I/we will comply with all provisions of the Internal Revenue Code relating to filing my/our returns and paying my/our required taxes for 5 years from the date IRS accepts the offer. This condition does not apply to offers based on Doubt as to Liability.

(e) I/we waive and agree to the suspension of any statutory periods of limitation (time limits provided for by law) for IRS assessment and collection of the tax liability for the tax periods identified in item (5).

(f) IRS will keep all payments and credits made, received, or applied to the amount being compromised before this offer was submitted. IRS may keep any proceeds from a levy served prior to submission of the offer, but not received at the time the offer is submitted. If I/we have an installment agreement prior to submitting the offer, I/we must continue to make the payments as agreed while this offer is pending. Installment agreement payments will not be applied against the amount offered.

(g) IRS will keep any refund, including interest, due to me/us because of overpayment of any tax or other liability, for tax periods extending through the calendar year that IRS accepts the offer. *I/we may not designate a refund, to which the IRS is entitled, to be applied to estimated tax payments for the following year.* This condition doesn't apply if the offer is based only on Doubt as to Liability.

(h) I/we will return to IRS any refund identified in (g) received after submission of this offer. This condition doesn't apply if the offer is based only on Doubt as to Liability.

(i) The total amount IRS can collect under this offer can not be more than the full amount of the tax liability.

(j) I/we understand that I/we remain responsible for the full amount of the tax liability, unless and until IRS accepts the offer in writing and I/we have met all the terms and conditions of the offer. IRS won't remove the original amount of the tax liability from its records until I/we have met all the terms of the offer.

(k) I/we understand that the tax I/we offer to compromise is and will remain a tax liability until I/we meet all the terms and conditions of this offer. If I/we file bankruptcy before the terms and conditions of this offer are completed, any claim the IRS files in the bankruptcy proceeding will be a tax claim.

(l) Once IRS accepts the offer in writing, I/we have no right to contest, in court or otherwise, the amount of the tax liability.

(m) The offer is pending starting with the date an authorized IRS official signs this form and accepts my/our waiver of the statutory periods of limitation. The offer remains pending until an authorized IRS official accepts, rejects or acknowledges withdrawal of the offer in writing. If I/we appeal the IRS decision on the offer, IRS will continue to treat the offer as pending until the Appeals Office accepts or rejects the offer in writing. If I/we don't file a protest within 30 days of the date IRS notifies me/us of the right to protest the decision, I/we waive the right to a hearing before the Appeals office about the offer in compromise.

(n) The waiver and suspension of any statutory periods of limitation for assessment and collection of the amount of the tax liability described in item (5), continues to apply: while the offer is pending (see (m) above), during the time I/we have not paid all of the amount offered, during the time I/we have not completed all terms and conditions of the offer, and for one additional year beyond each of the time periods identified in this paragraph.

(o) If I/we fail to meet any of the terms and conditions of the offer, the offer is in default, then IRS may: immediately file suit to collect the entire unpaid balance of the offer; immediately file suit to collect an amount equal to the original amount of the tax liability as liquidating damages, minus any payments already received under the terms of this offer; disregard the amount of the offer and apply all amounts already paid under the offer against the original amount of tax liability; or file suit or levy to collect the original amount of the tax liability, without further notice of any kind.

IRS will continue to add interest as required by section 6621 of the Internal Revenue Code, on the amount IRS determines is due after default. IRS will add interest from the date the offer is defaulted until I/we completely satisfy the amount owed.

Item 9

If I/we submit this offer on a substitute form, I/we affirm that this form is a verbatim duplicate of the official Form 656, and I/we agree to be bound by all the terms and conditions set forth in the official Form 656.

Under penalties of perjury, I declare that I have examined this offer, including accompanying schedules and statements, and to the best of my knowledge and belief, it is true, correct and complete.

Russell Retired
(9a) Signature of Taxpayer-proponent

7/10/98
Date

_____
(9b) Signature of Taxpayer-proponent

_____
Date

For Official Use Only

I accept waiver of the statutory period of limitations for the Internal Revenue Service.

Signature of authorized Internal Revenue Service Official

_____
Title

_____
Date

C A S E   S T U D Y

Finalizing the Offer

Here Russell owes $73,000 in back taxes as a result of his assessment two years ago. Because 60 months is less than the IRS has to collect (10 years), use 60 months as the time factor.

   Based on his Form 433-A, Russell can pay only $125 a month (due to a small income) (see Figure 8.2). This, multiplied by 60 months, is $7,500 to be paid to the IRS. The present value calculation adds in the interest from the present value tables for 9 percent interest. $7,500 would be worth $11,500. Add onto this the $24,500 in net realizable equity and the minimum offer Russell should make is $36,000.

   Russell offers a $10,000 deposit payment and promises to pay $26,000 (out of a home equity loan) upon the IRS's acceptance of his offer. The IRS accepts the offer, Russell complies with the terms, and he has cut his back taxes from $73,000 to $36,000—a savings of more than 50 percent.

to arrive at the final figure, but this is not the way it works. The IRS also must factor in the present value of the money and calculate what the future value would be.

   In order to calculate this number, you can either use a calculator with a "PV" (present value) function, or simply call the IRS at 800-TAX-FORM and ask for the IRS's present value tables. Don't get nervous, this sounds harder than it really is. The IRS tables assume interest rates to be from about 7 to 12 percent and periods from 1 month to 120 months (ten years). But remember, the IRS limits its calculation to five years (60-months), so ignore the tables past the 60 month period.

   To arrive at the figure representing how much the IRS could get from you in a particular case, plug the following two figures into the IRS tables:

   1. Rate Factor—the IRS interest rate at the time you make your offer (assume for the case study that Russell will be making his offer when the rate is 9 percent).

Figure 8.2 Sample IRS Form 433-A, Collection Information Statement for Individuals

Form **433-A**
(Rev. September 1995)

Department of the Treasury — Internal Revenue Service

Collection Information Statement for Individuals

NOTE: Complete all blocks, except shaded areas, Write "N/A" *(not applicable)* in those blocks that do not apply.
Instructions for certain line items are in Publication 1854.

1. Taxpayer(s) name(s) and address	2. Home phone number ( )	3. Marital status
County _____	4.a. Taxpayer's social security number	b. Spouse's social security number

Section I.   Employment Information

5. Taxpayer's employer or business *(name and address)*	a. How long employed	b. Business phone number ( )	c. Occupation
	d. Number of exemptions claimed on Form W-4 _____	e. Pay period: ☐ Weekly ☐ Bi-weekly ☐ Monthly ☐ _____ Payday: _____ (Mon - Sun)	f. *(Check appropriate box)* ☐ Wage earner ☐ Sole proprietor ☐ Partner
6. Spouse's employer or business *(name and address)*	a. How long employed	b. Business phone number ( )	c. Occupation
	d. Number of exemptions claimed on Form W-4 _____	e. Pay period: ☐ Weekly ☐ Bi-weekly ☐ Monthly ☐ _____ Payday: _____ (Mon - Sun)	f. *(Check appropriate box)* ☐ Wage earner ☐ Sole proprietor ☐ Partner

Section II.   Personal Information

7. Name, address and telephone number of next of kin or other reference	8. Other names or aliases	9. Previous address(es)

10. Age and relationship of dependents living in your household *(exclude yourself and spouse)*

11. Date of Birth ▸	a. Taxpayer	b. Spouse	12. Latest filed income tax return *(tax year)*	a. Number of exemptions claimed	b. Adjusted Gross Income

Section III.   General Financial Information

13. Bank accounts *(include savings & loans, credit unions, IRA and retirement plans, certificates of deposit, etc.)* Enter bank *loans* in item 28.

Name of Institution	Address	Type of Account	Account No.	Balance
			Total *(Enter in Item 21)*	

Cat. No. 20312N

Form **433-A** (Rev. 9-95)

2. Time Factor—how many months the IRS has left to collect or 60 months, whichever is less.

The Nuts and Bolts of Offers in Compromise Based on Doubt as to Liability

The IRS does not require a collection information statement for Offers in Compromise based on doubt as to liability. However, in an offer based on doubt as to liability, you must include tangible evidence and a thorough discussion of all reasons why the tax or penalty may be doubtful from a legal perspective. If you have the ability to understand the complexities of the tax code, you may attempt to provide this discussion yourself with a review by your lawyer or CPA. However, the overwhelming majority of doubt as to liability cases requires some professional assistance in preparation.

Step-by-Step: Filling Out IRS Form 656—Offer in Compromise

1. Obtain IRS Form 656 (Rev. 1-97), Offer in Compromise, from your CPA, attorney, another tax professional (such as an enrolled agent), or your local IRS service center. It may be more difficult to find this form than you might expect. The IRS has not placed this form on its Web site nor in the binders distributed to public libraries (you can draw your own conclusions). Phone the IRS form hotline (800-TAX-FORM) or ask the revenue officer assigned to your case for the form. Be sure the far bottom right-hand corner reads Form 656 (Rev.1-97). This means that the IRS last revised this form in January 1997 and any form with that date or later is *acceptable*. The IRS will *reject* your Offer in Compromise if you use a form with a date earlier than 1-97.

2. In Item 1, write your full name (as it traditionally appears on your tax return) and your current address.

3. If this offer applies to your individual debt, you should fill in your Social Security number in Item 2. If it is a joint liability debt (for you and your spouse for example), then use the Social Security number that you used on the tax return(s) in question. If this is an offer for your small business that has its own employer identification number (EIN), then fill in only

Item 3. Whichever box you fill out, any blank box must be filled in with "N/A" (not applicable). This is true throughout this and other Offer in Compromise forms.

4. Figure the type of tax you owe and for what years you owe it. If you're not sure, recheck the correspondence you collected for Step 1 of this book. Check the appropriate box in Item 5 of the form and fill in the tax periods that are applicable. If you do not have the information required to fill out this item, do not estimate. If you are wrong, it will be grounds for the IRS to reject your offer as "unprocessable." Rather, call the phone number on any of your IRS correspondence and ask what type of tax you owe and for what tax year(s). Fill in this information and be sure to include all tax years to make sure that you're completely covered. If the type of tax owed is not preprinted on the form, insert it in the "other" blank along with the relevant tax-reporting period.

5. In Item 6, check the appropriate box for your Offer in Compromise category: collectibility or liability.

6. From your calculation of your minimum offer, insert the total amount you will offer (not just the deposit amount) into Item 7. Because most Offers in Compromise involve more than one payment, the IRS has provided several alternatives and even narrative lines in this section for you to explain how you will pay your offer amount. You may divide your offer amount any way you like, but be sure not to spread it out too long. The idea is to get the IRS to accept your offer, pay it off, and start over with a clean slate. An offer to pay out a few hundred dollars a year for five or six years and then pay a large lump sum from your future lottery win has little chance of being accepted by the IRS. Also, don't promise money you haven't already lined up for payment. You should have tried to collect as much as you can prior to submitting the offer, but you can use reasonable assumptions about your income in the future or on promises by relatives. If you go through the offer process and then not cannot make your payments, the IRS may assume you simply used the Offer in Compromise as a delay tactic. It may immediately employ its powerful collection methods such as emptying out your bank accounts through levy. Restudy the case study and Figure 8.1 for an example of how to complete this item properly.

7. Sign and date the form in Item 9 immediately after you have completed it. If it is not signed, the IRS will reject it without even looking at it.
8. Proofread the form for any missing or wrong information.

D O N ' T   F O R G E T . . .

✔ Figure the minimum amount the IRS will accept using the two-prong formula in this step.

✔ If your offer is based on doubt as to liability, be sure to have documented proof of why you are not liable for the taxes assessed.

✔ Fill out Form 656 using the step-by-step method in this step.

Determine Your Need for a Collateral Agreement

When submitting an Offer in Compromise, it is often wise to sweeten the deal with the IRS by promising some additional terms in the form of a collateral agreement. This is particularly true when yours is a borderline case (where you have submitted an Offer in Compromise based on doubt as to collectibility, but the amount offered is below the collection potential). In some cases, the IRS will require a collateral agreement after you have submitted your Offer in Compromise.

In a nutshell, a collateral agreement is an integral part of your Offer in Compromise contract with the IRS. The agreement provides for collection from future income or restricts future tax benefits from assets that are involved in the offer. There are three major types of collateral agreements: future income, waiver of losses, and waiver of deductions.

Future Income Collateral Agreement

The most common collateral agreement promises some percentage of your future income over a negotiated number of years. The IRS usually is happy with five years (but may go as high as ten years in some circumstances). This type of collateral agreement can be proposed by either the taxpayer or the IRS, but including a collateral agreement in your Offer in Compromise package helps to show the IRS that you are serious about wanting to pay off your tax debt.

When your income stream is sufficiently steady, the IRS views this as a reason not to accept your Offer in Compromise under the theory that they can simply wait out the collection period and have you pay the full amount of the tax. There are significant risks to the IRS if they wait because of the deadlines imposed on the IRS to collect the tax (known as the statute of limitations). By submitting the collateral agreement with the Offer in Compromise, you will be tempting the IRS to accept a lump sum deposit, and at the same time promising a percentage of your future income. In addition, the IRS's interests will be protected if you should inherit a large sum of money or if there is a significant increase in your income in some other fashion.

The percentage of income you promise to pay is based on your adjusted gross income over a certain level. In order to establish a baseline to start the collateral agreement, the amount of your ordinary and necessary expenses are first added up. The IRS wants you to promise a percentage of your income above your ordinary and necessary expenses to live (see Step 7 for more information on ordinary and necessary living expenses). For example, if you and the IRS agree that according to the IRS guidelines your ordinary and necessary living expenses add up to $30,000 annually, you could promise to pay the IRS 10 percent of any income above your $30,000 expenses. However, the IRS expects you to promise a higher percentage for higher levels of income. This means that you should usually submit this collateral agreement to pay out future income as a stepped program. In addition to the 10 percent step, you could agree to pay the IRS 20 percent of your after-expenses income above $40,000, 30 percent of your after-expenses income over $50,000, and so on.

If you choose this collateral agreement, the IRS will require you to submit IRS Form 3439 (Statement of Annual Income) every year in order to monitor your compliance with the Offer in Compromise and collateral agreement contracts.

Agreement-to-Waive-Losses Collateral Agreement

If you have net operating losses, capital losses, or unused investment credits, the IRS can require you to waive the carryback or carryover tax benefits resulting from the losses. If you have large carryover losses that may be carried forward to years after the Offer in Compromise is accepted, the IRS will be anxious to have you agree to waive those losses if it accepts your offer. Again, if you know you have the carryovers, don't wait for the IRS to require the waiver as a condition of the offer. Submit IRS Form 2261-C (Collateral Agreement—Waiver of Net Operating Losses and Capital Losses) as part of your Offer in Compromise package.

Agreement to Waive Deductions

You also may agree to waive certain deductions (such as a "bad debt" deduction or a "loss" deduction) as part of your Offer in Compromise. Typically, the IRS will require these deductions to be waived for the filing year in which the Offer in Compromise is accepted.

Other Miscellaneous Collateral Agreements

In addition to the three most common collateral agreements listed above, you also may want to consider the following types of agreements that apply to a more narrow group of taxpayers:

- Agreement to reduce the basis in a particular asset
- Co-obligor agreements in which one of the parties owning a joint tax liability is allowed to compromise that liability while protecting the IRS's interest in the other party's liability

Step-by-Step: Filling Out IRS Form 2261, Collateral Agreement

1. Fill in your name, address, and Social Security number at the top of Form 2261 (see Figure 9.1). Remember to use only your name if it is an individual liability and to use both your and your spouse's name in the case of joint liability. For businesses, use Form 2261-B.
2. Insert your total offer amount in Section 1 (first line).
3. In the second line of Section 1, fill in the years this collateral agreement will cover (usually five years from the date of offer).
4. Fill in the baseline amount in Section 1(a). This is the amount that will establish the beginning of your collateral agreement to pay. You are agreeing with the IRS that you will pay nothing until you exceed that floor amount.

Figure 9.1 Sample IRS Form 2261, Collateral Agreement

Form **2261**
(Rev. 04-95)

DEPARTMENT OF THE TREASURY — INTERNAL REVENUE SERVICE
Collateral Agreement
Future Income — Individual

Names and Address of Taxpayers

Andrew Assistant

Anytown, USA

Social Security and Employer
Identification Numbers

123-00-4567

To: Commissioner of Internal Revenue

The taxpayers identified above have submitted an offer dated ___1/10/97___ in the amount of $ ___9,000___ to

compromise unpaid ___Income___ tax liability, plus statutory additions, for the taxable periods ___1996___

The purpose of this collateral agreement (hereinafter referred to as this agreement) is to provide additional consideration for acceptance of the offer in compromise described above. It is understood and agreed:

1. That in addition to the payment of the above amount of $ ___9,000___ , the taxpayers will pay out of annual income for the years ___1997___ to ___2002___ , inclusive

   (a) Nothing on the first $ ___25,000___ of annual income.

   (b) ___25___ percent of annual income more than $ ___25,000___ and not more than $ ___35,000___ .

   (c) ___30___ percent of annual income more than $ ___35,000___ and not more than $ ___45,000___ .

   (d) ___40___ percent of annual income more than $ ___45,000___

2. That the term annual income, as used in this agreement, means adjusted gross income as defined in section 62 of the Internal Revenue Code (except losses from sales or exchanges of property shall not be allowed), plus all nontaxable income and profits or gains from any source whatsoever (including the fair market value of gifts, bequests, devises, and inheritances), minus (a) the federal income tax paid for the year for which annual income is being computed, and (b) any payment made under the terms of the offer in compromise (Form 656), as shown in item 5, for the year in which such payment is made. Annual income shall not be reduced by any overpayments waived in item 7g, Form 656. The annual income shall not be reduced by net operating losses incurred before or after the period covered by this agreement. However, a net operating loss for any year during such period may be deducted from annual income for the following year only. It is also agreed that annual income shall include all income and gains or profits of the taxpayers, regardless of whether these amounts are community income under state law.

3. That in the event close corporations are directly or indirectly controlled or owned by the taxpayers during the existence of this agreement, the computation of annual income shall include their proportionate share of the total corporate annual income in excess of $10,000. The term corporate annual income, as used in this agreement, means the taxable income of the corporation before net operating loss deduction and special deductions (except, in computing such income, the losses from sales or exchanges of property shall not be allowed), plus all nontaxable income, minus (a) dividends paid, and (b) the federal income tax paid for the year for which annual income is being computed. For this purpose, the corporate annual income shall not be reduced by any net operating loss incurred before or after the periods covered by this agreement, but a net operating loss for any year during such period may be deducted from the corporate annual income for the following year only.

4. That the annual payment provided for in this agreement (including interest at the rate established under section 6621 of the Internal Revenue Code (compounded under Code section 6622(a)) on delinquent payments computed from the due date of such payment) shall be paid to the Internal Revenue Service, without notice, on or before the 15th day of the 4th month following the close of the calendar or fiscal year, such payments to be accompanied by a sworn statement and a copy of the taxpayers' federal income tax return. The statement shall refer to this agreement and show the computation of annual income in accordance with items 1, 2, and 3 of this agreement. If the annual income for any year covered by this agreement is insufficient to require a payment under its terms, the taxpayers shall still furnish the Internal Revenue Service a sworn statement of such income and a copy of their federal income tax return. All blocks, records, and accounts shall be open at all reasonable times for inspection by the Internal Revenue Service to verify the annual income shown in the statement. Also, the taxpayers hereby expressly consent to the disclosure to each other of the amount of their respective annual income and of all books, records, and accounts necessary to the computation of their annual income for the purpose of administering this agreement. The payment (if any), the sworn statement, and a copy of the federal income tax return shall be transmitted to:
   Address:

Cat. No. 18243R   *(Over)*   Form **2261** (Rev. 04-95)

Figure 9.1 Sample IRS Form 2261, Collateral Agreement (Continued)

5. That the aggregate amount paid under the terms of the offer in compromise and the additional amounts paid under the terms of this agreement shall not exceed an amount equivalent to the liability covered by the offer plus statutory additions that would have become due in the absence of the compromise.

6. That payments made under the terms of this agreement shall be applied first to tax and penalty, in that order, due for the earliest taxable period, then to tax and penalty, in that order, for each succeeding taxable period with no amount to be allocated to interest until the liabilities for taxes and penalties for all taxable periods sought to be compromised have been satisfied.

7. That upon notice to the taxpayers of the acceptance of the offer in compromise of the liability identified in this agreement, the taxpayers shall have no right, in the event of default in payment of any installment of principal or interest due under the terms of the offer and this agreement or in the event any other provision of this agreement is not carried out in accordance with its terms, to contest in court or otherwise the amount of the liability sought to be compromised; and that in the event of such default or noncompliance or in the event the taxpayers become the subject of any proceeding (except a proceeding under the Bankruptcy Act) whereby their affairs are placed under the control and jurisdiction of a court or other party, the United States, at the option of the Commissioner of Internal Revenue or a delegated official, may (a) proceed immediately by suit to collect the entire unpaid balance of the offer and this agreement, or (b) proceed immediately by suit to collect as liquidated damages an amount equal to the tax liability sought to be compromised, minus any payments already received under the terms of the offer and this agreement, with interest at the rate established under section 6621 of the Internal Revenue Code (compounded under Code section 6622(a)) from the date of default, or (c) disregard the amount of such offer and this agreement, apply all amounts previously paid thereunder against the amount of the liability sought to be compromised and, without further notice of any kind, assess and collect by levy or suit (the restrictions against assessment and collection being waived) the balance of such liability. In the event the taxpayers become the subject of any proceeding under the Bankruptcy Act, the offer in compromise and this agreement may be terminated. Upon such termination, the tax liability sought to be compromised, minus any payments already received under the terms of the offer and this agreement, shall become legally enforceable.

8. That the taxpayers waive the benefit of any statute of limitations applicable to the assessment and collection of the liability sought to be compromised and agree to the suspension of the running of the statutory period of limitations on assessment and collection for the period during which the offer in compromise and this agreement are pending, or the period during which any installment under the offer and this agreement remains unpaid, or any provision of this agreement is not carried out in accordance with its terms, and for 1 year thereafter.

9. That when all sums, including interest, due under the terms of the offer in compromise and this agreement, except those sums which may become due and payable under the provisions of item 1 of this agreement, have been paid in full, then and in that event only, all federal tax liens at that time securing the tax liabilities which are the subject of the offer shall be immediately released. However, if, at the time consideration is being given to the release of the federal tax liens, there are any sums due and payable under the terms of item 1, they must also be paid before the release of such liens.

This agreement shall be of no force or effect unless the offer in compromise is accepted.

Taxpayer's Signature	Date
Andrew Assistant	1/10/97
Taxpayer's Signature	Date

I accept the waiver of statutory period of limitations for the Internal Revenue Service.

Signature and Title	Date

Cat. No. 18243R   Form **2261** (Rev. 04-95)

5. Fill in Section 1 (b–d) consistent with your step plan established earlier in this chapter.

6. Read the information in Sections 2–9, which is the basis for your collateral agreement with the IRS. If you violate the terms of the agreement, you will be back at Step 1. Unfortunately, at this point you will have lost all of the goodwill from the revenue officer. This agreement is a contract with the government, so read it closely like any other contract. If you have any questions, ask your attorney, CPA, or even the revenue officer handling your case.

7. Sign and date the form and submit it along with your Offer in Compromise package.

C A S E   S T U D Y

Anatomy of a Successful Offer in Compromise with Collateral Agreement

After Andrew was graduated from college, he had a difficult time finding a job. He started to do odd jobs for neighbors to earn some income while he continued his job search. Eventually, as Andrew started to earn a pretty good living, he began advertising his services outside his neighborhood and in a few weeks he was bringing in a steady stream of income from his work. Unfortunately, times became tighter and Andrew started to report to the IRS only half of what he actually earned. The IRS assessed taxes as follows:

Type	Tax Owed	Interest/Penalty
Income Tax 1996	$10,000	$2,750
Income Tax 1997	$11,000	$3,500
TOTAL TAX OWED:	**$27,250**	

The IRS properly assessed Andrew the taxes, and sent proper notice of the tax bill. Andrew's assets and liabilities are minimal:

Available Cash	$5,000
Car (Equity)	1,000
Furniture/Jewelry	2,000
Other Personal Property	1,000

Other Important Facts

- Andrew also is now employed full-time at an annual salary of $25,000. After taxes, Andrew brings home about $1,500 per month

- Andrew's rent and other living expenses total $1,300 per month. These expenses all fall within the national and local standards articulated by IRS guidelines.

- Andrew's parents have indicated their willingness to lend him some money to resolve his IRS debt.

- Andrew checked all of the IRS's calculations and assumptions and has determined that there are no errors.

Possible Solutions

Offer Based on Doubt as to Liability

Because Andrew has determined that the IRS was correct in its assessment, he cannot submit an offer based on doubt as to liability.

Installment Agreement

More than likely, the IRS revenue officer will be looking toward an installment agreement at first. This may temporarily relieve the pressure on Andrew and will be a way to make sure that no enforcement action is taken, such as levying his bank accounts. But the payments will make his living expenses much tighter.

Moreover, he will end up having to pay all the taxes, penalties, and ongoing interest. Because the IRS has not filed a Notice of Federal Tax Lien or tried to levy the bank accounts, Andrew still has time to submit an Offer in Compromise, though with fear that he will be subject to collections while he is preparing the offer package.

Offer Based on Doubt as to Collectibility

Because the forced sale of Andrew's assets will only yield a collection potential of $9,000, he will be best served by submitting an offer based on doubt as to collectibility. This is the IRS's potential collection and it could be submitted as the full amount owed. If the IRS were to accept the offer, it would result in the elimination of $27,250 worth of back tax debt and Andrew would start with a clean slate.

Potential Reason for Rejection—Collateral Agreement Requirement

Andrew will face an uphill battle with the IRS as he arguably has significant income earning potential. Although Andrew passes the "equity in assets being lower than tax owed" test with flying colors, he has good earning potential and will probably not meet the "other methods of collection test" (see Step 5 for more details on the criteria). The IRS will most likely require a collateral agreement for future income. Because Andrew is a young, college-educated taxpayer, the IRS will view him as having the ability to pay more if it is simply willing to wait a little longer to receive the tax owed. Taking into consideration Andrew's current income and expenses, he could propose the following installment agreement schedule:

- $1,500 as a deposit/first-time payment (from Andrew's savings)

- $7,500 (borrowed from parents) to be paid within 30 days from the IRS's acceptance of his Offer in Compromise.

- 20 percent of Andrew's income above $25,000. Therefore, if Andrew's income is $30,000 in the year after his offer is submitted, the IRS would get an additional $1,000.

- 30 percent of Andrew's income over and above $35,000. If Andrew earns $40,000 in the year after his offer was submitted, the IRS would get an additional $1,500.

This Offer in Compromise package protects Andrew in that if he were to lose his job or have to take a lower-paying position, he would not be responsible for paying out any other money other than his initial lump sum payment. In any case, Andrew's debt with the IRS would be settled for good so long as he kept current on his taxes and filings. In the end, Andrew will have saved himself as much as $18,250 and plenty of aggravation.

DON'T FORGET...

✔ Decide if you will need a collateral agreement to submit with your offer.

✔ Using your minimum offer calculations, determine how much of your future income you can realistically pledge.

Submitting Your Offer in Compromise Package

It's time to relax a little, but not to be careless. The hard part is over and you've followed all of the steps leading you to eliminating your back tax debt once and for all. But before you pat yourself on the back, carefully go through the Offer in Compromise package.

Avoiding the Most Common Mistakes

Because the IRS is a bureaucracy, Offers in Compromise may be rejected for "form" as opposed to "substance." That is, other than one defect in the form of the submission, the Offer in Compromise would be acceptable. Here are five of the most common mistakes and surefire ways to avoid them:

1. *Using expired forms.* The IRS changes some of its forms often and some forms go decades without a change. Be sure to use the updated Form 656 (Rev. 1-97) Offer in Compromise. An old form will be rejected. Call the IRS's toll-free forms hotline (800-TAX-FORM) and ask the call taker to identify the current revision of any forms you may use. If you don't have the current version of any form, ask that it (they) be mailed to you.
2. *Submitting an offer below collection potential.* Many taxpayers think that negotiating with the IRS is akin to negotiating a business deal. While this

is a good attitude, you must realize that generally the IRS has all of the cards and your negotiating power is minimal. In a business negotiation, you will generally start with a low offer, the other side starts high, and the two of you meet in the middle. The IRS frowns on this type of negotiation and instructs its revenue officers not to engage in a game of "High ball–low ball." If you offer less than the amount that your calculations from Step 6 reveal, your chances of having the offer accepted are minimal. If your offer is so low that it doesn't even come close to collection potential, you are in danger of giving the IRS the impression that you are stalling. Using the Offer in Compromise program as a stalling or delay tactic, without any serious attempt to resolve the tax liability, will result in the IRS becoming more aggressive about collecting the debt. While technically the IRS is not prohibited from taking collection action in a case while the offer is being reviewed, the *Internal Revenue Manual* instructs revenue officers to suspend collection activity while the offer is being reviewed unless the revenue officer has cause to believe that the offer is a delaying tactic.

3. *Lack of supporting documents.* Your Offer in Compromise package should contain documentation for as much of your financial history as possible. Submit copies (never originals) documenting:
   - Bank statements
   - Titles to vehicles
   - Sources of income other than your full-time job
   - Leases, mortgage papers, promissory notes
   - Documents proving that someone else has a first-position lien ahead of the IRS on your property (mortgage company, home equity loan company, etc.)
   - Unpaid bills or other evidence of your debt
   - Any other documents that evidence a liability or asset

4. *Math errors.* Offers may be rejected because the taxpayer's calculations are wrong. Recheck your math on the Offer in Compromise package and pay particular attention to the collection information statements (Form 433-A and Form 433-B).

5. *Improper submission format.* This covers common mistakes such as:
   - Not signing the form
   - Not dating the form

- Social Security number missing
- Submitting information that doesn't match the information the IRS has (e.g., the tax year in question differs from the year on your offer)

Any one of these (or similar mistakes) can be grounds for the IRS to reject your Offer in Compromise package.

Nuts and Bolts of Filing

There are generally two levels of review when you submit an Offer in Compromise package. Depending on where you stand with the IRS, you should either submit the package to the revenue officer assigned to handle your case or directly to the Offer in Compromise unit in your region (check Appendix A for the address). If your case is in collection mode (see Step 1, "Determine How Much the IRS Claims You Owe"), then your offer should first be submitted to the local field office where your revenue officer is located.

The first level of review in a collection case is performed by the revenue officer to check whether the offer is processable. Once it has passed the processability test at the local level, it is sent to the Offer in Compromise unit for review.

Step-by-Step: Packaging and Formatting Your Offer in Compromise Package

1. Use the Final Checklist at the end of this chapter for one final review, then have a trusted friend or relative review the offer package for mistakes.
2. Photocopy all original documents you will be submitting (mortgage bills, etc.) in support of your offer and place the copies in your package. Make one extra copy of the whole package for your own records.
3. Place the documents in the following order:
   a. Form 656, Offer in Compromise
   b. Form 433-A and/or Form 433-B
   c. Supplements and explanations for your Form 433
   d. Copies of your supporting documentation
   e. Form 886, Collateral Agreement
   f. Supplements and explanations for your Form 886

4. Mail the package by certified mail, return receipt requested. This will verify that you have mailed the Offer in Compromise and will come in handy if the IRS claims it never received your offer. The IRS loses more documents than they would like to admit and some people (even tax lawyers) send all documents to the IRS via certified mail—including their own tax returns!
5. Begin to line up the financing for the offer as soon as possible. You don't want to risk losing the goodwill you have created by backing out on an accepted offer because you couldn't raise the money in time.

How and When the IRS Responds

If your Offer in Compromise is not processable (the first level of review), the IRS will reject your package promptly and you will receive it back within a week or so. This is very common, and despite your adherence to the steps in this book, you may still have to correct a simple error and resubmit the package to the IRS. If your offer is drastically lower than your collection potential, you will receive the offer back promptly and the IRS will respond "offered amount does not reflect collection potential." This is a more serious problem and you should start again at Step 1 of this book and calculate an appropriate offer.

If your Offer in Compromise package is reviewed and marked "processable," you can expect to wait from three months to a year for the IRS to make a determination. If you have an existing installment agreement, you must still make payments and you absolutely must keep current on income taxes you owe. While the Offer in Compromise unit has guidelines to follow and levels of review within its office, an Offer in Compromise is still a highly subjective animal. Some offers are rejected simply because the IRS believes that some money will be due to the taxpayer before the statutory collection period runs out. On the other hand, some offers of less than 20 percent of the tax owed are accepted. If you make your Offer in Compromise package easy to read and show the IRS you are serious about paying your tax debt as soon as possible, your chances of having the offer accepted grow substantially.

During the investigation phase, you can expect the IRS to verify everything you have submitted in your financial statements. This sometimes may include a site visit by the revenue officer assigned to your case. If you've concealed your assets or misrepresented your liabilities, the IRS will stop the investigation, reject the offer, and begin collection immediately.

What to Do If the IRS Rejects Your Offer

What should you do if the IRS has rejected your first Offer in Compromise? Try, try again, of course. Assuming that you've submitted the Offer in Compromise in good faith, try to determine why the offer was rejected. If your offer is rejected, the IRS is required to give you a rejection letter. Generally, the IRS has stated that it has two major bases for rejection:

1. A too-low offer (most common)
2. Public policy concerns (e.g., you are a known tax cheat or have been convicted of a serious crime)

The IRS also has unstated reasons for rejecting your offer that you should know about. Perhaps the most universal is that time is on the IRS's side. If you are either beginning or well into your career, the IRS believes it can collect more from you by waiting than by accepting your offer. Younger taxpayers often find themselves in this situation and the IRS rejects their offer as "not reflecting collection potential."

Once you have received notice that your offer has been rejected, ask the revenue officer what would be an acceptable amount. You should also obtain a copy of the report the IRS used internally to evaluate your Offer in Compromise package. It lists the factors that caused the rejection. If the revenue officer won't give it to you (which is unlikely), file another Freedom of Information Act request using the information you learned in Step 2 of this book.

After you have determined what the problem was with the original offer, fill out a new Form 656 with appropriate amounts and resubmit the entire package. If the revenue officer won't help, contact the special procedures officer in your local service center for more help.

Remember too that there is no nationally accepted standard used by all IRS employees for acceptance of an Offer in Compromise. The attitudes and acceptance rate vary greatly from field office to field office and the very best way to figure out how to get an offer accepted is to review the Offers in Compromise that have already been submitted and accepted in your district. Offers in Compromise are public records for one year from the date of acceptance and you are free to review the offers in your district. Call your local district's Collection Division (see Appendix A) and request that you be permitted to set up a time to review the Offers in Compromise that were accepted in the past year. This is a very unusual request, so be patient but persistent. While you do have the right to examine the accepted offers, you do not have the right to march in at any time of day and demand that you be able to inspect offers on the spot.

The Appeal

If your Offer in Compromise is rejected, but you still believe that the revenue officer is giving you a raw deal, consider appealing through internal IRS channels. The nest way to negotiate an acceptance is directly with the revenue officer, but some revenue officers will not negotiate or give you any help with your Offer in Compromise. You have 30 days to appeal the rejection and you may appeal the rejection of any offer. Simply send a copy of your Offer in Compromise package with a protest letter and request a conference. The protest letter should contain the following:

- Your name (and your spouse's name if a joint return)
- Your Social Security number, address, and telephone number
- The reason why you disagree with the IRS's decision to reject the offer
- Copies of the IRS's rejection letter and a statement of why you were told the offer was rejected
- Your signature and a penalty clause (see the case study below)

CASE STUDY

The Protest Letter

After having his carefully crafted Offer in Compromise package rejected for being too low, Thomas reevaluated his offer and found that he met both tests under the collectibility standard and was thus eligible for the program. The revenue officer assigned to Thomas's case told him that his financial information statement indicated that he had enough equity in his house to cover more than the amount offered. But Thomas knew that he had no equity in his house because he had borrowed against the equity to pay bills. Since this was not yet recorded in the public record, the revenue officer added the equity to the pool of assets.

After a discussion with the revenue officer, Thomas decided to file an appeal. He sent this letter:

January 5, 1998

District Director (Appeal)
IRS, Philadelphia, PA
RE:Offer in Compromise Appeal of Thomas _____

Dear Sir/Madam:

I wish to appeal the IRS's determination letter rejecting my Offer in Compromise that I submitted on December 1, 1997. The reason I wish to appeal is because the revenue officer incorrectly added equity in my house to my assets pool. I have no equity in my house and therefore my net assets are $14,000. My collection potential is $11,000 and therefore I am offering $25,001 consistent with the terms of my Form 656.

I request a conference. I may be reached at 215-123-4567 during the day. Under penalty of perjury, I declare that the facts presented in this appeal and any accompanying documents are true and complete to the best of my belief and knowledge.

Sincerely,

Thomas _____ (SS# 123-45-6789)

Enclosed: Original Offer in Compromise Package

Final Checklist: Rejection-Proofing Your Offer in Compromise

1. _____ Complete Form 656 and leave no blanks.
2. _____ Complete Form 433-A and/or Form 433-B and leave no blanks (write N/A in blanks).
3. _____ Recalculate your actual tax liability from Step 3.
4. _____ Recalculate all of the assets and liabilities in Step 7.
5. _____ Attach supporting documents for each asset or liability in Step 7.
6. _____ Recalculate your minimum acceptable offer in Step 8.
7. _____ Redetermine your need for a collateral agreement. If unsure, file anyway.
8. _____ Include Form 2261, Collateral Agreement, if applicable.
9. _____ Check each form to make sure it is signed and dated.
10. _____ Photocopy all original documents (sending only copies).
11. _____ Send by certified mail, return receipt requested.
12. _____ Attach forms with paper clips, not staples.
13. _____ Keep a copy of all forms and documents submitted.
14. _____ Give the entire package a "once over" proofreading for errors.
15. _____ Recheck your Social Security number and relevant tax years.

IRS Service Centers and District Problem Resolution Offices

Service Center Offices

Correspondence should be addressed to:
Problem Resolution Office
Internal Revenue Service Center *with the appropriate address from the following list:*

Andover Service Center
310 Lowell Street (Stop 122)
Andover, MA 05501

Atlanta Service Center
P.O. Box 48-549 (Stop 29-A)
Doraville, GA 30362

Austin Service Center
P.O. Box 834
(Stop 1005 AUSG)
Austin, TX 78768

Austin Compliance Center
P.O. Box 2986
(Stop 1005 AUSG)
Austin, TX 78767

Brookhaven Service Center
P.O. Box 960 (Stop 102)
Haftsville, NY 11742

Cincinnati Service Center
P.O. Box 267 (Stop 11)
Covington, KY 41019

Fresno Service Center
P.O. Box 2161
Fresno, CA 93776

Kansas City Service Center
P.O. Box 24551
Kansas City, MO 64131

Memphis Service Center
P.O. Box 30309 AMF
(Stop 77)
Memphis, TN 38130

Ogden Service Center
P.O. Box 9941 (Stop 1005)
Ogden, UT 84409

Philadelphia Service Center
P.O. Box 16053
Philadelphia, PA 19114

District Offices

*Correspondence and facsimile
transmissions should be addressed to:*
Problem Resolution Office
Internal Revenue Service Center
*with the appropriate address
from the following list:*

Aberdeen District
115 4th Avenue, S.E.
Aberdeen, SD 57401
605-226-7278
FAX: 605-226-7270

Albany District
Leo O'Brien Federal Bldg.
Clinton Ave. & N. Pearl St.
Albany, NY 12207
518-472-4482
FAX: 518-472-3626

Albuquerque District
P.O. Box 1040 (Stop 1005)
Albuquerque, NM 87103
505-766-3760
FAX: 505-766-1317

Anchorage District
P.O. Box 101 500
Anchorage, AK 99510
907-261-4228 or 4230
FAX: 907-261-4413

Atlanta District
P.O. Box 1065
Room 1520 (Stop 202-D)
Atlanta, GA 30370
404-331-5232
FAX: 404-730-3438

Augusta District
220 Main Mall Road
South Portland, ME 04106
207-780-3309
FAX: 207-780-3515

Austin District
P.O. Box 1863 (Stop 1005)
Austin, TX 78767
512-499-5875
FAX: 512-499-5687

Baltimore District
P.O. Box 1553, Room 620A
Baltimore, MD 21203
301-962-2082
FAX: 301-962-9572

Birmingham District
500 22nd Street South
(Stop 316)
Birmingham, AL 35233
205-731-1177
FAX: 205-731-0017

Boise District
550 West Fort Street
Box 041
Boise, ID 83724
208-334-1324
FAX: 208-334-9663

Boston District
JFK P.O. Box 9103
Boston, MA 02203
617-565-1857
FAX: 617-565-4959

Brooklyn District
G.P.O. Box R
Brooklyn, NY 11202
718-780-6511
FAX: 718-780-6045

Buffalo District
P.O. Box 500
Niagara Square Station
Buffalo, NY 14201
716-846-4574
FAX: 716-846-5473

Burlington District
Courthouse Plaza
199 Main Street
Burlington, VT 05401
802-860-2008
FAX: 802-860-2006

Cheyenne District
308 West 21st Street
(Stop 1005)
Cheyenne, WY 82001
307-772-2489
FAX: 307-772-2488

Chicago District
230 S. Dearborn Street
Room 3214
Chicago, IL 60604
312-886-4396
FAX: 312-886-1564

Cincinnati District
P.O. Box 1818
Cincinnati, OH 45201
513-684-3094
FAX: 513-684-2445

Cleveland District
P.O. Box 99709
Cleveland, OH 44199
216-522-7134
FAX: 216-522-2992

Columbia District
P.O. Box 386, MDP03
Columbia, SC 29202-0386
803-765-5939
FAX: 803-253-3910

Dallas District
P.O. Box 50008
(Stop 1005)
Dallas, TX 75250
214-767-1289
FAX: 214-767-2178

Denver District
P.O. Box 1302 (Stop 1005)
Denver, CO 80201
303-844-3178
FAX: 303-844-4900

Des Moines District
P.O. Box 1337 (Stop 2)
Des Moines, IA 50305
515-284-4780
FAX: 515-284-4299

Detroit District
P.O. Box 330500 (Stop 7)
Detroit, MI 48232-6500
313-226-7899
FAX: 313-226-3502

Fargo District
P.O. Box 8
Fargo, ND 58107
701-239-5141
FAX: 701-239-5644

Ft. Lauderdale District
P.O. Box 17167
Plantation, FL 33318
305-424-2385
FAX: 305-424-2483

Greensboro District
320 Federal Place
Room 214B
Greensboro, NC 27401
919-333-5061
FAX: 919-333-5630

Hartford District
135 High Street (Stop 219)
Hartford, CT 06103
203-240-4179
FAX: 203-240-4023

Helena District
Federal Building
301 S. Park Avenue
Helena, MT 59626-0016
406-449-5244
FAX: 206-449-5342

Honolulu District
P.O. Box 50089
Honolulu, HI 96850
808-541-3300
FAX: 808-541-1117

Houston District
1919 Smith Street
(Stop 1005)
Houston, TX 77002
713-653-3660
FAX: 713-653-3708

Indianapolis District
P.O. Box 44687 (Stop 11)
Indianapolis, IN 46244
317-226-6332
FAX: 317-226-6110

Assistant Commissioner
(International)
950 L'Enfant Plaza
Washington, DC 20024
202-447-1020
FAX: 202-287-4466

Jackson District
100 West Capitol Street
Suite 504 (Stop 31)
Jackson, MS 39269
601-965-4800
FAX: 601-965-5796

Jacksonville District
P.O. Box 35045
(Stop D:PRO)
Jacksonville, FL 32202
904-791-3440
FAX: 904-791-2266

Laguna Niguel District
P.O. Box 30207
Laguna Niguel, CA
92607-0207
714-643-4182
FAX: 714-643-4436

Las Vegas District
4750 West Oakey Blvd.
Las Vegas, NV 89102
702-455-1099
FAX: 702-455-1009

Little Rock District
P.O. Box 3778 (Stop 3)
Little Rock, AR 72203
501-324-6260
FAX: 502-324-5109

Los Angeles District
P.O. Box 1791
Los Angeles, CA 90053
213-894-6111
FAX: 213-894-6365

Louisville District
P.O. Box 1735 (Stop 120)
Louisville, KY 40201
502-582-6030
FAX: 502-582-5580

Manhattan District
P.O. Box 408
Church Street Station
New York, NY 10008
212-264-2850
FAX: 212-264-6949

Milwaukee District
P.O. Box 386, Room M-28
Milwaukee, WI 53201
414-297-3046
FAX: 414-297-1640

Nashville District
P.O. Box 1107 (MDP 22)
Nashville, TN 37202
615-736-5219
FAX: 615-736-7489

New Orleans District
600 S. Maestri Place
(Stop 12)
New Orleans, LA 70130
504-589-3001
FAX: 504-589-3112

Newark District
Problem Resolution Unit
P.O. Box 1143
Newark, NJ 07101
201-645-6698
FAX: 201-645-3323

Oklahoma City District
P.O. Box 1 G40 (Stop 1005)
Oklahoma City, OK 73101
405-231-5125
FAX: 405-231-4929

Omaha District
106 S. 15th Street (Stop 2)
Omaha, NE 68102
402-221-4181
FAX: 402-221-4030

Parkersburg District
P.O. Box 1388
Parkersburg, WV 26102
304-420-6616
FAX: 304-420-6699

Philadelphia District
P.O. Box 12010
Philadelphia, PA 19106
215-597-3377
FAX: 215-440-1456

Phoenix District
2120 N. Central Avenue
(Stop 1005)
Phoenix, AZ 85004
602-379-3604
FAX: 602-379-3530

Pittsburgh District
P.O. Box 705
Pittsburgh, PA 15230
412-644-5987
FAX: 412-644-2769

Portland District
P.O. Box 3341
Portland, OR 97208
503-326-4166
FAX: 503-326-5453

Providence District
380 Westminster Mall
Providence, RI 02903
603-433-0571
FAX: 603-528-4646

Richmond District
P.O. Box 10113, Room 5502
Richmond, VA 23240
804-771-2643
FAX: 804-771-2008

Sacramento District
P.O. Box 2900
(Stop SA 5043)
Sacramento, CA 95812
916-978-4079
FAX: 916-978-5052

St. Louis District
P.O. Box 1548 (Stop 002)
St. Louis, MO 63188
314-539-6770
FAX: 314-539-3990

St. Paul District
P.O. Box 64599
St. Paul, MN 55164
612-290-3077
FAX: 612-290-4236

Salt Lake City District
P.O. Box 2069 (Stop 1005)
Salt Lake City, UT 84110
801-524-6287
FAX: 801-524-6080

San Francisco District
P.O. Box 36136 (Stop 4004)
450 Golden Gate Avenue
San Francisco, CA 94102
415-556-5046
FAX: 514-556-4456

San Jose District
P.O. Box 100
San Jose, CA 95103
408-291-7132
FAX: 408-291-7109

Seattle District
P.O. Box 2207 (Stop 405)
Seattle, WA 98111
206-442-7393
FAX: 206-442-1176

Springfield District
P.O. Box 19201 (Stop 22)
Springfield, IL 62794-9201
217-492-4517
FAX: 217-492-4073

Wichita District
P.O. Box 2907 (Stop 2005)
Wichita, KS 67201
316-291-6506
FAX: 316-291-6557

Wilmington District
844 King Street, Room 3402
Wilmington, DE 19801
302-573-6052
FAX: 302-573-6309

National Office
1111 Constitution Ave., N.W.
Room 3003 C:PRP
Washington, DC 20224
202-566-6475
FAX: 202-377-6154

Excerpts from the *Internal Revenue Manual,* IRM 57(10)

57(10)0 *(2-26-92)*
Offers in Compromise

57(10)1 *(2-26-92)*
Introductions

The Service, like any other business, will encounter situations where an account receivable cannot be collected in full or there is a dispute as to what is owed. It is an accepted business practice to resolve these collection and liability issues through a compromise. Additionally, the compromise process is available to provide delinquent taxpayers with a fresh start toward future compliance with the tax laws.

57(10)1.1 *(2-26-92)*
Offer Policy

Policy Statement P-5-100 sets forth the Service's position on using compromises. "The Service will accept an Offer In Compromise when it is unlikely that the tax liability can be collected in full and the amount offered reasonably reflects collection potential. An offer in compromise is a legitimate alternative to declaring a case as currently not collectible or to a protracted installment agreement. The goal is to achieve collection of what is potentially collectible at the earliest possible time and at the least cost to the government.

"In cases where an Offer In Compromise appears to be a viable solution to a tax delinquency, the Service employee assigned the case will discuss the compromise alternative with the taxpayer and, when necessary, assist in preparing the required forms. The taxpayer will be responsible for initiating the first specific proposal for compromise.

"The success of the compromise program will be assured only if taxpayers make adequate compromise proposals consistent with their ability to pay and the Service makes prompt and reasonable decisions. Taxpayers are expected to provide reasonable documentation to verify their ability to pay. The ultimate goal is a compromise which is in the best interest of both the taxpayer and the Service. Acceptance of an adequate offer will also result in creating, for the taxpayer, an expectation of and a fresh start toward compliance with all future filing and payment requirements."

57(10)1.2 *(2-26-92)*
Compromise Objectives

(1) To resolve accounts receivable which cannot be collected in full or on which there is a legitimate dispute as to what is owed.

(2) To effect collection of what could reasonably be collected at the earliest time possible and at the least cost to the government.

(3) To give taxpayers a fresh start to enable them to voluntarily comply with the tax laws.

(4) To collect funds which may not be collectible through any other means.

57(10)1.3 *(4-12-95)*
Public Policy

(1) Policy Statement P-5-89, of IRM 1218, Policies of the Internal Revenue Service Handbook, sets forth the Service's position that offers may be rejected because they are contrary to public policy. "If acceptance of an offer might in

any way be detrimental to the Government's interests, it may be rejected even though it is shown conclusively that the amounts offered are greater than could reasonably be collected in any other manner."

(2) A decision to reject an offer for public policy considerations should be extremely rare. It should be made only where a clear and convincing case can be made that public reaction to the acceptance would be so negative that future voluntary compliance by the public would be diminished.

(3) An offer will not be rejected on public policy grounds solely because it would generate considerable public interest, some of it critical.

(4) An offer will not be rejected solely because a taxpayer was criminally prosecuted for a tax or non-tax violation. However, an offer may be rejected when it is suspected that the financial benefits of the criminal activity are concealed or the criminal activity is continuing. Also, an offer may be rejected where the criminal activity was so egregious that the public would be outraged and our acceptance would affect voluntary compliance.

(5) Offers in Compromise from federal employees with delinquent tax obligations will be considered, but based upon public policy considerations, acceptances should be rare.

(6) If an offer is to be rejected for public policy reasons, the specific reasons should be fully documented in the case file.

(7) The authority to reject offers in compromise for public policy reasons is restricted to District Directors, Service Center Directors, and Director, Austin Compliance Center. See Delegation Order No. 11. as revised, of IRM 1229. Handbook of Delegation Orders.

57(10)1.4 *(9-22-94)*
Liabilities to Be Compromised

57(10)1.41 *(9-22-94)*
Taxes, Penalties and Interest Constitute One Liability

A compromise is effective for the entire liabilities penalty, and interest for the years or periods covered by the offer. All questions of tax liability for the year(s) or period(s) covered by such offer in compromise are conclusively settled. Neither the taxpayer nor the government can reopen the case unless there was falsification or concealment of assets, or a mutual mistake of a material fact was made which would be sufficient to set aside or reform a contract.

57(10)1.42 *(9-22-94)*
Compromise of Unassessed Liability

Taxpayers may submit an offer to compromise taxes which have not yet been assessed. IRS has no statutory authority to compromise unassessed taxes. Therefore, before the offer can be accepted, the taxes must be assessed. However, this does not preclude consideration of an offer prior to assessment.

57(10)1.43 *(9-22-94)*
Compromise of Substitute for Return Assessments

(1) When considering to compromise this type of liability the Substitute for Return (SFR) tax return must be reviewed to determine if all the taxpayer's income is included in the assessment. If the offer investigation reveals additional income not included in the SFR assessment, the taxpayer will be required to file an amended return to include the income.

(2) Offers in Compromise based on doubt as to collectibility submitted on SFR eases will be worked following the same IRMA guidelines as for other offers.

(3) Offers submitted based on doubt as to liability on SFR cases will be forwarded to Examination Division.

57(10)1.5 *(2-26-92)*
Compromise of Expired Tax Liability

The Service will not accept an offer in compromise of a tax which has become unenforceable able by reason of lapse of time unless the taxpayer is fully aware of the feet that the collection of the tax is barred. Where such a situation exists, the offer itself (or a separate letter over the signature of the taxpayer) should show that he/she has been advised of the expiration of the statutory period for collection, but, notwithstanding such fact, still desires to have the offer accepted. In this type of ease, no collateral agreement is necessary.

57(10)1.6 *(9-22-94)*
Commissioner's Delegation of Authority to Accept, Reject, and Acknowledge withdrawal of Offers in Compromise

Delegation Order No. 11 redelegates the compromise authority vested in the Commissioner. See IRM 1229.

57(10)1.7 *(2-26-92)*
Jurisdictional Responsibility

57(10)1.71 *(9-22-94)*
District Collection Function

(1) District Collection functions have jurisdictional responsibility for the following:

(a) Consideration of all offers in compromise based on doubt as to collectibility as well as preparation of the necessary documents and letters. This includes offers to compromise proposed liabilities which are still the subject of settlement negotiations in the district Examination function or Appeals Office.

(b) Consideration of penalty only offers. The service center will normally handle these except, in cases where service center management believes they should be considered in the district The district also has jurisdiction on penalty offers where the issue is in doubt as to collectibility.

(c) Consideration of all offers to compromise Trust Fund Recovery penalty and Personal Liability for Excise Tax (IRC 4103) assessments based either on doubt as to liability or doubt as to collectibility. Collection will not be responsible for working doubt as to liability offers submitted on either Trust Fund Recovery Penalty or Personal Liability for Excise Tax cases when Appeals has previously worked the penalty appeal and either sustained the penalty in part or in whole. Collection will forward these cases to be worked in Appeals. Collection will follow these procedures:

    1 process in the cases and make the processability determination,

    2 send the taxpayer a letter informing them that the case is going to be determined in Appeals, and

    3 be responsible for all of the inputs. The cases will be counted in open inventory pending the Appeals decision and will not be counted for purposes of determining age of disposal.

(d) Consideration of all offers in default, regardless of whether the basic offer was based on doubt as to liability or doubt as to collectibility.

(e) Offers in compromise based on both doubt as to liability and doubt as to collectability will be assigned initially to the Collection function for a collectibility determination. If it is determined that the taxpayer may be able to pay an amount in excess of the amount offered, processing of the offer should be discontinued. The offer and copies of related documents should be forwarded through district channels to the service center and/or transferred to the Examination function as a doubt as to liability case. In either case the service center will be notified of the change in jurisdiction and the Form 2515 so notated.

(f) Consideration of all offers to compromise based on doubt as to collectibility or doubt as to liability for employment tax deficiencies arising from Employment Tax Examinations (ETE).

57(10)1.72 *(9-22-94)*
District Examination Function

(1) The district Examination function has jurisdictional responsibility for investigation and processing of tax offers based solely on doubt as to liability, including preparation of the necessary documents and letters to effect their disposition.

(2) Offers in compromise received in the district Examination function will be processed in accordance with established Examination procedures. Any requests for information from Collection records should be coordinated through the appropriate Collection function This may include information on liens, suits, judgments, bankruptcy or decedent estates.

(3) Offers based solely on doubt as to liability, if not submitted to compromise the liabilities described in IRM 57(10)1.71:(1)(c) and 57(10)1.71:(1)(f), will be transferred to Examination for consideration. Such eases will be

counted as transfers on Form 4196, Collection Monthly Report of Offer in Compromise Activity.

57(10)1.8 *(2-26-92)*
Determination of Liability

(1) Liability Less than Offer—If during the investigation of an offer, the liability is found to be equal to or less than the offer, the amount of the assessment in excess of the liability should be abated, and the taxpayer should be requested to withdraw the offer, or the offer should be rejected. The taxpayer will be advised to pay the correct liability.

(2) Liability Greater than Offer—If during the investigation of an offer, liability is found to be greater then the offer, but less than the amount assessed, the excess amount of the assessment should be abated. The taxpayer will be informed of the re-determined liability and be advised to pay the correct liability.

(3) Definite Determination Cannot be Made—If a definite determination of the liability cannot be made, but there is a doubt about the liability, the degree of doubt may be measured and the case closed by compromise. The amount acceptable will depend upon the degree of doubt found in the particular case.

(4) The Examination function will dispose of completed offer investigations in essentially the same manner as the Collection function, except that:

(a) The processing performed in the Collection function will be performed by the Quality Review Staff in accordance with existing Examination procedures.

(b) Cases shall be referred to the Criminal Investigation function for concurrence if the following conditions exist:

    1 the merits of the ad valorem fraud or negligence penalty are involved;

    2 the case is one in which the Special Agent had recommended assertion of such a penalty in the final report in the case; and

    3 the district Examination function is recommending acceptance of the offer.

(c) If the Criminal Investigation function concurs in the recommended disposition of the case, concurrence should be made and by memorandum the entire file resumed to the district Examination function for processing. If the Criminal Investigation function does not concur and no agreement can be reached with the Examination function as to the disposition of the offer, the entire file shall be forwarded to the district director for resolution. Thereafter, the case will be processed in accordance with established procedures. This is applicable only to cases in which no prosecution has been recommended or the question of prosecution has been settled and the criminal case closed.

(d) In those offers accepted by the Examination function, the appropriate Form 7249, Offer Acceptance Report, should be forwarded to Collection for inclusion in the public inspection file.

(e) If the offer was rejected or withdrawn, Form 1271, Rejection and Withdrawal Memorandum, and accompanying memorandum should be forwarded to Collection.

57(10)1.9 *(2-26-92)*
Cases Pending in District Examination Function

When an offer to compromise a proposed liability is submitted on the basis of inability to pay during the examination process, the offer should be considered by the district office in the same manner as any other inability to pay case. If it appears to be an acceptable amount based on a preliminary analysis of the taxpayer's financial statement, the Examination function will secure from the taxpayer conditional agreement on a definite liability. The agreement form should be held in escrow pending final action on the offer. If the offer is accepted by a delegated official, action will then be taken to have the tax assessed. The acceptance letter should not be mailed to the taxpayer until the assessment has been made. It should be noted that if a statutory notice of deficiency has been sent, the period for filing a petition with the Tax Court is not suspended.

57(10)1.(10) *(2-26-92)*
Jurisdiction of the Appeals Offices

(1) When an offer is based in whole or in part on doubt as to liability and the Appeals Office has determined the liability or the case is pending before the Appeals Office, the district director will forward the offer to Appeals for consideration.

(2) If an offer in compromise based on doubt as to liability is pending in the Appeals Office, the Appeals Office may call upon the district director to conduct any investigation deemed necessary to reach a conclusion on the merits of the case. These investigations should be conducted as expeditiously as possible.

(3) If any offer is submitted only on doubt as to collectibility and the liability was previously determined by Appeals, the acceptability of the offer will be determined by the district office.

(4) If an offer is submitted only on doubt as to collectibility and the liability is pending in Appeals, the Appeals Office will be notified and asked whether there is any objection to consideration. The Appeals Office will respond within 30 days. The actual investigation of the offer will be deferred during that period pending the response of the Appeals Office. The Appeals Office will inform the district director of any objection by memorandum.

(5) If there are no objections and the offer is to be investigated, the Appeals Office will normally secure the taxpayer's conditional agreement to the liability or to the revised amount determined to be due. If the offer is accepted, the Appeals Office will be notified and it will arrange to have the liability assessed. The acceptance letter should not be mailed until the assessment has been made.

(6) If the offer is rejected, Appeals will be notified so that they can again consider the merits of the liability.

(7) It should be noted that the filing of an offer does not stay the running of the 90-day period set forth in a deficiency notice.

57(10)1.(11) *(9-22-94)*
Tax Court Cases

(1) Procedures for handling Appeals cases will be followed.

(2) When an offer is to be investigated, Appeals will normally secure a stipulation agreement to the proposed liability. This will normally be held in escrow.

(3) If the offer is recommended for rejection, Appeals will be notified. Appeals will have 10 days to provide the district office with any information that should be weighed in making the final decision. However, the district office will decide whether to reject the offer and provide the taxpayer with the necessary appeal rights.

(4) If the offer is accepted by the district office, Appeals will take the necessary action to get the stipulation filed with the Tax Court. The Appeals Office will then take steps to have the tax assessed. The acceptance letter should not be issued until the tax is assessed.

57(10)1.(12) *(2-26-92)*
Appeal of Rejected Offers

(1) When Appeals decides that an offer is to be accepted, Appeals will take all the appropriate acceptance procedures. After the required reports have been signed by the delegated official, the case will be returned to the district office for processing.

(2) When Appeals sustains the proposed rejection of the offer, Appeals will notify the taxpayer and the offer file will be returned to the district office for processing.

57(10)1.(13) *(9-22-94)*
Cases Under Jurisdiction of Department of Justice

(1) The Service does not have the authority to accept an offer in compromise in the following types of cases:

(a) An offer covering a liability "in suit".

(b) Cases where the liability has been reduced to judgment.

(c) Cases in which recommendation for prosecution is pending in the Department of Justice or United States Attorney's Offices including cases in which criminal proceedings have been instituted but not disposed of.

(d) Cases in which a recommendation for prosecution is pending in the Office of the Chief Counsel, and in related cases in which offers in compromise have been submitted.

(e) Cases in which the acceptance of an offer by the Service is dependent upon the acceptance of a related offer or upon a settlement under the jurisdiction of the Department of Justice.

(2) The Chief Counsel will ordinarily be called upon for views and a recommendation on the acceptability of an offer on a liability under the jurisdiction of the Department of Justice. The district director will usually be requested to conduct an investigation of the taxpayer's financial condition and to make a recommendation regarding acceptance. The investigation will be conducted as quickly as possible. In no event will the Service's response take longer than 90 days unless the Department of Justice advises that the investigation may take longer. Additionally, we will comply with any shorter time frame requested by the Department of Justice because a court will not allow more time. Any amounts received by the district in payment of an offer or related collateral agreement accepted by the Department of Justice, should be forwarded directly to the appropriate service center for posting.

(3) The Service will comply with all special instructions from the Department of Justice for processing the offer, releasing the lien and default notification.

57(10)2 *(2-26-92)*
Management of the Offer Program

57(10)2.1 *(9-22-94)*
General

(1) Management has the following responsibilities under the offer program

(a) To ensure that the spirit and intent of Policy Statement P-5-100 are adhered to.

(b) The Regions, Districts, and Service Centers will develop a procedure plan to define the manner in which offers will be processed. This plan will include the following:

1 Making the processability determination,

2 Preparing the Form 2515 or other core. computer version,

3 Input TC 48X,

4 Input/reverse of Status 71,

5 Request for transcripts,

6 Maintenance of information necessary to complete Form 4196, Collection Quarterly Report of Offer in Compromise Activity

(c) District management has the responsibility to establish a plan for the assignment, control, review, and approval of offer investigations.

(d) The procedural plan should be designed to ensure the following:

1 Timely processing, to ensure offers are completed within a reasonable timeframe. Absent unusual circumstance it is the expectation that offer investigations be completed within six months. It is expected that offer investigations will be completed within six months unless extraordinary circumstances exist which dictate a longer completion time frame. An across the board extension of the six month time frame may not be made. The six month time

frame is determined by the following: the start date is the date the waiver on Form 656 is signed in as processable, which is the same date entered on Item 2 of the Form 2515 and also the date of the TC 480 on the TXMOD; the end date is the date of the acceptance letter, Pattern Letter 673, the date of the proposed rejection letter, pattern Letter P-238, or the date on the Service's letter acknowledging the taxpayer's withdrawal, Pattern Letter P-241. The date the original offer is signed in as processable is used to compute overage, not the date on an amended offer.

2 Quality investigation limited to what is actually necessary

3 Limited review

4 Development of methods/initiatives to further streamline the offer process.

5 Use of clerical and paraprofessional resources for case-building activities (i.e., conducting research, requesting RTVUE, contact with taxpayer to clarify information on the Collection information Statement, etc.). Employees in the Automated Collection System (ACS) and Service Center Collection Branch (SCCB) may be assigned to conduct case building activities in connection with investigation of an OIC.

6 Investigation of the offer by the revenue officer (if any) currently assigned the account, if within his or her assigned duties. Local management may assign the offer investigation to another employee if workload considerations dictate.

7 There is no requirement that the Special Procedures function be involved in this process.

(e) The Service Center Collection Branch should be advised in writing by each district of the organizational unit to receive all offer referrals and questions for that particular district.

57(10)2.2 *(9-22-94)*
Follow-up on Pending Offer

No later than February 1st of each year, the service center will prepare and forward to the office having jurisdiction, a list of all pending offers in compromise more than 12 months old. The receiving office will report whether the case is opened or closed, resuming a copy of the list to the service center within 30 days of its receipt.

57(10)3 *(9-22-94)*
(Reserved)

57(10)4 *(9-22-94)*
Collection Activity Reporting Instructions of Offer in Compromise Activity

In order to evaluate the Offer in Compromise program and disposition of cases, the National Office requires monthly reporting on Form 4196, Collection Monthly Report of Offer in Compromise Activity (Report Symbol NO-5000-108). Instructions for the preparation and submission of the form are contained on the reverse of Form 4196.

57(10)5 *(2-26-92)*
Advising Taxpayers of Offer Provisions

57(10)5.1 *(9-22-94)*
General

(1) When criminal proceedings are not contemplated and an analysis of the taxpayer's assets, liabilities, income and expenses show that a tax liability cannot be realistically collected in full, the possibility of an offer in compromise will be discussed with the taxpayer (See 7(10)1 of LEM V). There may be situations where we would reject an offer due to Public Policy, see IRM 57(10)1.3. In these situations, we would not want to initiate a discussion of the Offer Program with the taxpayer.

(2) The taxpayer will be advised what an offer is, what the Service procedures and policies are with respect to offers, what forms must be completed, and what benefits the taxpayer will receive from an offer acceptance. The taxpayer should be instructed to read the entire Form 656 including the instructions carefully. When necessary, the Service employee will assist the taxpayer in preparing the required forms.

(3) Taxpayers will also be advised that collection will normally be withheld unless it is determined that the offer is a delaying tactic and collection is in jeopardy. However, if the taxpayer is making payments under an installment payment agreement, the taxpayer should be told to continue the payments.

(4) Before an offer is submitted, the taxpayer will not be told what specifically to offer. The taxpayer will be responsible for initiating the first specific proposal for compromise. However, the taxpayer should be advised that the proposal should not be a "fishing expedition" but a legitimate compromise proposal based on the ability to pay. The taxpayer should be advised that the service does not operate on the theory that "something is better than nothing."

(5) The taxpayer should be encouraged to submit a deposit as a sign of good faith. However, lack of a deposit does not make an offer unprocessable. Furthermore, no requirement should be imposed to tender a deposit or to sign Form 3040, Authorization to Apply Offer in Compromise Deposit to Liability, as a condition for processing or for any other aspect of an offer. The taxpayer will be advised that the deposit check will be cashed, will not beer interest, and will not constitute acceptance of the offer. Refer the taxpayer to Form 656 (Revision 9/93), pages 5 and 6, for instructions regarding what constitutes an acceptable offer. The offer deposit may be returned at any time at the request of the taxpayer. The taxpayer should be advised that if the offer is rejected, the Service will return the deposit unless the taxpayer authorizes in writing that the deposit may be applied to the liability.

(a) See IRC 7809(b) for legal authority to place offer deposits in a deposit fund separate from collected amounts and for the requirement to return me deposit if the offer is not accepted.

(b) See Regulation 301.7122-1(d) (4) for the basis for not paying interest on the deposit.

(6) The Revenue Officer should determine what information (e.g. evaluation, bank statements etc.) is still needed to verify the ability to pay. The taxpayer should be encouraged to submit the information with the offer since the sooner this information is available the sooner the Service can make a decision.

(7) The taxpayer should be advised that submission of an offer does not constitute acceptance. No offer is accepted until the appropriate delegated official approves acceptance and the taxpayer is notified by letter that the offer has been accepted.

(8) The taxpayer will be advised that no abatement will be made or tax liens released until the total amount offered, including interest on any deferred payments, has been paid in full.

(9) On doubt as to collectibility offers, the taxpayer will be advised that acceptance will require the taxpayer to comply fully with all filing and paying requirements of the law for five years. The taxpayer will also be advised that default of this condition shall be treated the same as a default in payment. On doubt as to liability offers, the five (5) year compliance provision does not apply. The provision will be deleted from Form 656 prior to recommending acceptance.

(10) Taxpayers will also be advised that they waive certain refunds or credits they may otherwise be entitled to receive.

(11) The taxpayer will be advised that after the offer amount is paid, accrued interest on any deferred amount must also be paid. Interest is due from the date of acceptance until the amount offered is paid in full. The interest provision of deferred payment offers should be explained and the taxpayer should be advised that Letter 277(C) will be sent by the service center advising of the amount of interest due and requesting payment.

57(10)5.2 *(2-26-92)*
Sources of Offer Funds

(1) When discussing offer possibilities with the taxpayer, sources of potential funds should be discussed. Some potential sources could be:

(a) A non-liable spouse who has property which he/she may be interested in utilizing to secure a compromise of a spouse's tax debt.

(b) Relatives or friends
(c) Lending institutions
(d) Employers
(e) Suppliers
(f) Customers

57(10)5.3 *(9-22-94)*
Liens on Pending Assessments

If the offer is to provide for deferred payments and no lien has been filed, it is advisable to inform the taxpayer that to protect the government's interest, a lien will be filed after a proposed posed liability is assessed. This will avoid any misunderstanding. However, care should be taken to ensure that the lien will not adversely impact the taxpayers ability to raise the funds necessary to satisfy the offer. If a lien will be filed, the taxpayer must be notified as required by Policy Statement P-5-47.

57(10)6 *(2-26-92)*
Preparation of the Offer (Form 656)

57(10)6.1 *(2-26-92)*
Name and Address of Taxpayer

The full name, address, Social Security Number, and/or Employer Identification Number of the taxpayer must be entered on Form 656. If the liability is joint and both parties wish to make the offer, both names must be shown. If the taxpayer is singly liable for a liability (e.g., employment taxes) and jointly liable for a liability (e.g., income taxes) and only one person is submitting the offer, only one offer must be submitted. If the taxpayer is singly liable for one liability and jointly liable for another and both joint parties are submitting the offer, two offers must be submitted, one for the separate liability and one for the joint liability.

57(10)6.2 *(9-22-94)*
Total Liability on Form 656, Offer in Compromise

(1) A taxpayer must list all unpaid tax liabilities sought to be compromised in item (4) on Form 656. The type of tax and the period of the liability must be specifically identified by checking the block next to the appropriate pre-printed description on the form.

(2) When the block for Trust Fund Recovery is used the period(s) ended will be the corporate quarterly periods for which the Trust Fund Recovery assessment is based. The period(s) ending of the Trust Fund Recovery penalty should not be used.

57(10)6.3 *(9-22-94)*
Amount of Offer

(1) The total amount offered should be shown. If any amount is to be paid on notice of acceptance of the offer or at any later date, the taxpayer must include in item (5) as follows:

(a) The amount, if any, deposited at the time of filing the offer.

(b) Any amount deposited on a prior offer which is to be applied on the offer. (This does not include any amount the taxpayer previously authorized the Service to apply directly to the tax liability.)

(c) The amount of any subsequent payment and the date on which each payment is to be made.

57(10)6.4 *(9-22-94)*
Terms of Payment

(1) In the spirit of Policy Statement P-5-100 the amount offered should be paid as quickly as possible.

(2) A cash offer is one where the total amount offered is paid within 90 days of acceptance.

(3) A deferred payment offer is one where any part of the amount offered is to be paid at any date(s) more than 90 days after acceptance of the offer. As a general rule, deferred payment should not be extended beyond two years. However, the following must be considered:

(a) A longer or shorter period of time may be acceptable if extraordinary circumstances exist and are documented in the case file. However, regions or districts may not establish a general rule to require payment within a specific time frame.

(b) If the amount of the offer is acceptable and will be paid within two years, an offer will not be rejected unless exceptional circumstances are clearly documented which establish why a shorter period of time for payment is appropriate (e.g., the money to be paid will come from a specific, predictable event such as sale of an asset).

(4) The terms of a deferred payment offer should be precisely stated so there can be no doubt as to the taxpayer's intent if the offer is accepted. The due date of each payment should be specified, as in the following examples:

(a) $5,000.00 deposited with the offer and the balance of $25,000.00 to be paid within 30 days after the date of notice of the offer's acceptance

(b) $103,000: to be paid within ninety (90) days from the date of acceptance.

(5) Designated Payment Code (DPC) 09 will be used for payments made on an accepted offer in compromise.

(6) The input of a TC 780 on a deferred payment offer will delay the issuance of all refunds to the taxpayer for a period of eight (8) weeks. Taxpayers must be advised to expect such delays.

57(10)6.5 *(9-22-94)*
Grounds for Offer

The taxpayer will indicate on Form 656 if the offer is being submitted on doubt as to collectibility doubt as to liability, or both, by placing an "X" in the appropriate block(s).

57(10)6.6 *(2-26-92)*
Signing the Offer

(1) Where a husband and wife seek to compromise a joint liability, both must sign to ensure that the waiver and other provisions bind both parties. In the case of a corporation, the corporate name must be entered on the first line and the signature of the president or other authorized officer on the second line.

(2) An offer submitted by a qualified fiduciary of the estate of a deceased taxpayer will be binding on the taxpayer's estate to the extent that it would be binding on a tax-

payer who submits an offer on his/her own behalf. The fiduciary should submit evidence of his/her qualifications.

(3) A Form 2848 is sufficient to allow complete representation for an offer in compromise with the exception of Appeals. (See Circular 230 for complete representation requirements of Appeals). Form 2848 does not have to specifically grant the authority to execute Form 656.

57(10)6.7
Overpayments

(1) The taxpayer waives certain refunds or credits he or she may otherwise be entitled to receive or actually receives after submitting the offer. These overpayments of any tax or other liability, including interest and penalties, cover periods that end before, within, or as of the end of the calendar year in which the offer is accepted. Offset of any overpayment would be limited to the difference between the tax liability, including statutory additions, and the amount paid on the offer.

(2) The overpayment of one spouse may not be applied against the separate liability of the other spouse unless a written consent to credit is obtained. Often consents to credit or the waiver of refunds are executed by related taxpayers with the express condition that they be made only if the offer is accepted.

(3) Under no circumstances will this waiver provision be deleted in the case of a taxpayer who seeks a compromise on grounds of doubt as to collectability.

(4) Under no circumstances will the taxpayer be asked to return to IRS any refunds or overpayments which he or she received before submitting the offer.

57(10)7 *(2-26-92)*
Statutory Waiver

57(10)7.1 *(2-26-92)*
Suspension of Statute of Limitations

(1) The compromise agreement on Form 656, Offer in Compromise, provides that the taxpayer agrees to the suspension of the running of the statutory period of limitations on both assessment and collection for the period that the offer is pending, or the period that any installment remains unpaid, and for one year thereafter. This includes the period of time in which the offer is being considered by Appeals. For the suspension provisions to be effective, both the taxpayer and the authorized Service employee must sign the offer before the expiration of the statutory period, and the date the employee signs the waiver must be filled in.

(2) Where multiple offers are filed by one taxpayer, the effect of the waivers on the offers is cumulative. It should be noted, however, that when an offer is filed within one year after rejection or withdrawal of a previous offer, the overlapping period should only be counted once in determining the suspension of the statutory period of limitations. While there are various methods to determine the new expi-

ration date, only the method shown in Exhibit 5700-21 all be used for uniformity in these calculations.

(3) Where an offer is submitted by a proponent other than the taxpayer, who is not authorized to act for the taxpayer, the statutory period for assessment and collection are not suspended unless the taxpayer's signature is secured. The service center or district office, whichever discovers this fact first, will flag the offer in order to alert the examining officer of the possible need to protect both statutory periods.

(4) Unless a significant error or omission exists which requires return of the offer to the proponent, to ensure that the waiver provisions are effective, the waiver acceptance in the lower left comer of Form 656 will be signed at the earliest possible time after receipt. If possible, waiver acceptance will be signed on the date a processable offer is received by a delegated employee fin accordance with Delegation Order 42) in the district office or at the service center. The offer is considered pending from the date the delegated Service employee signs and dates the acceptance of the waiver of the statutory period of limitations on Form 656, until it is accepted, rejected or withdrawn. The same procedure will be followed for collateral agreements. (See IRC 6501 and 6502). The Service employee authorized to sign the receipt of the waiver in IMF cases only will place the appropriate alpha collection statute expiration code "P" (primary), "S" (secondary) or "B" (both) in red in the far right of the date box at the bottom of Form 656 to identity which taxpayer the extension applies to.

57(10)7.2 *(2-26-92)*
Collection Waivers—Form 656, Offer in Compromise Vis-à-Vis Form 900, Tax Collection Waiver

(1) The Service takes the position that in any case where the taxpayer and the Service have agreed, by the execution of Form 900, Tax Collection Waiver, to extend the collection statute to a specific date, the acceptance of the waiver of the statute of limitations by an authorized Service employee when an offer is submitted will suspend the running of the statute of limitations. This will effectively extend the date specified on Form 900 by the number of days that the offer and any related collateral agreements are pending or by the number of days that any installments under the offer remain unpaid or that any other provisions of the offer are not carried out and for one year thereafter.

(2) This position is not governing in the Fifth Circuit (covering Texas, Louisiana and Mississippi) or the Eleventh Circuit (covering Georgia, Florida and Alabama) where the decision in *United States v. Newman*, 405 F. 2d 189 (5th Cir. 1968), is controlling law. It should be noted that the rule established in *United States v. Newman*, 405 F. 2d 189 (5th Cir. 1968) states that a Form 900 waiver replaces the statutory period of limitation with a date certain beyond which the Government's cause of action is barred. The Form 900

waiver now provides that the date certain specified therein is to be further extended by any offer in compromise.

57(10)8 *(9-22-94)*
Preparing the Financial Statement

A taxpayer seeking to compromise a liability based on doubt as to collectibility, must submit a Form 433-A Financial Statement for Individuals, Form 433-B, Collection Information Statement for Business, and/or any other financial statement prepared by the taxpayer as long as it conforms with the information provided in the Form 433A/B and is signed under penalties of perjury. If a taxpayer is self-employed, both financial statements are required. The taxpayer's financial statement must reflect "N/A" (not applicable) in those blocks that do not affect the taxpayer.

57(10)9 *(2-26-92)*
Receipt and Processing

57(10)9.1 *(9-22-94)*
General

(1) When an offer in compromise is received from the taxpayer, it will be date stamped and a determination will be made whether the offer is processable. The earliest date stamp will be used to calculate the number of days for a processability determination to be made. Offers which are unprocessable and returned to the taxpayer may be corrected and resubmitted on the same form. If this is the case, a new date stamp will be required and the new date stamp will be considered the earliest date used to determine time frames.

(2) If an offer is not processable the waiver acceptance should not be executed and the Form 656 will be returned to the taxpayer within 14 calendar days from receipt. The offer will be returned to the taxpayer specifying what must be corrected or added before offer processing can begin. The taxpayer may correct an unprocessable offer by either: 1) entering and initialing the change on the Form 656 submitted, or 2) filing a new Form 656. See Exhibit 5700-17 for the letter used to notify the taxpayer.

(3) An offer is unprocessable if:

(a) The taxpayer is not identified
(b) The liabilities to be compromised are not identified
(c) No amount is offered
(d) Appropriate signatures are not present
(e) Financial statement is not provided
(f) The offer does not reasonably reflect net equity in assets from Forms 433-A, Collection Information Statement for Individuals, line 30 and 433-B, Collection Information Statement for Businesses, line 27, and amounts recoverable from future income sources, as reflected on financial statements. In addition, on cash offers or deferred offers which will be paid within 90 days of acceptance of the offer, the present value computation should be used. (See IRM 57(10)(13).(10)) However, judgment should be exercised when deciding whether to return an offer as

unprocessable for this reason alone. It may be desirable to receive an offer into inventory which does not technically meet this criterion. This would apply if the amount offered is close enough to the sum of net equity from Forms 433-A and 433-B, and amounts recoverable from future income sources that successful negotiation with the taxpayer could be pursued.

(g) An obsolete Form 656 has been used. Only Form 656 (Rev. 9-93) or later may be used.

(h) The taxpayer alters the terms on Form 656, Offer in Compromise. An offer will not be considered if any of the preprinted terms have been altered or deleted. However, on doubt as to liability offers, it is acceptable to delete the waiver of refund provision on Form 656.

(4) Local deviation from the criteria for processability reviews, as stated in (3) above, may not be made without first requesting and receiving National Office approval. For example, under no circumstances will an offer be returned solely on the basis that the cost of investigation does not justify consideration of the offer or that the taxpayer is not current with filing and payment requirements. When it is obvious that the existing liability cannot be paid, building the level of voluntary compliance is working with the taxpayer to cure noncompliance. Making the offer nonprocessable may result in the further expansion of the noncompliance.

(5) As described above, the offer may be returned to the taxpayer as unprocessable. However, in the spirit of "one stop service," we should go farther. It makes little sense for the taxpayer to receive the offer back and still be faced with the necessity of contacting another Service employee to resolve payment problems. Therefore the information submitted with the offer should be reviewed and an installment agreement entered into, if appropriate.

(6) Within 14 calendar days of receipt, a letter will be sent to the taxpayer acknowledging that the offer was received and processed. It will also inform the taxpayer that we will contact him or her within 30-45 calendar days. See Exhibit 5700-27 for the letter used to notify the taxpayer.

57(10)9.2 *(9-22-94)*
Timely Processing of Offer Deposits

57(10)9.21 *(9-22-94)*
Local Deposit Versus Service Center Deposit

(1) Deposits which are received with Form 656, Offer in Compromise, or received during the time the offer is pending, must be deposited timely.

(2) Regional management is responsible for deciding whether the most effective method for accomplishing this goal is to deposit the funds Locally or to send the remittance to the service center via overnight delivery for processing and deposit there.

57(10)9.22 *(9-22-94)*
Local Deposit by District Office

(1) The district employee (revenue officer or offer examiner) making the processability determination (or the employee receiving the deposit, if it is a subsequent offer deposit), will prepare Form 3244, Payment Posting Voucher, or Form 809, Receipt for Payment of Taxes, the same day the remittance is received.

(a) Form 3244 will be completed in triplicate. The following statement will be entered in the remarks section: "OIC pending, apply to 20X6879 (4710 account)."

(b) If the taxpayer submits cash, Form 809 will have to be annotated with "20X6879" in the "Other TC" box. To identify the remittance as an OIC deposit, the "other" block will have to be checked, with "OICPN" written next to it.

(2) The revenue officer or offer examiner will annotate the Form 795 remittance entry with appropriate identification (20X6879) that it is an offer remittance.

(3) The revenue officer or offer examiner will send the original Form 3244 and one copy (or Form 809 and one photocopy) by overnight mail to Collection Support function (CFf) with remittance the same day the remittance is received.

(4) The same day, the revenue officer or offer examiner will also send the remaining copy of Form 3244 (or Form 809) to Service Center Collection Branch (SCC8) with Form 2515, Record of Offer in Compromise, and Form 656.

57(10)9.23 *(9-22-94)*
Deposit by Service Center

(1) The employee making the processability determination or receiving subsequent deposits will prepare the remittance for transmittal to SCCB.

(2) The same day the offer is determined to be processable or the same day the subsequent deposit is received, Form 2515, Record of Offer in Compromise, and Form 656, will be sent via overnight delivery to the service center function designated by regional management.

57(10)9.3 *(9-22-94)*
Withholding Collection on Accounts Sought to be Compromised

(1) Collection activity will be withheld on any open accounts if it is determined that the offer merits consideration and there is no reason to believe that collection of the tax liability will be in jeopardy. The term "jeopardy" means the same as when used in jeopardy levy or jeopardy assessments situations. See IRM 5313.1:(3). As an example, should collection be withheld when the taxpayer submits information with the offer that documents the existence of assets which were not disclosed previously? In most cases, collection should be withheld. The fact that a Collection Information Statement submitted with an offer discloses an asset that was not previously disclosed is not significant unless other factors are present. The facts should be ana-

lyzed to determine whether the offer was filed solely for the purpose of delaying collection of the liability or the interests of the government would be placed in jeopardy by withholding collection. If the answer is affirmative, collection should not be withheld and it may be appropriate to proceed against the taxpayer's assets. including the asset not previously disclosed. If there is no indication that jeopardy exists, collection should be withheld and no enforced collection may be taken. If there is any indication that the filing of an offer in compromise was solely for the purpose of delaying collection of the liability or that the delay would jeopardize the government's interest, immediate steps should be taken to collect the unpaid liability. (See Treasury Regulation 301.7122-1(d)(2) and Policy Statement P-5-97.)

(2) If the taxpayer is currently paying under the term of an installment agreement, the taxpayer should be told to continue those payments.

(3) Where the grounds for the offer are strictly doubt as to liability and there is no evidence that filing the offer was sorely for the purpose of delaying collector or that the delay would jeopardize the government's interest, collector will be withheld.

(4) The input of the TC 480 and Status 71 should be done as quickly as possible to prevent notices or unnecessary action from being taken against the taxpayer. Prior to input of the TC 480 and Status 71, IDRS/CFOL will be researched to determine the taxpayer's entire outstanding liability. Upon input of the TC 480, accounts will be updated to Status 89 if NMF or Status 71 if Master File in the following situations:

(a) all notice status accounts

(b) status 22 (ACS)

(c) status 24 (queue)

(d) status 53 (CNC)

(5) Accounts will be updated to status 71 upon receipt of notification of the TC 480 if a decision has been made to withhold collection.

(6) A status 71 should not be input if one of the co-obligors has not submitted an offer on a joint liability.

(7) Form 657, Revenue Officer Report, will be prepared only when collection action will continue or when the offer will be investigated by someone other than the revenue officer who has the taxpayer's account. Group manager approval will be required only when Form 657 is prepared to continue collector activity.

(8) When collection is to be withheld the TDA's covering accounts sought to be compromised will be retained with the offer.

(9) If an offer is rejected and the taxpayer submits a protest, collector will be withheld during the appeal period if it was or should have been withheld during the time the offer was being investigated. However, if it is determined that a jeopardy situation exists as described in (1) above, prepare Form 657 and pursue collection. This should be coordinated with appeals to ensure they are aware collection is resumed. Note that jeopardy levies are also appealable.

57(10)9.4 *(9-22-94)*
Taxpayer Contact

(1) Within 30-45 calendar days from the date the waiver is signed, the taxpayer will be contacted. Contact could be by telephone, correspondence, or in person. If contact with the taxpayer cannot be made within 30-45 calendar days of the date of the letter, another letter will be sent prior to the expiration of that time period. The second letter will explain the delay and estimate when contact will be made. The taxpayer should be notified of any information that is needed to make a decision. The request should be reasonable and the taxpayer should be given a reasonable time to comply. However, a specified date must be given. The taxpayer will be notified that the offer will be rejected if the information is not supplied.

(2) If the taxpayer does not comply, the offer should be rejected absent unusual circumstances. As outlined in Policy Statement P-5-100 the offer process cannot work if the taxpayer does not cooperate.

57(10)9.5 *(9-22-94)*
Emergency Processing

(1) In some cases, the taxpayer may have entered into a contract or business agreement which requires him or her, as a condition of the contract or agreement, to resolve a tax liability by a specific date. If the tax liability must be resolved before the business transaction is completed and the liability to be compromised is at least $100,000 the taxpayer may request expedited processing.

(2) The taxpayer should indicate such a request by marking the top margin of Form 656, page 1, "Emergency Processing Requested."

(3) If all necessary appraisals or other proofs of asset and liability valuation are submitted with the offer, the taxpayer will be notified of our decision within 90 days from the date we receive the offer.

(4) If it is necessary to request additional documentation, the taxpayer will be advised that additional time may be required. However, every attempt will be made to meet the 90 day time frame.

57(10)(10) *(2-26-92)*
Adequate Offer

57(10)(10).1 *(9-22-94)*
Determination of Adequate Offer

(1) An offer is adequate if it reasonably reflects collection potential. An acceptable offer is made up of the following components:

(a) the amount collectable from the taxpayer's assets;

(b) the amount collectible from the taxpayer's present and future income;

(c) the amount collectible from third parties, e.g., trust fund recovery penalty and transferee; and

(d) the amount the taxpayer should reasonably be expected to raise from assets in which he or she has an interest but the interest is beyond the reach of the government. For example, property located outside the U.S. or property owned by tenancy by the entirety.

(2) The starting point in the consideration of an offer submitted based on doubt as to collectibility is the value of the taxpayer's assets less encumbrances which have priority over the federal tax lien. Ordinarily, the liquidating or quick sale value of assets should be used. Quick sale or liquidating value is the amount which would be realized from the sale of an asset in a situation where financial pressures cause the taxpayer to sell in a short period of time. It should be recognized, however, that the acceptance of an offer serves the best interest of the government. Therefore, it would not be unreasonable in a given case to use minimum bid in determining collection potential. Minimum bid should be determined in accordance with Policy Statement P-5-35 and IRM 56(13)5.1 No lower value may be used by collection. Since valuations of property, except cash or cash equivalents, are not scientifically exact, care should be exercised to avoid inflexible, non-negotiable values.

(3) Under the current legal definition of doubt as to collectibility, all assets must be considered in determining the amount collectible from the taxpayer. Assets may not be eliminated or valued at $0 simply because we would not take enforcement action against the asset, even though the net result might be rejection of the offer and reporting the case as currently not collectible. The Attorney General has ruled that we cannot legally accept an offer because of equity, hardship, or any other issue which coos not have a direct bearing on our legal ability to collect from the taxpayer. In determining the taxpayer's equity in property a range of alternatives from quick sale through forced sale to minimum bid price are acceptable options. Quick sale value is defined as a value greater than forced sale value with forced sale value defined as no less than 75% of fair market value. To determine forced sale value and minimum bid price follow instructions in IRM 56(13)5, Establishment of Minimum Bid.

(4) The Service also takes into consideration the amount that can be collected from the taxpayer's future income. In evaluating those future prospects, the taxpayer's education, profession or trade, age and experience, health, past and present income will be considered. In evaluating future income potential an evaluation must be made of the likelihood that any increase in real income will be available to pay the delinquent taxes. The Service needs to take into consideration the increasing cost of living as a factor in determining amounts potentially collectible from future income. In determining necessary living expenses, the procedures in IRM 5323 will be used.

(5) Rejection of an offer solely based on narrow asset and income evaluation should be avoided. The Service should attempt to negotiate offer agreements which are in the best interest of all parties. Included in determining the government's interests are the cost of collection.

57(10)(10).2 *(9-22-94)*
Negotiating an Acceptable Offer

(1) Service personnel should determine what would be an acceptable offer. The taxpayer will be given an opportunity to increase the offer. Asset values are generally subject to market forces and interpretation. Therefore, a flexible negotiation position should be taken when negotiating an offer.

(2) Negotiation is not only limited to the dollar amount of the offer, but also involves issues such as:

    (a) terms of payments

    (b) benefits of earlier payment

        1 release of lien

        2 reduced interest charge

    (c) collateral agreements

(3) Since an offer will not be accepted if a taxpayer is not current in all filing and payment requirements, efforts should be directed towards bringing the taxpayer into compliance so the offer can be accepted.

(4) In the event the offer is not an acceptable resolution, negotiations should be directed toward other case alternatives (e.g., full payment, installment agreement).

57(10)(10).3 *(9-22-94)*
Identifying Open Examinations, Underreporter Cases and Amended or Duplicate Filed Returns

(1) When an offer is recommended for acceptance, CC AMDISA, CC TSUMYI, and CC IMFOLT/BMFOLT (Look for "L" freeze or unreversed TC 420—AIMS indicator) should be checked to determine if any tax years are being examined. The appropriate Examination, EP/EO, service center function, or Collection Employment Tax Examination function will be contacted and advised of the existence of the offer. Action deemed appropriate can then be coordinated between functions.

(2) Prior to acceptance of an offer, CC TXMOD or transcripts must be examined to identify the presence of an open Underreporter case. Underreporter cases are open if there is a TC 922 without a CP 2000 process code accompanying either the TC 922 or a TC 290 or 291. If an open case is identified, SCCB must be contacted and advised of the planned offer acceptance. SCCB will then contact Underreporter and give them an opportunity to close their case with the appropriate process code prior to signature of Form 7249, Offer Acceptance Report' by the delegated official. Underreporter will close the case by either making an additional assessment, or when they lack sufficient basis for an agent, closing the case "no change". The response from SCCB will be due within five calendar days of the district office request. If Underreporter does not take the requested action, processing of the acceptance report will not be delayed. If a tax increase will be assessed, the increased assessed bat balance must be shown on Form 7249.

(3) Prior to acceptance of an offer, CC TXMOD or transcripts must be examined to identify the presence of either amended or duplicate returns. Amended or duplicate returns are identified in the system by the presence of a TC 976 or TC 977 on the module. If an amended or duplicate return is present, verify that the balance is still greater than the amount of the offer.

(4) The above checks in (1) and (2) above will help prevent unpostable codes from posting to modules containing unreversed TC 780s.

Offer in Compromise
Filing Forms

Department of Treasury
Internal Revenue Service

Form 656 (Rev. 1-97)
Catalog Number 16728N

Form 656

Offer in Compromise

Item 1

Taxpayer's Name and Home or Business Address

Name

Street Address

City   State   Zip Code

Mailing Address (if different from above)

City   State   Zip Code

Item 2

Social Security Numbers

(a) Primary

(b) Secondary

Item 3

Employer Identification Number (Included in offer)

Item 4

Other Employer Identification Numbers (Not included in offer)

Item 5

To: Commissioner of Internal Revenue Service

I/we (includes all types of taxpayers) submit this offer to compromise the tax liabilities plus any interest, penalties, additions to tax, and additional amounts required by law (tax liability) for the tax type and period marked below: (Please mark an "X" for the correct description and fill-in the correct tax periods(s), adding additional periods if needed.)

☐ **1040/1120 Income tax**—Year(s)

☐ **941 Employer's Quarterly Federal Tax Return**—Quarterly Period(s)

☐ **940 Employer's Annual Federal Unemployment (FUTA) Tax Return**—Year(s)

☐ **Trust Fund Recovery Penalty** as a
responsible person of (enter corporation name)

for failure to pay withholding and Federal Insurance Contributions Act Taxes (Social Security taxes)—Period(s)

☐ **Other Federal taxes** (specify type and periods(s),

Item 6

I/we submit this offer for the reason(s) checked below:

☐ **Doubt as to Liability**— "I do not believe I owe this amount." You *must* include a detailed explanation of the reasons you believe you do not owe the tax.

☐ **Doubt as to Collectibility**--"I have insufficient assets and income to pay the full amount." You *must* include a complete financial statement (Form 433-A and/ or Form 433-B).

Item 7

I/We offer to pay $

☐ **Paid in full with this offer.**
☐ **Deposit of $**   **with this offer.**
☐ **No deposit.**
Check one of the following boxes.

☐ Balance to be paid in ☐ 10, ☐ 30, ☐ 60, or ☐ 90 days from notice of acceptance of the offer. If more than one payment will be paid during the time frame checked, provide the amount of the payment and date to be paid on the line below.

☐ Other proposed payment terms. Enter the specific dates (mm/dd/yy format) and dollar amounts of the the payment terms you propose on the lines below.

In addition to the above amount, IRS will add interest from the date IRS accepts the offer until the date you completely pay the amount offered, as required by section 6621 of the Internal Revenue Code, IRS compounds interest daily, as required by section 6622 of the Internal Revenue Code.

Item 8

By submitting this offer, I/we understand and agree to the following conditions:

(a) I/we voluntarily submit all payments made on this offer.

(b) IRS will apply payments made under the terms of this offer in the best interest of the government.

(c) If IRS rejects the offer or I/we withdraw the offer, IRS will return any amount paid with the offer. If I/we agree in writing, IRS will apply the amount paid with the offer to the amount owed. If I/we agree to apply the payment, the date the offer is rejected or withdrawn will be considered the date of payment. I/we understand that IRS will not pay interest on any amount I/we submit with the offer.

(d) **I/we will comply with all provisions of the Internal Revenue Code relating to filing my/our returns and paying my/our required taxes for 5 years from the date IRS accepts the offer. This condition does not apply to offers based on Doubt as to Liability.**

(e) I/we waive and agree to the suspension of any statutory periods of limitation (time limits provided for by law) for IRS assessment and collection of the tax liability for the tax periods identified in item (5).

(f) IRS will keep all payments and credits made, received, or applied to the amount being compromised before this offer was submitted. IRS may keep any proceeds from a levy served prior to submission of the offer, but not received at the time the offer is submitted. If I/we have an installment agreement prior to submitting the offer, I/we must continue to make the payments as agreed while this offer is pending. Installment agreement payments will not be applied against the amount offered.

(g) **IRS will keep any refund, including interest, due to me/us because of overpayment of any tax or other liability, for tax periods extending through the calendar year that IRS accepts the offer. I/we may not designate a refund, to which the IRS is entitled, to be applied to estimated tax payments for the following year.** This condition doesn't apply if the offer is based only on Doubt as to Liability.

(h) I/we will return to IRS any refund identified in (g) received after submission of this offer. This condition doesn't apply if the offer is based only on Doubt as to Liability.

(i) The total amount IRS can collect under this offer can not be more than the full amount of the tax liability.

(j) I/we understand that I/we remain responsible for the full amount of the tax liability, unless and until IRS accepts the offer in writing and I/we have met all the terms and conditions of the offer. IRS won't remove the original amount of the tax liability from its records until I/we have met all the terms of the offer.

(k) I/we understand that the tax I/we offer to compromise is and will remain a tax liability until I/we meet all the terms and conditions of this offer. If I/we file bankruptcy before the terms and conditions of this offer are completed, any claim the IRS files in the bankruptcy proceeding will be a tax claim.

(l) Once IRS accepts the offer in writing, I/we have no right to contest, in court or otherwise, the amount of the tax liability.

(m) The offer is pending starting with the date an authorized IRS official signs this form and accepts my/our waiver of the statutory periods of limitation. The offer remains pending until an authorized IRS official accepts, rejects or acknowledges withdrawal of the offer in writing. If I/we appeal the IRS decision on the offer, IRS will continue to treat the offer as pending until the Appeals Office accepts or rejects the offer in writing. If I/we don't file a protest within 30 days of the date IRS notifies me/us of the right to protest the decision, I/we waive the right to a hearing before the Appeals office about the offer in compromise.

(n) **The waiver and suspension of any statutory periods of limitation for assessment and collection of the amount of the tax liability described in item (5), continues to apply: while the offer is pending (see (m) above), during the time I/we have not paid all of the amount offered, during the time I/we have not completed all terms and conditions of the offer, and for one additional year beyond each of the time periods identified in this paragraph.**

(o) If I/we fail to meet any of the terms and conditions of the offer, the offer is in default, then IRS may: immediately file suit to collect the entire unpaid balance of the offer; immediately file suit to collect an amount equal to the original amount of the tax liability as liquidating damages, minus any payments already received under the terms of this offer; disregard the amount of the offer and apply all amounts already paid under the offer against the original amount of tax liability; or file suit or levy to collect the original amount of the tax liability, without further notice of any kind.

IRS will continue to add interest as required by section 6621 of the Internal Revenue Code, on the amount IRS determines is due after default. IRS will add interest from the date the offer is defaulted until I/we completely satisfy the amount owed.

Item 9

If I/we submit this offer on a substitute form, I/we affirm that this form is a verbatim duplicate of the official Form 656, and I/we agree to be bound by all the terms and conditions set forth in the official Form 656.

Under penalties of perjury, I declare that I have examined this offer, including accompanying schedules and statements, and to the best of my knowledge and belief, it is true, correct and complete.

(9a) Signature of Taxpayer-proponent

_____

Date

_____

(9b) Signature of Taxpayer-proponent

_____

Date

_____

For Official Use Only

I accept waiver of the statutory period of limitations for the Internal Revenue Service.

Signature of authorized Internal Revenue Service Official

_____

Title

_____

Date

_____

Form **433-A**
(Rev. September 1995)

Department of the Treasury — Internal Revenue Service

Collection Information Statement for Individuals

NOTE: **Complete all blocks, except shaded areas, Write "N/A"** *(not applicable)* in those blocks that do not apply.
Instructions for certain line items are in Publication 1854.

1. Taxpayer(s) name(s) and address	2. Home phone number	3. Marital status
	( )	
	4.a. Taxpayer's social security number	b. Spouse's social security number
County _____		

Section I.   Employment Information

5. Taxpayer's employer or business *(name and address)*	a. How long employed	b. Business phone number ( )	c. Occupation
	d. Number of exemptions claimed on Form W-4 _____	e. Pay period: ☐ Weekly ☐ Bi-weekly ☐ Monthly ☐ _____ Payday: _____ (Mon - Sun)	f. *(Check appropriate box)* ☐ Wage earner ☐ Sole proprietor ☐ Partner
6. Spouse's employer or business *(name and address)*	a. How long employed	b. Business phone number ( )	c. Occupation
	d. Number of exemptions claimed on Form W-4 _____	e. Pay period: ☐ Weekly ☐ Bi-weekly ☐ Monthly ☐ _____ Payday: _____ (Mon - Sun)	f. *(Check appropriate box)* ☐ Wage earner ☐ Sole proprietor ☐ Partner

Section II.   Personal Information

7. Name, address and telephone number of next of kin or other reference	8. Other names or aliases	9. Previous address(es)

10. Age and relationship of dependents living in your household *(exclude yourself and spouse)*

11. Date of Birth ▶	a. Taxpayer	b. Spouse	12. Latest filed income tax return *(tax year)*	a. Number of exemptions claimed	b. Adjusted Gross Income

Section III.   General Financial Information

13. Bank accounts *(include savings & loans, credit unions, IRA and retirement plans, certificates of deposit, etc.)* Enter bank loans in item 28.

Name of Institution	Address	Type of Account	Account No.	Balance
		Total *(Enter in Item 21)*		

Cat. No. 20312N

Form **433-A** (Rev. 9-95)

Section III - *continued*   General Financial Information

14. Charge cards and lines of credit from banks, credit unions, and savings and loans. List all other charge accounts in item 28.

Type of Account or Card	Name and Address of Financial Institution	Monthly Payment	Credit Limit	Amount Owed	Credit Available
	Totals *(Enter in Item 27)* ▶				

15. Safe deposit boxes rented or accessed *(List all locations, box numbers, and contents)*

16.	**Real Property** *(Brief description and type of ownership)*	Physical Address
a.		County _____
b.		County _____
c.		County _____

17.	**Life Insurance** *(Name of Company)*	Policy Number	Type	Face Amount	Available Loan Value
			☐ Whole ☐ Term		
			☐ Whole ☐ Term		
			☐ Whole ☐ Term		
			Total *(Enter in Item 23)* ▶		

18. Securities *(stocks, bonds, mutual funds, money market funds, government securities, etc.):*

Kind	Quantity or Denomination	Current Value	Where Located	Owner of Record

19. Other information relating to your financial condition. If you check the yes box, please give dates and explain on page 4, Additional Information or Comments:

a. Court proceedings	☐ Yes ☐ No	b. Bankruptcies	☐ Yes ☐ No
c. Repossessions	☐ Yes ☐ No	d. Recent sale or other transfer of assets for less than full value	☐ Yes ☐ No
e. Anticipated increase in income	☐ Yes ☐ No	f. Participant or beneficiary to trust, estate, profit sharing, etc.	☐ Yes ☐ No

Form **433-A**   **page 2**   (Rev. 9-95)

Section IV.   Assets and Liabilities

Description	Current Market Value	Current Amount Owed	Equity in Asset	Amount of Monthly Payment	Name and Address of Lien/Note Holder/Lender	Date Pledged	Date of Final Payment
20. Cash							
21. Bank accounts *(from Item 13)*							
22. Securities *(from Item 18)*							
23. Cash or loan value of insurance							
24. Vehicles *(model, year, license, tag#)*							
a.							
b.							
c.							
25. Real property *(From Section III, item 16)* a.							
b.							
c.							
26. Other assets							
a.							
b.							
c.							
d.							
e.							
27. Bank revolving credit *(from Item 14)*							
28. Other Liabilities *(Including bank loans, judgments, notes, and charge accounts not entered in Item 13.)* a.							
b.							
c.							
d.							
e.							
f.							
g.							
29. Federal taxes owed (prior years)							
30. **Totals**			$	$			

Internal Revenue Service Use Only Below This Line

Financial Verification/Analysis

Item	Date Information or Encumbrance Verified	Date Property Inspected	Estimated Forced Sale Equity
Personal Residence			
Other Real Property			
Vehicles			
Other Personal Property			
State Employment *(Husband and Wife)*			
Income Tax Return			
Wage Statements *(Husband and Wife)*			
Sources of Income/Credit *(D&B Report)*			
Expenses			
Other Assets/Liabilities			

Form **433-A**   **page 3**   (Rev. 9-95)

Form **433-B**
(Rev. June 1991)
Department of the Treasury
Internal Revenue Service

Collection Information Statement for Businesses

(If you need additional space, please attach a separate sheet.)

Note: Complete all blocks, except shaded areas. Write "N/A" *(not applicable)* **in those blocks that do not apply.**

1 Name and address of business	2 Business phone number ( )
	3 (Check appropriate box)
	☐ Sole proprietor ☐ Other *(specify)*
	☐ Partnership
County	☐ Corporation

4 Name and title of person being interviewed	5 Employer identification number	6 Type of business

7 Information about owner, partners, officers, major shareholder, etc.

Name and Title	Effective Date	Home Address	Phone Number	Social Security Number	Total Shares or Interest

Section I   **General Financial Information**

8 Latest filed income tax return ▶	Form	Tax year ended	Net income before taxes

9 Bank accounts *(List all types of accounts including payroll and general, savings, certificates of deposit, etc.)*

Name of Institution	Address	Type of Account	Account Number	Balance
		Total *(Enter in item 17)* . . . . ▶		

10 Bank credit available *(Lines of credit, etc.)*

Name of Institution	Address	Credit Limit	Amount Owed	Credit Available	Monthly Payments
Totals *(Enter in items 24 or 25 as appropriate)* . . . . ▶					

11 Location, box number, and contents of all safe deposit boxes rented or accessed

Cat. No. 16649P   Form **433-B** (Rev. 6-91)

Form 433-B (Rev. 6-91)   Page **2**

Section I (continued)   **General Financial Information**

12   Real property

Brief Description and Type of Ownership	Physical Address
a	County ....
b	County ....
c	County ....
d	County ....

13   Life insurance policies owned with business as beneficiary

Name Insured	Company	Policy Number	Type	Face Amount	Available Loan Value
Total (Enter in item 19). . . . . ▶					

14a   Additional information regarding financial condition *(Court proceedings, bankruptcies filed or anticipated, transfers of assets for less than full value, changes in market conditions, etc. Include information regarding company participation in trusts, estates, profit-sharing plans, etc.)*

b   If you know of any person or organization that borrowed or otherwise provided funds to pay net payrolls:

(i)   Who borrowed funds?

(ii)   Who supplied funds?

15   Accounts/notes receivable *(Include current contract jobs, loans to stockholders, officers, partners, etc.)*

Name	Address	Amount Due	Date Due	Status
		$		
Total (Enter in item 18). . . . . ▶	$			

Form 433-B (Rev. 6-91) Page **3**

Section II					**Asset and Liability Analysis**		
(a) **Description**	**(b)** Cur. Mkt. Value	**(c)** Liabilities Bal. Due	**(d)** Equity in Asset	**(e)** Amt. of Mo. Pymt	**(f)** Name and Address of Lien/Note Holder/Obligee	**(g)** Date Pledged	**(h)** Date of Final Pymt.
16 Cash on hand							
17 Bank accounts							
18 Accounts/Notes receivable							
19 Life insurance loan value							
20 Real property *(from item 12)* a							
b							
c							
d							
21 Vehicles *(model, year, and license)* a							
b							
c							
22 Machinery and equipment *(specify)* a							
b							
c							
23 Merchandise inventory *(specify)* a							
b							
24 Other assets *(specify)* a							
b							
25 Other liabilities *(including notes and judgments)* a							
b							
c							
d							
e							
f							
g							
h							
26 Federal taxes owed							
27 Total							

Form 433-B (Rev. 6-91)　　　　　　　　　　　　　　　　　　　　　　　　　　　　Page **4**

Section III		**Income and Expense Analysis**	

The following information applies to income and expenses during the period _____ to _____		Accounting method used	
Income		**Expenses**	
28 Gross receipts from sales, services, etc.	$	**34** Materials purchased	$
29 Gross rental income		(Number of employees ....) **35** Net wages and salaries	
30 Interest		**36** Rent	
31 Dividends		*(IRS use only)* **37** Allowable installment payments	
32 Other income *(specify)*		**38** Supplies	
		39 Utilities/telephone	
		40 Gasoline/oil	
		41 Repairs and maintenance	
		42 Insurance	
		43 Current taxes	
		44 Other *(specify)*	
33 Total income　▶	$	**45** Total expenses *(IRS use only)*　▶	$
		46 Net difference *(IRS use only)*　▶	$

Certification: Under penalties of perjury, I declare that to the best of my knowledge and belief this statement of assets, liabilities, and other information is true, correct, and complete.

47 Signature	**48** Date

Internal Revenue Service Use Only Below This Line

Financial Verification/Analysis

Item	Date Information or Encumbrance Verified	Date Property Inspected	Estimated Forced Sale Equity
Sources of income/credit (D&B report)			
Expenses			
Real property			
Vehicles			
Machinery and equipment			
Merchandise			
Accounts/notes receivable			
Corporate information, if applicable			
U.C.C.: senior/junior lienholder			
Other assets/liabilities			

Explain any difference between item 46 (or P&L) and the installment agreement payment amount:

Name of originator and IDRS assignment number	Date

	Department of the Treasury — Internal Revenue Service
Form **2261-A** (Rev. 10-94)	**Collateral Agreement** Future Income — Individual

Name of Corporation	Employer Identification Number

To: Commissioner of Internal Revenue

The taxpayers identified above has submitted an offer dated _____ in the amount of $ _____ to compromise unpaid _____ tax liability, plus statutory additions, for the taxable periods _____

The purpose of this collateral agreement (hereinafter referred to as this agreement) is to provide additional consideration for acceptance of the offer in compromise described above. It is understood and agreed:

1. That in addition to the payment of the above amount of $ _____ , the taxpayers will pay out of annual income for the years _____ to _____ , inclusive

    (a) Nothing on the first $ _____ of annual income.

    (b) _____ percent of annual income more than $ _____ and more than $_____ .

    (c) _____ percent of annual income more than $ _____ .

2. That the term annual income, as used in this agreement, means adjusted gross income before net operating loss deduction and special deductions (except losses from sales or exchanges of property shall not be allowed), plus all nontaxable income, minus (a) the federal income tax paid for the year for which annual income is being computed, and (b) any payment made under the terms of the offer in compromise (Form 656), as shown in item 5, form 656, for the year in which such payment is made. Annual income shall not be reduced by any overpayments waived in item 7g, Form 656. The annual income shall not be reduced by net operating losses incurred before or after the period covered by this agreement. However, a net operating loss for any year during such period may be deducted from annual income for the following year only.

3. That net operating losses sustained for years ending before the calendar year in which this offer is accepted shall not be claimed as a net operating loss carry over in computing federal income tax.

4. That the annual payment provided for in this agreement (including interest at the annual rate as established under sections 6621(a) and 6622 of the Internal Revenue Code (subject to adjustments s provided by Code section 6621(b)) on delinquent payments computed from the due date of such payments) shall be paid to the Internal Revenue Service on or before the 15th day of the 3rd month following the close of the calendar or fiscal year, such payments to be accompanied by a sworn statement and a copy of the taxpayer's federal income tax return. The statement shall refer to this agreement and show the computation of annual income in accordance with items 1, and 2 of this agreement. If the annual income for any year covered by this agreement is insufficient to require a payment under its terms, the taxpayers shall still furnish the Internal Revenue Service a sworn statement of such income and a copy of their federal income tax return. All blocks, records, and accounts shall be open at all reasonable times for inspection by the Internal Revenue Service to verify the annual income shown in the statement. The payment (if any), the sworn statement, and a copy of the federal income tax return shall be transmitted to:

    Address:

5. That the aggregate amount paid under the terms of the offer in compromise and the additional amounts paid under the terms of this agreement shall not exceed an amount equivalent to the liability covered by the offer plus statutory additions that would become due in the absence of the compromise.

6. That payments made under the terms of this agreement shall be applied first to tax and penalty, in that order, due for the earliest taxable period, then to tax and penalty, in that order, for each succeeding taxable period with no amount to be allocated to interest until the liabilities for taxes and penalties for all taxable periods sought to be compromised have been satisfied.

7. That upon notice to the taxpayers of the acceptance of the offer in compromise of the liability identified in this agreement, the taxpayers shall have no right, in the event of default in payment of any installment of principal or interest due under the terms of the offer and this agreement or in the event any other provision of this agreement is not carried out in accordance with its terms, to contest in court or otherwise the amount of the liability sought to be compromised; and that in the event of such default or noncompliance or in the event the taxpayers become the subject of any proceeding (except a proceeding under the Bankruptcy Act) whereby their affairs are placed under the control and jurisdiction of a court or other party, the United States, at the option of the Commissioner of Internal Revenue or a delegated official, may (a) proceed immediately by suit to collect the entire unpaid balance of the offer and this agreement, or (b) proceed immediately by suit to collect as liquidated damages an amount equal to the tax liability sought to be compromised, minus any payments already received under the terms of the offer and this agreement, with interest at the annual rate established under sections 6621(a) and 6622 of the Internal Revenue Code (subject to adjustments as provided by Code section 6621(b)) from the date of default, or (c) disregard the amount of such offer and this agreement, apply all amounts previously paid thereunder against the amount of the liability sought to be compromised and, without further notice of any kind, assess and collect by levy or suit (the restrictions against assessment and collection being waived) the balance of such liability. In the event the taxpayers becomes the subject of any proceeding under the Bankruptcy Act, the offer in compromise and this agreement may be terminated. Upon such termination, the tax liability sought to be compromised, minus any payments already received under the terms of the offer and this agreement, shall become legally enforceable.

8. That the taxpayer waives the benefit of any statute of limitations applicable to the assessment and collection of the liability sought to be compromised and agrees to the suspension of the running of the statutory period of limitations on assessment and collection for the period during which the offer in compromise and this agreement are pending, or the period during which any installment under the offer and this agreement remains unpaid, or any provision of this agreement is not carried out in accordance with its terms, and for 1 year thereafter.

9. That when all sums, including interest, due under the terms of the offer in compromise and this agreement, except those sums which may become due and payable under the provisions of item 1 of this agreement, have been paid in full, then and in that event only, all federal tax liens at that time securing the tax liabilities which are the subject of the offer shall be immediately released. However, if, at the time consideration is being given to the release of the federal tax liens, there are any sums due and payable under the terms of item 1, they must also be paid before the release of such liens.

This agreement shall be of no force or effect unless the offer in compromise is accepted.

Name of Corporation	Signature and Title of Officer	Date

I accept the waiver of statutory period of limitations for the Internal Revenue Service.

Signature and Title		Date

*U.S. GPO: 1994-387-109/01880

Form **2261-A** (Rev. 10-94)

Form **2261-B** (Rev. May 1988)	DEPARTMENT OF THE TREASURY — INTERNAL REVENUE SERVICE **Collateral Agreement** Adjusted Basis of Specific Assets
Names and Address of Taxpayers	Social Security and Employer Identification Numbers

To: Commissioner of Internal Revenue

The taxpayers identified above have submitted an offer dated _____ in the amount of S _____

to compromise unpaid _____ tax liability, plus statutory additions, for the

taxable periods _____ .

The purpose of this collateral agreement (hereinafter referred to as this agreement) is to provide additional consideration for acceptance of the offer in compromise described above. It is understood and agreed:

1. That for the purpose of computing income taxes of the taxpayers for all taxable years beginning after _____ , the basis for certain assets under the existing law for computing depreciation and the gain or loss upon sale, exchange, or other disposition shall be as follows:

Name of asset	*Basis*
	$

2. That in no event shall the basis shown in item 1, above, be in excess of the basis that would otherwise be allowable for tax purposes except for this agreement.

3. That the aggregate amount paid under the terms of the offer in compromise and the additional amounts of taxes paid as the result of the reduction of the basis of the assets described above shall not exceed an amount equivalent to the liability covered by the offer plus statutory additions that would have become due in the absence of the compromise.

Cat. No. 18245N   (Over)   Form **2261-B** (Rev. 5-88)

4. That upon notice to the taxpayers of the acceptance of the offer in compromise of the liability identified in this agreement, the taxpayers shall have no right, in the event of default in payment of any installment of principal or interest due under the terms of the offer and this agreement or in the event any other provision of this agreement is not carried out in accordance with its terms, to contest in court or otherwise the amount of the liability sought to be compromised; and that in the event of such default or noncompliance or in the event the taxpayers become the subject of any proceeding (except a proceeding under the Bankruptcy Act) whereby their affairs are placed under the control and jurisdiction of a court or other party, the United States, at the option of the Commissioner of Internal Revenue or a delegated official, may (a) proceed immediately by suit to collect the entire unpaid balance of the offer and this agreement, or (b) proceed immediately by suit to collect as liquidated damages an amount equal to the tax liability sought to be compromised, minus any payments already received under the terms of the offer and this agreement, with interest at the rate established under section 6621 of the Internal Revenue Code from the date of default, or (c) disregard the amount of such offer and this agreement, apply all amounts previously paid thereunder against the amount of the liability sought to be compromised and, without further notice of any kind, assess and collect by levy or suit (the restrictions against assessment and collection being waived) the balance of such liability. In the event the taxpayers become the subject of any proceeding under the Bankruptcy Act, the offer in compromise and this agreement may be terminated. Upon such termination, the tax liability sought to be compromised, minus any payments already received under the terms of the offer and this agreement, shall become legally enforceable.

5. That the taxpayers waive the benefit of any statute of limitations applicable to the assessment and collection of the liability sought to be compromised and agree to the suspension of the running of the statutory period of limitations on assessment and collection for the period during which the offer in compromise and this agreement are pending, or the period during which any installment under the offer and this agreement remains unpaid, or any provision of this agreement is not carried out in accordance with its terms, and for 1 year thereafter.

6. That when all sums, including interest, due under the terms of the offer in compromise and this agreement, except those sums which may become due and payable under the provisions of item 1 of this agreement, have been paid in full, then and in that event only, all Federal tax liens at that time securing the tax liabilities which are the subject of the offer shall be immediately released. However, if, at the time consideration is being given to the release of the Federal tax liens, there are any sums due and payable under the terms of item 1, they must also be paid before the release of such liens.

This agreement shall be of no force or effect unless the offer in compromise is accepted.

Taxpayer's Signature	Date
Taxpayer's Signature	Date

I accept the waiver of statutory period of limitations for the Internal Revenue Service.

Signature and Title	Date

Form **2261-B** (Rev. 5-88)

Form **2261-C** (Rev. May 1988)	DEPARTMENT OF THE TREASURY — INTERNAL REVENUE SERVICE **Collateral Agreement** Waiver of Net Operating Losses, Capital Losses, and Unused Investment Credits
Names and Address of Taxpayers	Social Security and Employer Identification Numbers

To: Commissioner of Internal Revenue

The taxpayers identified above have submitted an offer dated _____ in the amount of $ _____ to compromise unpaid _____ tax liability, plus statutory additions, for the taxable periods _____ .

The purpose of this collateral agreement (hereinafter referred to as this agreement) is to provide additional consideration for acceptance of the offer in compromise described above. It is understood and agreed that for the purpose of computing the taxpayers' Federal income tax for all taxable years beginning after _____ :

1. That any net operating losses sustained for the years _____ to _____ , inclusive, shall not be claimed as net operating loss deductions under the provisions of section 172 of the Internal Revenue Code.

2. That any net capital losses sustained for the years before _____ shall not be claimed as carryovers or carrybacks under the provisions of section 1212 of the Internal Revenue Code.

3. That any unused investment credits for the years _____ to _____ , inclusive, shall not be claimed as investment credit carrybacks or carryovers under the provisions of Internal Revenue Code section 39 or 46, as applicable.

4. That the aggregate amount paid under the terms of the offer in compromise and the additional amounts of taxes paid as the result of the waiver of the losses and credits involved in this agreement shall not exceed an amount equivalent to the liability covered by the offer plus statutory additions that would become due in the absence of the compromise.

5. That upon notice to the taxpayers of the acceptance of the offer in compromise of the liability identified in this agreement, the taxpayers shall have no right, in the event of default in payment of any installment of principal or interest due under the terms of the offer and this agreement or in the event any other provision of this agreement is not carried out in accordance with its terms, to contest in court or otherwise the amount of the liability sought to be compromised; and that in the event of such default or noncompliance or in the event the taxpayers become the subject of any proceeding (except a proceeding under the Bankruptcy Act) whereby their affairs are placed under the control and jurisdiction of a court or other party, the United States, at the option of the Commissioner of Internal Revenue or a delegated official, may (a) proceed immediately by suit to collect the entire unpaid balance of the offer and this agreement, or (b) proceed immediately by suit to collect as liquidated damages an amount equal to the tax liability sought to be compromised, minus any payments already received under the terms of the offer and this agreement, with interest at the rate established under section 6621 of the Internal Revenue Code from the date of default, or (c) disregard the amount of such offer and this agreement, apply all amounts previously paid thereunder against the amount of the liability sought to be compromised and, without further notice of any kind, assess and collect by levy or suit (the restrictions against assessment and collection being waived) the balance of such liability. In the event the taxpayers become the subject of any proceeding under the Bankruptcy Act, the offer in compromise and this agreement may be terminated. Upon such termination, the tax liability sought to be compromised, minus any payments already received under the terms of the offer and this agreement, shall become legally enforceable.

6. That the taxpayers waive the benefit of any statute of limitations applicable to the assessment and collection of the liability sought to be compromised and agree to the suspension of the running of the statutory period of limitations on assessment and collection for the period during which the offer in compromise and this agreement are pending, or the period during which any installment under the offer and this agreement remains unpaid, or any provision of this agreement is not carried out in accordance with its terms, and for 1 year thereafter.

7. That when all sums, including interest, due under the terms of the offer in compromise and this agreement, except those sums which may become due and payable under the provisions of items 1, 2, and 3 of this agreement, have been paid in full, then and in that event only, all Federal tax liens at that time securing the tax liabilities which are the subject of the offer shall be immediately released. However, if, at the time consideration is being given to the release of the Federal tax liens, there are any sums due and payable under the terms of items 1, 2, and 3, they must also be paid before the release of such liens.

This agreement shall be of no force or effect unless the offer in compromise is accepted.

Taxpayers's Signature	Date
Taxpayer's Signature	Date

I accept the waiver of statutory period of limitations for the Internal Revenue Service.

Signature and Title	Date

*U.S. GPO: 1993-301-643/92144   Form **2261-C** (Rev. 5-88)

DEPARTMENT OF THE TREASURY—INTERNAL REVENUE SERVICE

Form **2261-D**
(Rev. October 1982)

**COLLATERAL AGREEMENT
DELINQUENCY PENALTY OFFER—INCOME TAX**

Carryback of Net Operating Loss or Investment Credit

Names and Address of Taxpayers

Social Security and Employer
Identification Numbers

TO: **Commissioner of Internal Revenue**

_____ , submitted an offer dated
(Type or Print Taxpayers' Names)
_____ in the amount of $ _____ to
compromise an unpaid penalty assessed because of the delinquent filing of income tax
returns for the years _____ .

The purpose of this agreement is to clarify the offer referred to above:

It is understood and agreed that no refund will be made or claimed for
any part of the tax, including additions to the tax, previously assessed
and collected for the years covered by the offer, by reason of carryback
of a net operating loss or an investment credit for a later taxable period
or year.

The offer is confirmed in all other respects.

Taxpayers' Signatures

Date

Catalog No. 18247J   *U.S. GPO: 1990-517-016/22452   Form **2261-D** (Rev.10-82)

Sample Offer in Compromise Package

Department of Treasury
Internal Revenue Service

Form 656 (Rev. 1-97)
Catalog Number 16728N

Form 656

Offer in Compromise

Item 1

Taxpayer's Name and Home or Business Address

John J. Red
Name

100 Main Street
Street Address

Maintown,   PA   19355
City   State   Zip Code

P.O. Box III
Mailing Address (if different from above)

Maintown, PA 19355

_____
City   State   Zip Code

Item 2

Social Security Numbers

(a) Primary____111-22-3333_____

(b) Secondary_____N/A_____

Item 3

Employer Identification Number (included in offer)

N/A

Item 4

Other Employer Identification Numbers (Not included in offer)

23-111411 (Business Assets)

_____

_____

_____

Item 5

To: Commissioner of Internal Revenue Service

I/we (includes all types of taxpayers) submit this offer to compromise the tax liabilities plus any interest, penalties, additions to tax, and additional amounts required by law (tax liability) for the tax type and period marked below: (Please mark an "X" for the correct description and fill-in the correct tax periods(s), adding additional periods if needed.)

☒ **1040/1120 Income tax**—Year(s) __1988, 1989, 1990__

☐ **941 Employer's Quarterly Federal Tax Return**—Quarterly Period(s) _____

☐ **940 Employer's Annual Federal Unemployment (FUTA) Tax Return**—Year(s) _____

☐ **Trust Fund Recovery Penalty** as a responsible person of (enter corporation name) _____

for failure to pay withholding and Federal Insurance Contributions Act Taxes (Social Security taxes)—Period(s) _____

☐ **Other Federal taxes** (specify type and periods(s). _____

Item 6

I/we submit this offer for the reason(s) checked below:

☐ **Doubt as to Liability**— "I do not believe I owe this amount." You *must* include a detailed explanation of the reasons you believe you do not owe the tax.

☐ **Doubt as to Collectibility**—"I have insufficient assets and income to pay the full amount." You *must* include a complete financial statement (Form 433-A and/ or Form 433-B).

Item 7

I/We offer to pay $ __71,001__

☐ **Paid in full with this offer.**
☒ **Deposit of $** __7,000.⁰⁰__ **with this offer.**
☐ **No deposit.**
Check one of the following boxes.
☒ Balance to be paid in ☐ 10, ☐ 30, ☐ 60, or ☐ 90 days from notice of acceptance of the offer. If more than one payment will be paid during the time frame checked, provide the amount of the payment and date to be paid on the line below.

$30,000 120 days from notice of acceptance

☐ Other proposed payment terms. Enter the specific dates (mm/dd/yy format) and dollar amounts of the the payment terms you propose on the lines below.

$34,001 within 6 months of

acceptance

In addition to the above amount, IRS will add interest from the date IRS accepts the offer until the date you completely pay the amount offered, as required by section 6821 of the Internal Revenue Code. IRS compounds interest daily, as required by section 6622 of the Internal Revenue Code.

Item 8

By submitting this offer, I/we understand and agree to the following conditions:

(a) I/we voluntarily submit all payments made on this offer.

(b) IRS will apply payments made under the terms of this offer in the best interest of the government.

(c) If IRS rejects the offer or I/we withdraw the offer, IRS will return any amount paid with the offer. If I/we agree in writing, IRS will apply the amount paid with the offer to the amount owed. If I/we agree to apply the payment, the date the offer is rejected or withdrawn will be considered the date of payment. I/we understand that IRS will not pay interest on any amount I/we submit with the offer.

(d) I/we will comply with all provisions of the Internal Revenue Code relating to filing my/our returns and paying my/our required taxes for 5 years from the date IRS accepts the offer. This condition does not apply to offers based on Doubt as to Liability.

(e) I/we waive and agree to the suspension of any statutory periods of limitation (time limits provided for by law) for IRS assessment and collection of the tax liability for the tax periods identified in item (5).

(f) IRS will keep all payments and credits made, received, or applied to the amount being compromised before this offer was submitted. IRS may keep any proceeds from a levy served prior to submission of the offer, but not received at the time the offer is submitted. If I/we have an installment agreement prior to submitting the offer, I/we must continue to make the payments as agreed while this offer is pending. Installment agreement payments will not be applied against the amount offered.

(g) IRS will keep any refund, including interest, due to me/us because of overpayment of any tax or other liability, for tax periods extending through the calendar year that IRS accepts the offer. I/we may not designate a refund, to which the IRS is entitled, to be applied to estimated tax payments for the following year. This condition doesn't apply if the offer is based only on Doubt as to Liability.

(h) I/we will return to IRS any refund identified in (g) received after submission of this offer. This condition doesn't apply if the offer is based only on Doubt as to Liability.

(i) The total amount IRS can collect under this offer can not be more than the full amount of the tax liability.

(j) I/we understand that I/we remain responsible for the full amount of the tax liability, unless and until IRS accepts the offer in writing and I/we have met all the terms and conditions of the offer. IRS won't remove the original amount of the tax liability from its records until I/we have met all the terms of the offer.

(k) I/we understand that the tax I/we offer to compromise is and will remain a tax liability until I/we meet all the terms and conditions of this offer. If I/we file bankruptcy before the terms and conditions of this offer are completed, any claim the IRS files in the bankruptcy proceeding will be a tax claim.

(l) Once IRS accepts the offer in writing, I/we have no right to contest, in court or otherwise, the amount of the tax liability.

(m) The offer is pending starting with the date an authorized IRS official signs this form and accepts my/our waiver of the statutory periods of limitation. The offer remains pending until an authorized IRS official accepts, rejects or acknowledges withdrawal of the offer in writing. If I/we appeal the IRS decision on the offer, IRS will continue to treat the offer as pending until the Appeals Office accepts or rejects the offer in writing. If I/we don't file a protest within 30 days of the date IRS notifies me/us of the right to protest the decision, I/we waive the right to a hearing before the Appeals office about the offer in compromise.

(n) The waiver and suspension of any statutory periods of limitation for assessment and collection of the amount of the tax liability described in item (5), continues to apply: while the offer is pending (see (m) above), during the time I/we have not paid all of the amount offered, during the time I/we have not completed all terms and conditions of the offer, and for one additional year beyond each of the time periods identified in this paragraph.

(o) If I/we fail to meet any of the terms and conditions of the offer, the offer is in default, then IRS may: immediately file suit to collect the entire unpaid balance of the offer; immediately file suit to collect an amount equal to the original amount of the tax liability as liquidating damages, minus any payments already received under the terms of this offer; disregard the amount of the offer and apply all amounts already paid under the offer against the original amount of tax liability; or file suit or levy to collect the original amount of the tax liability, without further notice of any kind.

IRS will continue to add interest as required by section 6621 of the Internal Revenue Code, on the amount IRS determines is due after default. IRS will add interest from the date the offer is defaulted until I/we completely satisfy the amount owed.

Item 9

If I/we submit this offer on a substitute form, I/we affirm that this form is a verbatim duplicate of the official Form 656, and I/we agree to be bound by all the terms and conditions set forth in the official Form 656.

Under penalties of perjury, I declare that I have examined this offer, including accompanying schedules and statements, and to the best of my knowledge and belief, it is true, correct and complete.

John J. Red

(9a) Signature of Taxpayer-proponent

7-10-87

Date

(9b) Signature of Taxpayer-proponent

Date

For Official Use Only

I accept waiver of the statutory period of limitations for the Internal Revenue Service.

Signature of authorized Internal Revenue Service Official

Title

Date

Form **433-A**
(Rev. September 1995)

Department of the Treasury — Internal Revenue Service

Collection Information Statement for Individuals

NOTE: Complete all blocks, except shaded areas, Write "**N/A**" *(not applicable)* in those blocks that do not apply.
Instructions for certain line items are in Publication 1854.

1. Taxpayer(s) name(s) and address	2. Home phone number	3. Marital status
John J. Red 100 Main Street Maintown, PA 19355 County _Main_	(215) 555-1111	Married - Separated
	4.a. Taxpayer's social security number N/A	**b.** Spouse's social security number N/A

Section I.   Employment Information

5. Taxpayer's employer or business *(name and address)*	a. How long employed	b. Business phone number	c. Occupation
Domestic Company, Inc. 200 Main Street Maintown, PA 19355	4 years	(215) 555-2222	Sales

d. Number of exemptions claimed on Form W-4 1	e. Pay period: ☐ Weekly ☒ Bi-weekly ☐ Monthly ☐ Payday: _____ (Mon - Sun)	f. *(Check appropriate box)* ☒ Wage earner ☐ Sole proprietor ☐ Partner

6. Spouse's employer or business *(name and address)*	a. How long employed	b. Business phone number ( )	c. Occupation

d. Number of exemptions claimed on Form W-4 _____	e. Pay period: ☐ Weekly ☐ Bi-weekly ☐ Monthly ☐ Payday: _____ (Mon - Sun)	f. *(Check appropriate box)* ☐ Wage earner ☐ Sole proprietor ☐ Partner

Section II.   Personal Information

7. Name, address and telephone number of next of kin or other reference	8. Other names or aliases	9. Previous address(es)
Jason J. Red (215) 555-1414	N/A	N/A

10. Age and relationship of dependents living in your household *(exclude yourself and spouse)*

11. Date of Birth ▶	a. Taxpayer 1/1/60	b. Spouse N/A	12. Latest filed income tax return *(tax year)* 1998	a. Number of exemptions claimed 1	b. Adjusted Gross Income $40,000

Section III.   General Financial Information

13. Bank accounts (include savings & loans, credit unions, IRA and retirement plans, certificates of deposit, etc.) Enter bank *loans* in item 28.

Name of Institution	Address	Type of Account	Account No.	Balance
Prime Bank	100 E. Lancaster Ave. Wanye, PA	check	141-001	$500
			Total *(Enter in Item 21)*	

Cat. No. 20312N   Form **433-A** (Rev. 9-95)

Section V. **Monthly Income and Expense Analysis**

Total Income			Necessary Living Expenses		
Source	**Gross**			**Claimed**	*(IRS use only)* **Allowed**
31. Wages/Salaries *(Taxpayer)*	$ 3,300		42. National Standard Expenses[1]	$	$
32. Wages/Salaries *(Spouse)*	– 0 –		43. Housing and utilities[2]	950	
33. Interest - Dividends	– 0 –		44. Transportation[3]	200	
34. Net business income *(from Form 433-B)*	– 0 –		45. Health care	50	
35. Rental Income	– 0 –		46. Taxes *(income and FICA)*	200	
36. Pension *(Taxpayer)*	– 0 –		47. Court ordered payments	– 0 –	
37. Pension *(Spouse)*	– 0 –		48. Child/dependent care	– 0 –	
38. Child Support			49. Life insurance	10	
39. Alimony	– 0 –		50. Secured or legally-perfected debts *(specify)*	– 0 –	
40. Other	– 0 –		51. Other expenses *(specify)*		
			Credit Cards	340	
41. Total Income	$ 3,300		**52. Total Expenses**	$ 1,750	$
			53. *(IRS use only)* Net difference *(income less necessary living expenses)*	$	

Certification Under penalties of perjury, I declare that to the best of my knowledge and belief this statement of assets, liabilities, and other information is true, correct, and complete.

54. Your signature	55. Spouse's signature *(if joint return was filed)*	56. Date
John Jr. Red		4/15/98

Notes

1. Clothing and clothing services, food, housekeeping supplies, personal care products and services, and miscellaneous.

2. Rent or mortgage payment for the taxpayer's principal residence. Add the average monthly payment for the following expenses if they are *not* included in the rent or mortgage payment: property taxes, homeowner's or renter's insurance, parking, necessary maintenance and repair, homeowner dues, condominium fees and utilities. Utilities includes gas, electricity, water, fuel oil, coal, bottled gas, trash and garbage collection, wood and other fuels, septic cleaning and telephone.

3. Lease or purchase payments, insurance, registration fees, normal maintenance, fuel, public transportation, parking and tolls.

Additional information or comments:

Internal Revenue Service Use Only Below This Line

Explain any difference between Item 53 and the installment agreement payment amount:

Name of originator and IDRS assignment number:	Date

Form **433-A** page 4 (Rev. 9-95)   ☆ U.S. GPO:1997-432-213/71716

Form **2261** (Rev. 04-95)	DEPARTMENT OF THE TREASURY — INTERNAL REVENUE SERVICE **Collateral Agreement** Future Income — Individual

Names and Address of Taxpayers Andrew Assistant	Social Security and Employer Identification Numbers 123 - 00 - 4567

To: Commissioner of Internal Revenue

The taxpayers identified above have submitted an offer dated __1/10/97__ in the amount of $ __9,000__ to

compromise unpaid __Income__ tax liability, plus statutory additions, for the taxable periods __1996__

The purpose of this collateral agreement (hereinafter referred to as this agreement) is to provide additional consideration for acceptance of the offer in compromise described above. It is understood and agreed:

1. That in addition to the payment of the above amount of $ __9,000__ , the taxpayers will pay out of annual income for the years __1997__ to __2002__ , inclusive

   (a) Nothing on the first $ __25,000__ of annual income.

   (b) __25__ percent of annual income more than $ __25,000__ and not more than $ __35,000__ .

   (c) __30__ percent of annual income more than $ __35,000__ and not more than $ __45,000__ .

   (d) __40__ percent of annual income more than $ __45,000__

2. That the term annual income, as used in this agreement, means adjusted gross income as defined in section 62 of the Internal Revenue Code (except losses from sales or exchanges of property shall not be allowed), plus all nontaxable income and profits or gains from any source whatsoever (including the fair market value of gifts, bequests, devises, and inheritances), minus (a) the federal income tax paid for the year for which annual income is being computed, and (b) any payment made under the terms of the offer in compromise (Form 656), as shown in item 5, for the year in which such payment is made. Annual income shall not be reduced by any overpayments waived in item 7g, Form 656. The annual income shall not be reduced by net operating losses incurred before or after the period covered by this agreement. However, a net operating loss for any year during such period may be deducted from annual income for the following year only. It is also agreed that annual income shall include all income and gains or profits of the taxpayers, regardless of whether these amounts are community income under state law.

3. That in the event close corporations are directly or indirectly controlled or owned by the taxpayers during the existence of this agreement, the computation of annual income shall include their proportionate share of the total corporate annual income in excess of $10,000. The term corporate annual income, as used in this agreement, means the taxable income of the corporation before net operating loss deduction and special deductions (except, in computing such income, the losses from sales or exchanges of property shall not be allowed), plus all nontaxable income, minus (a) dividends paid, and (b) the federal income tax paid for the year for which annual income is being computed. For this purpose, the corporate annual income shall not be reduced by any net operating loss incurred before or after the periods covered by this agreement, but a net operating loss for any year during such period may be deducted from the corporate annual income for the following year only.

4. That the annual payment provided for in this agreement (including interest at the rate established under section 6621 of the Internal Revenue Code (compounded under Code section 6622(a)) on delinquent payments computed from the due date of such payment) shall be paid to the Internal Revenue Service, without notice, on or before the 15th day of the 4th month following the close of the calendar or fiscal year, such payments to be accompanied by a sworn statement and a copy of the taxpayers' federal income tax return. The statement shall refer to this agreement and show the computation of annual income in accordance with items 1, 2, and 3 of this agreement. If the annual income for any year covered by this agreement is insufficient to require a payment under its terms, the taxpayers shall still furnish the Internal Revenue Service a sworn statement of such income and a copy of their federal income tax return. All blocks, records, and accounts shall be open at all reasonable times for inspection by the Internal Revenue Service to verify the annual income shown in the statement. Also, the taxpayers hereby expressly consent to the disclosure to each other of the amount of their respective annual income and of all books, records, and accounts necessary to the computation of their annual income for the purpose of administering this agreement. The payment (if any), the sworn statement, and a copy of the federal income tax return shall be transmitted to:
   Address:

Cat. No. 18243R	*(Over)*	Form **2261** (Rev. 04-95)

5. That the aggregate amount paid under the terms of the offer in compromise and the additional amounts paid under the terms of this agreement shall not exceed an amount equivalent to the liability covered by the offer plus statutory additions that would have become due in the absence of the compromise.

6. That payments made under the terms of this agreement shall be applied first to tax and penalty, in that order. due for the earliest taxable period, then to tax and penalty, in that order, for each succeeding taxable period with no amount to be allocated to interest until the liabilities for taxes and penalties for all taxable periods sought to be compromised have been satisfied.

7. That upon notice to the taxpayers of the acceptance of the offer in compromise of the liability identified in this agreement. the taxpayers shall have no right, in the event of default in payment of any installment of principal or interest due under the terms of the offer and this agreement or in the event any other provision of this agreement is not carried out in accordance with its terms, to contest in court or otherwise the amount of the liability sought to be compromised; and that in the event of such default or noncompliance or in the event the taxpayers become the subject of any proceeding (except a proceeding under the Bankruptcy Act) whereby their affairs are placed under the control and jurisdiction of a court or other party, the United States, at the option of the Commissioner of Internal Revenue or a delegated official, may (a) proceed immediately by suit to collect the entire unpaid balance of the offer and this agreement, or (b) proceed immediately by suit to collect as liquidated damages an amount equal to the tax liability sought to be compromised, minus any payments already received under the terms of the offer and this agreement, with interest at the rate established under section 6621 of the Internal Revenue Code (compounded under Code section 6622(a)) from the date of default. or (c) disregard the amount of such offer and this agreement, apply all amounts previously paid thereunder against the amount of the liability sought to be compromised and, without further notice of any kind, assess and collect by levy or suit (the restrictions against assessment and collection being waived) the balance of such liability. In the event the taxpayers become the subject of any proceeding under the Bankruptcy Act, the offer in compromise and this agreement may be terminated. Upon such termination, the tax liability sought to be compromised, minus any payments already received under the terms of the offer and this agreement, shall become legally enforceable.

8. That the taxpayers waive the benefit of any statute of limitations applicable to the assessment and collection of the liability sought to be compromised and agree to the suspension of the running of the statutory period of limitations on assessment and collection for the period during which the offer in compromise and this agreement are pending, or the period during which any installment under the offer and this agreement remains unpaid, or any provision of this agreement is not carried out in accordance with its terms, and for 1 year thereafter.

9. That when all sums, including interest, due under the terms of the offer in compromise and this agreement, except those sums which may become due and payable under the provisions of item 1 of this agreement, have been paid in full, then and in that event only, all federal tax liens at that time securing the tax liabilities which are the subject of the offer shall be immediately released. However, if, at the time consideration is being given to the release of the federal tax liens, there are any sums due and payable under the terms of item 1, they must also be paid before the release of such liens.

This agreement shall be of no force or effect unless the offer in compromise is accepted.

Taxpayer's Signature	Date
Andrew Assistant	1/10/97
Taxpayer's Signature	Date

I accept the waiver of statutory period of limitations for the Internal Revenue Service.

Signature and Title	Date

Cat. No. 18243R   Form **2261** (Rev. 04-95)

Important Tax Publications

The IRS produces many free publications to help you fill out your tax return and to answer your tax questions. All IRS publications and forms can be downloaded from the Internet or ordered at no charge by calling the IRS at 1-800-829-3676. You can also get forms faxed to you. See section IRS Tax Fax under Electronic Tax Products.

Tax Publications and Related Forms

You may want to get one or more of the publications listed below for information on a specific topic. Where the publication title may not be enough to describe the contents of the publication, there is a brief description. Forms and schedules related to the contents of each publication are shown after each listing.

Pub 1, *Your Rights as a Taxpayer* — explains your rights at each step in the tax process. To ensure that you always receive fair treatment in tax matters, you should know what your rights are.

Pub 1SP, *Derechos del Contribuyente* (**Your Rights as a Taxpayer**) — (Publication 1 in Spanish.)

Pub 3, *Armed Forces' Tax Guild* — gives information about the special tax situations of active members of the Armed Forces. This publication contains information on items that are included in and excluded from gross income, combat zone exclusion, alien status, dependency exemptions, sale of residence, itemized deductions, tax liability, extension of deadline, and filing returns. ALSO CONTAINS BOSNIA PROVISIONS.

Form 1040, 1040A, 1040EZ, 1040NR, 1040X, 1310, 2106, 2688, 2948, 3903, 3903F, 4868, W-2.

Pub 4, *Student's Guide to Federal Income Tax* — explains the federal tax laws that are of particular interest to high school and college students. It describes student's responsibilities to pay taxes and file returns and explains how to file and get help, if needed.

Forms 1040EZ, 4070, W-2, W-4.

Pub 15, *Employer's Tax Guide (Circular E)* — Forms 940, 941.

Pub 15A, *Employer's Supplemental Tax Guide*

Pub 51, *Agricultural Employer's Tax Guide (Circulary A)* — Form 943.

Pub 54, *Tax Guide for U.S. Citizens and Resident Aliens Abroad* — explains the special tax rules for U.S. citizens and resident aliens who live and work abroad or who have income earned in foreign countries. In particular, this publication explains the rules for excluding income and excluding or deducting certain housing costs.

Forms 1040 (Schedule SE), 1116, 2555, 2555EZ.

Pub 80, *Federal Tax Guide for Employers in the Virgin Islands, Guam, American Samoa, and the Commonwealth of Northern Mariana Islands (Circular SS)* — Forms 940, 941SS, 943.

Pub 179, *Guía Contributiva Federal Para Patronos Puertorriqueños (Circular PR)* (Federal Tax Guide for Employers in Puerto Rico) — Forms 940PR, 941PR, 943P, W-3PR.

Pub 225, *Farmer's Tax Guide* — identifies the kind of farm income you must report and the different deductions you can take.

Forms 1040 (Schedules D, E, SE), 4562, 4684, 4797.

Popular Publications

Pub 17, *Your Federal Income Tax (For Individuals)*—can help you prepare your individual tax return. This publication takes you step-by-step through each part of the return. It explains the tax laws in a way that will help you better understand your taxes so that you pay only as much as you owe and no more. *(Note to Practitioners only: There is a fee of $10.00 to order this publication.)*
    Forms 1040 (Schedules A, B, D, E, ETC. R.SE) 1040A, 1040EZ, 2106, 2119, 2441, 3903, W.2.

Pub 334, *Tax Guide for Small Business (For Individuals Who Use Schedule C or C-EZ)*—explains federal tax laws that apply to proprietorships and statutory employees. *(Note to Practitioners only: There is a fee of $6.50 for this publication.)*
    Forms 1040 (Schedules C, C-EZ, SE); 4562.

Pub 579SP, *Como Preparar la Declaracion de Impuesto Federal* **(How to Prepare the Federal Income Tax Return)**—Forms 1040, 1040A, (Schedules 1 and 2). 1040EZ, and Schedule EIC.

Pub 378, *Fuel Tax Credits and Refunds*—explains the credit or refund allowable for the federal excise taxes paid on certain fuels.
    Form 720, 4136, 8849.

Pub 463, *Travel, Entertainment, Gift and Car Expenses*—identifies business-related travel, entertainment, gift, and local transportation expenses that may be deductible.
    Form 2106, 2106EZ.

Pub 501, *Exemptions, Standard Deduction, and Filing Information*—Forms 2120, 8332.

Pub 502, *Medical and Dental Expenses*—explains which medical and dental expenses are deductible, how to deduct them, and how to treat insurance reimbursements you may receive for medical care.
    Form 1040 (Schedule A).

Pub 503, *Child and Dependent Care Expenses* — explains that you may be able to take a credit if you pay someone to care for your dependent who is under age 13, your disabled dependent, or your disabled spouse.

For purposes of the credit, "disabled" refers to persons physically or mentally unable to care for themselves. Tax rules covering benefits paid under a dependent care assistance plan are also explained.

See Publication 926 for information on the employment taxes you may have to pay if you are a household employer.

Forms 1040A (Schedule 2), 2441.

Pub 504, *Divorced or Separated Individuals* — Form 8332.

Pub 505, *Tax Withholding and Estimated Tax* — Forms 1040-ES, 2210, 2210F, W-4, W-4P, W-4S, W-4V.

Pub 508, *Educational Expenses* — identifies work-related educational expenses that may be deductible. Also discusses the exclusion for employer-provided educational assistance.

Forms 1040 (Schedule A), 2106, 2106EZ.

Pub 509, *Tax Calendars for 1997* — covers in detail the various federal excise taxes reported on Form 720. These include environmental taxes; facilities and service taxes on communications and air transportation; fuel taxes; manufacturers' taxes; vaccines; tax on heavy trucks, trailers, and tractors; luxury taxes; and tax on ship passengers. This publication briefly describes other excise taxes and which forms to use in reporting and paying the taxes.

Form 11-C, 637, 720, 730, 6197, 6627.

Pub 513, *Tax Information for Visitors to the United States* — briefly reviews the general requirements of U.S. income tax rules for foreign visitors who may have to file a U.S. income tax return during their visit. Most visitors who come to the United States are not allowed to work in this country. Check with the Immigration and Naturaliation Service before taking a job.

Forms 1040C, 1040-ES (NR), 1040 NR, 2063.

Pub 514, *Foreign Tax Credit for Individuals* — explains the foreign tax credit that is allowed for income taxes paid to a foreign government on income taxed by both the United States and a foreign country.

Form 1116.

Pub 515, *Withholding of Tax on Nonresident Aliens and Foreign Corporations*—provides information for withholding agents who are required to withhold and report tax on payments to nonresident aliens and foreign corporations. This publication includes information on required withholding upon the disposition of a U.S. real property interest by a foreign person. Also, it includes three tables listing U.S. tax treaties and some of the treaty provisions that provide for reduction of or exemption from withholding for certain types of income.
Forms 1001, 1042, 1042S, 1078, 4224, 8233, 8288, 8288-A, 8288-B, 8709, 8804, 8805, 8813, W-8.

Pub 516, *U.S. Government Civilian Employees Stationed Abroad*

Pub 517, *Social Security and Other Information for Members of the Clergy and Religious workers*—discusses Social Security and Medicare taxes for ministers and religious workers. This publication explains the income tax treatment of certain income items of interest to the clergy.
Forms 1040 (Schedules C-EZ, SE), 2106EZ, 4029, 4361.

Pub 519, *U.S. Tax Guide for Aliens*—gives guidelines on how aliens determine their U.S. tax status and figure their U.S. income tax.
Forms 1040, 1040C, 1040NR; 1040NR-EZ, 2063.

Pub 520, *Scholarships and Fellowships*—explains the tax rules that apply to U.S. citizens and resident aliens who study, teach or conduct research in the United States or abroad under scholarships and fellowship grants.
Forms 1040A, 1040EZ.

Pub 521, *Moving Expenses*—explains whether certain expenses of moving are deductible. For example, if you changed job locations last year or started a new job, you may be able to deduct your moving expenses. You also may be able to deduct expenses of moving to the United States if you retire while living and working overseas or if you are a survivor or dependent of a person who died while living and working overseas.
Forms 3903, 3903F, 4782.

Pub 523, *Selling Your Home*—explains how to treat any gain or loss from selling your main home.
Forms 2119, 8828.

Pub 524, *Credit for the Elderly or the Disabled* — explains who qualifies for the credit and how to figure this credit.
Forms 1040 (Schedule R), 1040A (Schedule 3).

Pub 525, *Taxable and Nontaxable Income*

Pub 526, *Charitable Contributions* — describes organizations that are qualified to receive charitable contributions. It also describes contributions you can (and cannot) deduct and explains deduction limits.
Forms 1040 (Schedule A), 8283.

Pub 527, *Residential Rental Property* — explains rental income and expenses and how to report them on your return. This publication also defines other special rules that apply to rental activity.
Forms 1040 (Schedule E), 4562, 4797.

Pub 529, *Miscellaneous Deductions* — identifies expenses you may be able to take as miscellaneous deductions on Form 1040 (Schedule A), such as employee business expenses and expenses of producing income. This publication does not discuss other itemized deductions, such as the ones for charitable contributions, moving expenses, interest, taxes, or medical and dental expenses.
Forms 1040 (Schedule A), 2106EZ.

Pub 530, *Tax Information for First-Time Homeowners* — Forms 1040 (Schedule A), 8396.

Pub 531, *Reporting Tip Income* — explains how tip income is taxes and the rules for keeping records and reporting tips to your employers. This publication focuses on employees of food and beverage establishments, but recordkeeping rules and other information may also apply to other workers who receive tips, such as hairdressers, cab drivers, and casino dealers. (See Publication 1244)
Forms 4070, 4070A.

Pub 533, *Self-Employment Tax* — explains how people who work for themselves figure and pay self-employment tax on their earned income. Self-employment tax consists of Social Security and Medicare taxes.
Form 1040 (Schedule SE).

Pub 534, *Depreciating Property Placed in Service Before 1987* — Form 4562.

Pub 535, *Business Expenses*

Pub 536, *Net Operating Losses* — Form 1045.

Pub 537, *Installment Sales* — explains the tax treatment of property sales arrangements (called installment sales) that provide part or all of the selling price to be paid in a later year. If you finance the buyer's purchase of your property, instead of having the buyer get a loan or mortgage from a bank (or other lender), you probably have an installment sale.
Form 6252.

Pub 538, *Accounting Periods and Methods*

Pub 541, *Partnerships* — Form 1065 (Schedules K, K-1).

Pub 542, *Corporations* — Form 1120, 1120A.

Pub 544, *Sales and Other Dispositions of Assets* — explains how to figure gain and loss on various transactions, such as trading, selling, or exchanging an asset used in a trade or business. This publication defines capital and noncapital assets and the tax results of different types of gains and losses.
Forms 1040 (Schedule D), 4797, 8824.

Pub 547, *Casualties, Disasters, and Thefts (Business and Nonbusiness)* — helps you identify a deductible disaster, casualty, or theft loss. This publication also explains how to figure and prove your loss and how to treat the reimbursement you receive from insurance or other sources.
Form 4684.

Pub 550, *Investment Income and Expenses* — covers investment income such as interest and dividends, expenses related to investments, and sales and trades of investment property including capital gains and losses.
Forms 1040 (Schedules B, D), 1099-DIV, 1099-INT, 4952, 6781, 8815.

Pub 551, *Basis of Assets* — explains how to determine the basis of property, which is usually its cost.

Pub 552, *Recordkeeping for Individuals* — highlights and serves as a ready reference on general recordkeeping for individual income tax filing.

Pub 553, *Older Americans' Tax Guide*—a guide to tax matters that may affect older Americans.
　　Forms 1040 (Schedules B, D, R), 1040A, 2119.

Pub 555, *Community Property*—provides helpful information to married tax-payers who reside in a community property state—Arizona, California, Idaho, Louisiana, Nevada, New Mexico, Texas, Washington, or Wisconsin. If you and your spouse file separate tax returns, you should understand how community property laws affect the way you figure your income on your federal income tax return.

Pub 556, *Examination of Returns, Appeal Rights, and Claims for Refund*—Forms 1040X, 1120X.

Pub 559, *Survivors, Executors, and Administrators*—provides helpful information of reporting and paying the proper federal income tax if you are responsible for settling a decedent's estate. This publication answers many questions that a spouse or other survivor faces when a person dies.
　　Forms 1040, 1041, 4810.

Pub 560, *Retirement Plans for the Self-Employed*—explains tax considerations relevant to retirement plans available to self-employed employers, such as the simplified employee pensions (SEPs) and Keogh (H.R. 10) plans.
　　Forms 5305-SEP, 5500EZ.

Pub 561, *Determining the Value of Donated Property*—defines fair market value and provides other guidance that may help you determine the value of property you donated to a qualified organization.
　　Form 8283.

Pub 564, *Mutual Fund Distributions*—explains the tax treatment of distributions paid or allocated to an individual shareholder of a mutual fund, and explains how to figure gain or loss on the sale of mutual fund shares.
　　Forms 1040 (Schedules B,D), 1099-DIV.

Pub 570, *Tax Guide for Individuals with Income from U.S. Possessions*—provides tax guidance for individuals with income from American Samoa, Guam, the Commonwealth of the Northern Mariana Islands, Puerto Rico, or the U.S. Virgin Islands. This publication also gives information and addresses for filing U.S. possession tax returns, if required.
　　Forms 1040, 1040-SS, 4563, 5074, 8689.

Pub 571, *Tax-Sheltered Annuity Programs for Employees of Public Schools and Certain Tax-Exempt Organizations* — explains the rules that apply to tax-sheltered annuities offered by qualified employers to eligible employees. Rules discussed include those affecting the deferral limit, the exclusion allowance, and the limit on employer contributions.
    Form 5330.

Pub 575, *Pension and Annuity Income (Including Simplified General Rule)* — explains how to report pension and annuity income and discusses the optional tax treatment you can choose to use for lump-sum distributions from pension, stock bonus, or profit-sharing plans. Also discusses rollovers from qualified retirement plans.
    Forms 1040, 1040A, 1099-R, 4972.

Pub 583, *Starting a Business and Keeping Records* — provides basic federal tax information for people who are starting a business. It also provides information on keeping records and illustrates a recordkeeping system.
    Forms 1040 (Schedule C), 4562.

Pub 584, *Nonbusiness Disaster, Casualty, and Theft Loss Workbook* — contains worksheets for listing contents of your residence that were lost due to casualty or theft. It also includes schedules to help you determine item losses.

Pub 584SP, *Registro de Perdidas Personales Causadas por Hechos Fortuitos (Imprevistos) o Robos* — (Publication 584 in Spanish)

Pub 587, *Business Use of Your Home (Including Use by Day-Care Providers)* — explains rules for claiming deductions for business use of your home and what expenses may be deducted.

Pub 590, *Individual Retirement Arrangements (IRAs)* — explains the tax rules that apply to IRAs and the penalties for not following them. Rules discussed include those affecting contributions, deductions, transfers (including rollovers) and withdrawals. This publication also includes tax rules for simplified employee pension (SEP) plans.
    Forms 1040, 1040A, 5329, 8606.

Pub 593, *Tax Highlights for U.S. Citizens and Residents Going Abroad*— provides a brief overview of various U.S. tax provisions that apply to U.S. citizens and resident aliens who live or work abroad and expect to receive income from foreign sources.

Pub 594, *Understanding the Collection Process* — defines your rights and duties as a taxpayer who owes federal taxes. This publication also explains how the IRS fulfills its legal obligation to collect these taxes.

Pub 594SP, *Comprendiendo el Proceso de Cobro (Understanding the Collection Process)* — (Publication 594 in Spanish.)

Pub 595, *Tax Highlights for Commercial Fishermen* — intended for sole proprietors who use Form 1040 (Schedule C) to report profit or loss from fishing. This publication does not cover corporations or partnerships.
    Forms 1040 (Schedule C), 1099-MISC, 4562.

Pub 596, *Earned Income Credit*—explains who may receive the credit, how to figure and claim the credit, and how to receive advance payments of the credit.
    Forms 1040, 1040A, Schedule EIC, EIC Worksheets, W-5.

Pub 596SP, *Credito por Ingreso del Trabajo (Earned Income Credit)* — (Publication 596 in Spanish.)

Pub 597, *Information on the United States–Canada Income Tax Treaty* — reproduces the text of the U.S.-Canada income tax treaty and defines its key provisions. This publication also explains certain tax problems that may be encountered by U.S. residents who temporarily work in Canada.

Pub 598, *Tax on Unrelated Business Income of Exempt Organizations* — explains the tax provisions that apply to most tax-exempt organizations, and explains that the tax may apply if an organization regularly operates a trade or business that is not substantially related to its exempt purposes.
    Form 990-T.

Pub 686, *Certification for Reduced Tax Rates in Tax Treaty Countries* — explains how U.S. citizens, residents, and domestic corporations may certify to a foreign country that they are entitled to tax treaty benefits.

Pub 721, *Tax Guide to U.S. Civil Service Retirement Benefits* — Forms 1040, 1040A.

Pub 850, *English-Spanish Glossary of Words and Phrases Used in Publications Issued by the Internal Revenue Service*

Pub 901, *U.S. Tax Treaties* — explains the reduced tax rates and exemptions from U.S. taxes provided under U.S. tax treaties with foreign countries. This publication provides helpful information for residents of those countries who received income from U.S. sources. It may be useful to U.S. citizens and residents with income from abroad.

Forms 1040NR, 1040NR-EZ, 8833.

Pub 907, *Tax Highlights for Persons with Disabilities* — briefly explains tax laws that apply to persons with disabilities and directs readers to sources of detailed information, such as Pub 502, *Medical and Dental Expenses,* Pub 503, *Child and Dependent Care Expenses;* Pub 524, *Credit for the Elderly or the Disabled;* Pub 525, *Taxable and Nontaxable Income;* and Pub 915, *Social Security and Equivalent Railroad Retirement Benefits.* For information on the disabled access credit, see Pub 334, *Tax Guide for Small Business.* For business tax information on deducting costs of removing architectural or transportation barriers, see Pub 535, *Business Expenses.*

Pub 908, *Bankruptcy Tax Guide* — Forms 982, 1040, 1041.

Pub 911, *Direct Sellers* — provides information on figuring income from direct sales and identifies deductible expenses. A direct seller is a person who sells consumer products to others on a person-to-person basis, such as door-to-door, at sales parties, or by appointment in someone's home.

Form 1040 (Schedules C, SE).

Pub 915, *Social Security and Equivalent Railroad Retirement Benefits* — Forms SSA-1042S and RRB-1042S, SSA-1099 and RRB-1099, Social Security Benefits Worksheets.

Pub 919, *Is My Withholding Correct for 1998?* — discusses Form W-4 and offers guidance for getting the right amount of tax withheld from your pay.

Form W-4.

Pub 925, *Passive Activity and At-Risk Rules* — Form 8582.

Pub 926, *Household Employer's Tax Guide* — identifies "household employers." You may be a household employer if you have a babysitter, maid, yard worker, or other person who works at your house. This publication explains what taxes to withhold and pay and what records to keep.
Forms 1040 (Schedule H), W-2, W-4, W-5.

Pub 929, *Tax Rules for Children and Dependents* — explains filing requirements and the standard deduction amount for dependents. This publication also explains when and how a child's parents may include their child's interest and dividend income on their return and when and how a child's interest, dividends, and other investment income are taxed at the parents' tax rate.
Forms 8615, 8814.

Pub 936, *Home Mortgage Interest Deduction* — Form 1040 (Schedule A).

Pub 938, *Real Estate Mortgage Investment Conduits (REMICs) Reporting Information* — explains reporting requirements for issuers of REMICs and Collateralized Debt Obligations (CDOs) and contains a directory of REMICs and CDOs to assist brokers and middlemen with their reporting requirements. Available electronically on the IRS-Martinsburg bulletin board only. Using a modem, dial 1-304-264-7070 and follow the instructions. This is not a toll free call.

Pub 939, *Pension General Rule (Nonsimplified Method)* — covers the General Rule for the taxation of pensions and annuities, which must be used if the Simplified General Rule does not apply or is not chosen. For example, this nonsimplified method must be used for payments under commercial annuities. The publication contains needed actuarial tables.

Pub 946, *How to Depreciate Property* — Form 4562.

Pub 947, *Practice Before the IRS and Power of Attorney* — explains who can represent a taxpayer before the IRS and what forms or documents are used to authorize a person to represent a taxpayer.
Forms 2848, 8821.

Pub 950, *Introduction to Estate and Gift Taxes* — outlines some of the topics covered in Publication 448, *Federal Estate and Gift Taxes.*

Pub 953, *International Tax Information for Business*—covers topics of interest to U.S. citizens and resident aliens with foreign investments and nonresident aliens who want to invest in U.S. businesses.

Pub 954, *Tax Incentives for Empowerment Zones and Enterprise Communities*

Pub 957, *Reporting Back Pay to the Social Security Administration*

Pub 967, *The IRS Will Figure Your Tax*—explains the procedures for choosing to have the IRS figure the tax on Forms 1040, 1040A, and 1040EZ.

Pub 1004, *Identification Numbers under ERISA*

Pub 1045, *Information for Tax Practitioners*

Pub 1212, *List of Original Issue Discount Instruments*—explains the tax treatment of original issue discount (OID) by brokers and other middlemen and by owners of OID debt instruments.

Pub 1244, *Employee's Daily Record of Tips and Report to Employers*— Forms 4070, 4070-A.

Pub 1542, *Per Diem Rates*

Pub 1544, *Reporting Cash Payments of over $10,000 (Received in a Trade or Business)*—explains when and how persons in a trade or business must file a Form 8300 when they receive cash payments of more than $10,000 from one buyer. It also discusses the substantial penalties for not filing the form.
    Form 8300.

Pub 1546, *How to Use the Problem Resolution Program of the IRS*

Installment Agreement Request (IRS Form 9465)

Form **9465**
(Rev. January 1996)
Department of the Treasury
Internal Revenue Service

Installment Agreement Request

▶ **See instructions below and on back.**

OMB No. 1545-1350

Note: *Do not file this form if you are currently making payments on an installment agreement. You must pay your other Federal tax liabilities in full or you will be in default on your agreement.*

If you can't pay the full amount you owe, you can ask to make monthly installment payments. If we approve your request, you will be charged a $43 fee. **Do not include the fee with this form.** We will deduct the fee from your first payment after we approve your request, unless you choose **Direct Debit** (see the line 13 instructions). We will usually let you know within 30 days after we receive your request whether it is approved or denied. But if this request is for tax due on a return you filed after March 31, it may take us longer than 30 days to reply.

To ask for an installment agreement, complete this form. Attach it to the front of your return when you file. If you have already filed your return or you are filing this form in response to a notice, see **How Do I File Form 9465?** on page 2. If you have any questions about this request, call 1-800-829-1040.

Caution: *A Notice of Federal Tax Lien may be filed to protect the government's interest until you pay in full.*

1	Your first name and initial	Last name	**Your social security number**
	If a joint return, spouse's first name and initial	Last name	**Spouse's social security number**
	Your current address (number and street). If you have a P.O. box and no home delivery, show box number.		Apt. number
	City, town or post office, state, and ZIP code. If a foreign address, show city, state or province, postal code, and full name of country.		

2 If this address is new since you filed your last tax return, check here . . . . ▶ ☐

3 (___) _____ _____
       Your home phone number   Best time for us to call

4 (___) _____ _____ _____
       Your work phone number   Ext.   Best time for us to call

5 Name of your bank or other financial institution:

Address

City, state, and ZIP code

6 Your employer's name:

Address

City, state, and ZIP code

7 Enter the tax return for which you are making this request (for example, Form 1040). But if you are filing this form in response to a notice, don't complete lines 7 through 9. Instead, attach the bottom section of the notice to this form and go to line 10. . . . . ▶ _____

8 Enter the tax year for which you are making this request (for example, 1995) . . . . . . ▶ _____

9 Enter the total amount you owe as shown on your tax return . . . . ▶ $ _____

10 Enter the amount of any payment you are making with your tax return (or notice). See instructions ▶ $ _____

11 Enter the amount you can paym each month. **Make your payments as large as possible to limit interest and penalty charges.** The charges will continue until you pay in full . . . . ▶ $ _____

12 Enter the date you want to make your payment each month. Do not enter a date later than the 28th ▶ _____

13 If you would like to make your monthly payments using **Direct Debit** (automatic withdrawals from your bank account), check here. . . . . ▶ ☐

Your signature	Date	Spouse's signature. If a joint return, BOTH must sign.	Date

Privacy Act and Paperwork Reduction Act Notice.—Our legal right to ask for the information on this form is Internal Revenue Code sections 6001, 6011, 6012(a), 6109, and 6159 and their regulations. We will use the information to process your request for an installment agreement. The reason we need your name and social security number is to secure proper identification. We require this information to gain access to the tax information in our files and properly respond to your request. If you do not enter the information, we may not be able to process your request. We may give this information to the Department of Justice as provided by law. We may also give it to cities, states, and the District of Columbia to carry out their tax laws.

Cat. No. 14842Y   Form **9465** (Rev. 1-96)

The time needed to complete and file this form will vary depending on individual circumstances. The estimated average time is: **Learning about the law or the form,** 2 min.; **Preparing the form,** 24 min.; and **Copying, assembling, and sending the form to the IRS,** 20 min.

If you have comments concerning the accuracy of this time estimate or suggestions for making this form simpler, we would be happy to hear from you. You can write to the Tax Forms Committee, Western Area Distribution Center, Rancho Cordova, CA 95743-0001. **DO NOT** send the form to this address. Instead, see **How Do I File Form 9465?** on this page.

General Instructions

If you cannot pay the full amount you owe shown on your tax return (or on a notice we sent you), you can ask to make monthly installment payments. But before requesting an installment agreement, you should consider other less costly alternatives, such as a bank loan.

You will be charged interest and may be charged a late payment penalty on any tax not paid by its due date, even if your request to pay in installments is granted. To limit interest and penalty charges, file your return on time and pay as much of the tax as possible with your return (or notice).

You will be charged a $43 fee if your request is approved. **Do not** include the fee with this form. We will send you a letter telling you your request has been approved, how to pay the fee, and how to make your first installment payment. After we receive each payment, we will send you a letter showing the remaining amount you owe, and the due date and amount of your next payment.

By approving your request, we agree to let you pay the tax you owe in monthly installments instead of immediately paying the amount in full. In return, you agree to make your monthly payments on time. **You also agree to meet all your future tax liabilities.** This means that you must have adequate withholding or estimated tax payments so that your tax liability for future years is paid in full when you timely file your return. If you do not make your payments on time or have an outstanding past-due amount in a future year, you will be in default on your agreement and we may take enforcement actions to collect the entire amount you owe.

Bankruptcy—Offer-in-Compromise.—If you are in bankruptcy or we have accepted your offer-in-compromise, **do not** file this form. Instead, call your local IRS District Office Special Procedures function. You can get the number by calling 1-800-829-1040.

Specific Instructions

Line 1

If you are making this request for a joint tax return, show the names and SSNs in the same order as on your tax return.

Line 10

Even if you can't pay the full amount you owe now, you should pay as much of it as possible to limit penalty and interest charges. If you are filing this form with your tax return, make the payment with your return. If you are filing this form by itself, for example, in response to a notice, include a check or money order payable to the Internal Revenue Service with this form. **Do not** send cash. On your payment, write your name, address, social security number, daytime phone number, and the tax year and tax return for which you are making this request (for example, "1995 Form 1040").

Line 11

You should try to make your payments large enough so that your balance due will be paid off by the due date of your next tax return.

Line 12

You can choose the date your monthly payment is due. For example, if your rent or mortgage payment is due on the first of the month, you may want to make your installment payments on the 15th. When we approve your request, we will tell you the month and date that your first payment is due. If we have not replied by the date you choose for your first payment, you may send the first payment to the Internal Revenue Service Center at the address shown on this page for the place where you live. Make your check or money order payable to the Internal Revenue Service. See the instructions for line 10 for what to write on your payment.

Line 13

Check the box on line 13 if you want your monthly payments automatically deducted (**Direct Debit**) from your bank account. If your installment agreement request is approved, we will send you the required Direct Debit enrollment form and you must include the $43 fee when you return it.

How Do I File Form 9465?

● If you haven't filed your return, attach Form 9465 to the front of your return.

● If you have already filed your return, you are filing your return electronically, or you are filing this form in response to a notice, mail it to the **Internal Revenue Service** center at the address shown below for the place where you live. No street address is needed.

If you live in:	Use this address:
Florida, Georgia, South Carolina	Atlanta, GA 39901
New Jersey, New York (New York City and counties of Nassau, Rockland, Suffolk, and Westchester)	Holtsville, NY 00501
New York (all other counties), Connecticut, Maine, Massachusetts, New Hampshire, Rhode Island, Vermont	Andover, MA 05501
Illinois, Iowa, Minnesota, Missouri, Wisconsin	Kansas City, MO 64999
Delaware, District of Columbia, Maryland, Pennsylvania, Virginia	Philadelphia, PA 19255
Indiana, Kentucky, Michigan, Ohio, West Virginia	Cincinnati, OH 45999
Kansas, New Mexico, Oklahoma, Texas	Austin, TX 73301
Alaska, Arizona, California (counties of Alpine, Amador, Butte, Calaveras, Colusa, Contra Costa, Del Norte, El Dorado, Glenn, Humboldt, Lake, Lassen, Marin, Mendocino, Modoc, Napa, Nevada, Placer, Plumas, Sacramento, San Joaquin, Shasta, Sierra, Siskiyou, Solano, Sonoma, Sutter, Tehama, Trinity, Yolo, and Yuba), Colorado, Idaho, Montana, Nebraska, Nevada, North Dakota, Oregon, South Dakota, Utah, Washington, Wyoming	Ogden, UT 84201
California (all other counties), Hawaii	Fresno, CA 93888
Alabama, Arkansas, Louisiana, Mississippi, North Carolina, Tennessee	Memphis, TN 37501
American Samoa Guam: Nonpermanent residents only* Puerto Rico (or if excluding income under section 933) Virgin Islands: Nonpermanent residents only* Foreign country (or if a dual-status alien): U.S. citizens and those filing Form 2555, 2555-EZ, or 4563 All APO and FPO addresses	Philadelphia, PA 19255

*Permanent residents of Guam and the Virgin Islands cannot use Form 9465.

Printed on recycled paper   *U.S. Government Printing Office: 1996 — 417-677/40245*

GLOSSARY

abate The cancellation of some or all of a particular tax liability or penalties and interest.

assess The IRS procedure for creating a tax liability after review of a taxpayer return or other information.

audit A review by the IRS of a particular taxpayer's return used for verifying the information reported to the IRS.

basis The original cost of an asset, which is generally adjusted for tax purposes by depreciation or upgrade.

collection division The division of the IRS responsible for collecting the tax liability of taxpayers.

Criminal Investigation Division (CID) The division of the IRS that investigates tax crimes such as fraud.

deduction Expenses subtracted from a taxpayer's gross income that are allowed by the Internal Revenue Code, thereby reducing the taxpayer's taxable income.

depreciation A common tax deduction for the use of an income-producing item such as equipment in a business or a rental property.

fair market value The value of a particular asset—what a typical buyer and a typical seller would agree is an appropriate price.

fraud Any action meant to deceive the IRS or to receive unjust enrichment of the taxpayer for the payment of a tax liability. Fraud is either civil or criminal.

fraud referral IRS jargon for a transfer of a taxpayer file from one division to the Criminal Investigation Division.

gross income All income from any source that is required to be reported to the IRS.

group manager The IRS supervisor in charge of a group of auditors or agents.

installment agreement A payment plan whereby a taxpayer agrees to pay a certain amount per month to the IRS towards the payment of a past tax liability.

Internal Revenue Code The tax law. CPAs and tax lawyers almost always call it the "code."

Internal Revenue Manual A handbook used by IRS employees that explains many IRS processes and procedures.

jeopardy assessment A quick step procedure for assessing and collecting taxes from flight risks or those who may try to hid assets.

levy The seizure of a taxpayer's property or wages to satisfy a tax debt after the taxpayer has failed to pay when requested.

lien An encumbrance on a particular asset that the IRS places on the public record to be sure that the asset is not sold without the IRS receiving payments for any back taxes owed.

penalties Civil fines that are added to a tax liability for taxpayers who have violated tax laws.

revenue agent An IRS employee who conducts audits.

revenue officer An IRS employee who is responsible for collecting delinquent taxes.

revenue rulings An IRS interpretation of a tax law when applied to a specific situation.

service center Large, regional facilities where tax returns are filed and processed by the IRS.

special agent An IRS agent from the Criminal Investigation Division.

statute of limitations Time deadlines imposed by law on how long the IRS has to assess and collect taxes due.

summons A legal command for a taxpayer (or other entity) to provide financial information to the IRS.

willful act Intentionally illegal conduct that can subject the taxpayer to criminal prosecution.

INDEX

ABOUT THE AUTHOR

Sean P. Melvin is a practicing attorney who advises individuals and businesses on business and tax aspects of starting, managing, and expanding their business ventures. In addition to his law practice at the law firm Fox, Rothschild, O'Brien & Frankel, LLP, he is a frequent contributor to a number of business and finance periodicals. He is also the author of *The Entrepreneur's Business Law Handbook* (Macmillan, 1997).

Mr. Melvin earned his Juris Doctorate at Rutgers Law School where he was awarded the American Jurisprudence Award. He is a frequent speaker at taxpayer problem resolution workshops and seminars, and he teaches for the Institute of Management Accountants. Prior to becoming a lawyer, he worked with troubled taxpayers in a Philadelphia region accounting firm.

He is admitted to the practice of law in Pennsylvania and New Jersey, and is a member of the American Bar Association. He lives in Malvern, Pennsylvania, with his wife and son.